Illicit and Unnatural Practices

For Mo
and in fond memory of Ziggy and Zapher

Illicit and Unnatural Practices

The Law, Sex and Society in Scotland since 1900

Roger Davidson

EDINBURGH
University Press

Edinburgh University Press is one of the leading university presses in the UK. We publish academic books and journals in our selected subject areas across the humanities and social sciences, combining cutting-edge scholarship with high editorial and production values to produce academic works of lasting importance. For more information visit our website: edinburghuniversitypress.com

Edinburgh University Press Ltd
The Tun – Holyrood Road
12 (2f) Jackson's Entry
Edinburgh EH8 8PJ

First published in hardback by Edinburgh University Press 2020

Typeset in 10.5/13pt Sabon by
Servis Filmsetting Ltd, Stockport, Cheshire and
printed and bound by CPI Group (UK) Ltd,
Croydon, CR0 4YY

A CIP record for this book is available from the British Library

ISBN 978 1 4744 4119 3 (hardback)
ISBN 978 1 4744 4120 9 (paperback)
ISBN 978 1 4744 4121 6 (webready PDF)
ISBN 978 1 4744 4122 3 (epub)

Contents

Figures and Tables

Acknowledgements

Many people have helped me in the preparation of this book. In my quest to explore the interaction of the law with some of the more illicit and unnatural sexual practices in twentieth- and twenty-first-century Scotland, I have received invaluable support from many archivists and librarians. In particular, I would like to thank the staff of the British Medical Association Archives, Church of Scotland Archives, Edinburgh City Archives, Lothian Health Services Archive, Royal College of Physicians of Edinburgh Archives, and The National Archives (Public Record Office, Kew). I owe a special debt to the staff of the National Records of Scotland for their efforts over many years in facilitating my research, and especially Alison Lindsay, Head of Historical and Legal Search Rooms, whose eye for source material directly inspired two of the chapters in this volume. Thanks are also due to the Keeper of Public Records and the Keeper of the Records of Scotland for permission to quote from central government records. In addition, I wish to thank the Lord Justice General for permission to consult and cite selected High Court trial processes and appeal papers held at the National Records of Scotland. I am indebted to Pennie Taylor for sharing with me material relating to Dora Noyce and the Danube Street brothel which forms the subject of Chapter 6 and to Bob McCulloch and Mark Taylor for agreeing to be interviewed for the purposes of my study.

I have benefited enormously from the shared experience of many historians and social scientists, in particular Lynn Abrams, Angela Bartle, Virginia Berridge, Allan Beveridge, Anne Crowther, Gayle Davis, Nicholas Duvall, Trevor Griffiths, Leslie Hall, Louise Jackson, Jane O'Neill, Louise Settle, and Steve Sturdy. On the issue of the criminalisation of the transmission of HIV, I received valuable advice from James Chalmers, Helen Coyle, Catherine Dodds, George Valiotis, and

Matthew Weait. Very special thanks are also due to Ian Glover for his tireless and meticulous assistance in the proofreading and preparation of the text as well as for his enduring support and encouragement.

Above all, I have to thank my wife, Mo, for all her loving patience and care during the research and writing of this book, without which it would not have been possible. As a sufferer from Parkinson's disease, I have hugely valued the empowerment that producing this volume has given me but it is largely due to Mo that I have been able to undertake the project and see it to completion.

Abbreviations

BMJ	*British Medical Journal*
CSA	Church of Scotland Archives
DOE	Department of the Environment
DORA	Defence of the Realm Act
ECA	Edinburgh City Archives
FCS	Free Church of Scotland
FOI	Freedom of Information
FPCS	Free Presbyterian Church of Scotland
HC	House of Commons
HCJ	High Court of Justiciary
HL	House of Lords
JC	Justiciary Cases
LA	Lord Advocate
NCCVD	National Council for Combating Venereal Disease
NRS	National Records of Scotland
NVLA	National Viewers' and Listeners' Association
PP	Parliamentary Papers
PRO	The National Archives, Public Record Office, Kew
PWC	Proceedings of the Wolfenden Committee on Homosexual Offences and Prostitution
RCPE	Royal College of Physicians of Edinburgh
RCVD	Royal Commission on Venereal Diseases
RWC	Report of the Wolfenden Committee on Homosexual Offences and Prostitution
SDD	Scottish Development Department
SHHD	Scottish Home and Health Department
SLT	*Scottish Law Times*
SSS	Secretary of State for Scotland
VD	Venereal Disease

1

Introduction

HISTORIOGRAPHY

In recent decades, the subject of sexuality and sexual practices in twentieth-century Scotland has become the focus of increasing, if somewhat disparate, research by historians and social scientists. Several, sometimes overlapping, areas of investigation may be discerned. Using quantitative data analysis of census and civil registration records, historical demographers have identified trends and regional variations in nuptiality, fertility and illegitimacy rates and their implications for interpreting shifts in sexual behaviour and reproductive strategies.[1] Meanwhile, using more qualitative evidence derived from memoirs and oral history, some sociologists and cultural historians have explored the impact of shifts in social norms and economic circumstances on the nature of intimacy in Scottish society and patterns of courtship, cohabitation and premarital sexual relations.[2] Other historians, sometimes from a feminist perspective, have explored the management of sexuality in the young as part of the gendered disciplinary framework of early twentieth-century Scottish society.[3] In addition, again using oral history testimony, recent research has focused on aspects of social change that influenced the acquisition of sexual (pre-eminently contraceptive) knowledge and opportunities for sexual initiation, and that served to shape sexual identities.[4] Finally, a strand of investigation, heavily reliant on the files of Scottish departments of state, has addressed the policy-making process with respect to a range of issues relating to sexual offences, reproduction, sexual health, sex education, and censorship in the period after 1950, designed to map the role of Scottish governance in these often contentious and contested areas of civil society.[5]

With few exceptions, however,[6] partly because of the paucity of

accessible Sheriff Court records and a variety of restrictions and clo-
sures imposed on High Court and Crown Office papers, there has been
relatively little use made of criminal prosecution and trial papers and
newspaper law reports to provide an insight into sexual behaviours and
ideologies after 1900 and how society and 'the law in action' responded
when confronted by what were deemed illicit and/or unnatural practices.

AIMS

The central aim of this volume is to make good this omission by exploring eight areas of sexual or sex-related practices that featured in Scottish
legal proceedings between 1900 and the early years of the new millennium: VD quackery, child sexual abuse, abortion, bestiality, brothel
keeping, homosexual acts, the operation of sex shops and the wilful
transmission of HIV. In so doing, it will seek to tease out key features
of the interaction of the law, sex, and society since 1900. How far, for
example, did the legal process and outcome reflect and/or reinforce
contemporary moral panics over sexual behaviours and popular aversion to sexual gratification and diversity? To what extent do the case
studies bear out the Foucauldian view that the law was not merely a set
of institutions dispensing justice but a powerful discourse that shaped
perceptions of sex and the normative boundaries of sexual behaviour?[7]
In what respects was the operation of the law shaped not by a uniform
code of practice but socially constructed within a multilayered network
of accusation, investigation and indictment, by the ideology and influence of individual law officers and forensic experts as well as particular
civic responses to sexual offences? What role did the medical profession
play in shaping the content and outcome of legal proceedings and how
significant were the tensions between medical conceptions of sexually
'deviant' and unlawful behaviour as a form of mental dysfunction and
judicial conceptions of it as purely a criminal act? How far in its response
to sexual offences over the period did the legal system help to preserve
ideals of masculinity? To what degree did it continue to embrace a
double moral standard and deny female witnesses and 'victims' agency
in presenting their version of sexual events? Finally, in what respects
did Scotland's distinctive legal identity and procedures shape the way in
which illicit and unnatural sexual acts were prosecuted, and affect the
outcome of the legal process?

SOURCES

Many of the case studies are heavily based on surviving precognitions and High Court trial papers. Precognitions are witness statements, including testimony from medical experts and the police, compiled by a procurator fiscal on behalf of the local magistrate and transmitted to the Crown Office, headed by the Crown Agent,[8] in Edinburgh. A decision will then be taken, in consultation with Crown Counsel,[9] on whether or not, and at what level, to proceed to trial. In addition, precognitions often contain papers relating to the arrest of suspects, printed indictments, and notes exchanged between the procurator fiscal and Crown Agent as to the construction and presentation of the prosecution case. In more contentious cases involving legal precedent the opinion of an Advocate Depute[10] or the Lord Advocate may also be recorded along with pencilled marginalia referencing the legal texts to be cited in court. The trial papers or 'processes' are the main record of a High Court trial. They usually include a copy of the indictment, depositions, and other information on the accused and the crime, together with information about witnesses and jurors. Most importantly, they list and sometimes contain the 'productions' – articles produced and lodged as evidence in court including medical reports and incriminating correspondence from the accused or from anonymous informants.

For a number of reasons the social historian needs to exercise considerable caution in interpreting and generalising from High Court records. It has to be acknowledged that the sexual behaviours of those prosecuted in the High Court were almost certainly abnormal and not typical of the general population. Moreover, it is uncertain how far the sexual narratives contained in these documents were representative of the vast majority of offences that were neither reported nor prosecuted, or were processed in the lower courts. It has also to be remembered that the precognitions were collected and transcribed by legal officials specifically for the purpose of constructing a prosecution case, and the evidence, therefore, was often limited to events immediately surrounding the offence and designed to establish culpability. As Stephen Robertson observes, by allowing sexual behaviour to be discussed only in terms of the law, accounts offered by witnesses become distorted. As a result, court records 'usually deal with sexual acts, shorn of the participant's motives and understandings of those acts and without reference to their lives beyond the moment in which the act took place'.[11] The questioning that shaped the precognitions, deploying a 'limited legal lexicon' for describing sexual relations, was formulaic and served to produce a stylised version of what was actually said in accordance with the requirements of the law.[12] For these reasons, social and cultural historians have emphasised the need constantly to read between the lines in order to tease out the 'actual experiences of the actors from the ritualised assertions' recorded in the witness statements.[13]

The absence of surviving transcripts of High Court trials, except in a very few of the cases that were appealed or that raised issues requiring a judicial ruling, is an additional problem. It renders it impossible to explore how evidence in court of sexual behaviours and predilections was presented and interrogated and how courtroom exchanges reflected and/or reinforced certain sexual and moral codes. It limits the extent to which the historian can differentiate between various layers of meaning within the judicial process as conveyed on the one hand by the somewhat formulaic narratives of the law and forensic medicine and, on the other, the relatively spontaneous narratives of those participating in or witnessing the offence. In addition, without access to the judge's closing remarks to the jury, it is difficult to capture the views of the judiciary on illicit and unnatural sexual practices and the social and legal ideology that underpinned their approach to such cases.

Nor, for much of the twentieth century, can newspaper reports make good this omission. Some of the more 'unsavoury' trials were held 'in camera', with the public and press excluded. At other times, except for a few trials where a prominent member of the community was involved, court proceedings were rarely reported in any detail. Thus, while Glasgow's North Court heard 'all the more printable forms of crime', the South Court, 'known familiarly to the crime reporters as "the dirty court", often went unreported'.[14] There was often a tacit agreement between court officials and reporters that only a brief summary of the charge and sentence would be published for fear of deterring witnesses from giving evidence. In addition, the Scottish press was reluctant to offend a readership that found such sexual transgressions distasteful and unworthy of being paraded in the media. It was feared that publishing the more sordid and salacious details of offences would seriously offend women subscribers, pander to the more prurient readership, and merely serve to advertise illicit and unnatural sexual practices to others in the community. The Judicial Proceedings (Regulation of Reports) Act 1926, making it unlawful to report any judicial proceedings deemed 'indecent' or 'calculated to injure public morals', served merely to reinforce such reticence.

Despite these caveats and limitations, however, it is arguable that Scottish High Court records, supplemented by law reports and by press coverage in the later twentieth century, comprise a valuable source in the reconstruction of past sexual behaviours and attitudes. As Robertson has argued, with careful content analysis, 'court records can take the researcher beyond the crime itself into the social and cultural world in which the act took place'.[15] For Matt Cook, legal testimony provides 'access to voices rarely heard in the public record' and a 'vantage point' from which to view private sexual codes and experiences.[16] Other historians stress the paradox that legal records reveal for the social historian intimate details of sexual practices which would normally be 'cloaked in silence' and that the law was expressly designed to suppress.[17] From an analysis of the precognitions and trial papers, a profile of offenders (and where appropriate, 'victims') can be drawn, including their age, sex, class, marital and occupational status, criminal record and sexual and reproductive history. In addition, social networks underpinning the sexual offence can be identified along with community responses to the crime. The vital role of forensic and other expert evidence in legal proceedings can also be detected, along with professional tensions relating to issues of confidentiality or contrasting medical and legal perceptions of illicit sexual behaviour. Meanwhile, notes and memoranda exchanged between the Crown Office and procurators fiscal in the process of initiating prosecutions, coupled with sentencing evidence, can throw important light on the attitude of the legal establishment towards particular offences and how far these were influenced by contemporary social anxieties and moral panics. These sources, along with appeal papers, also provide a valuable commentary on the distinctiveness of Scots law in its rules of evidence (especially those relating to corroboration) and their impact on when and whom to prosecute.

CONTENTS

The structure of this volume has been primarily shaped by two factors: first, a concern to document the interface between the legal process and sexual transgression in periods of perceived moral crisis in the British state; and secondly, the varying degree of availability of High Court and Crown Office papers. The book consists of two groups of case studies. The first four studies (Chapters 2–5), for which precognitions and trial papers are available, focus on the period 1900–30. As in many other countries, this was a period of increasing anxiety and concern in Scotland over the impact of war and rapid social change on existing norms of sexual conduct. Social Darwinists and social purity campaigners fuelled moral panic over the adverse effects on public order and racial progress of promiscuous and predatory behaviours, along with a growing desire to penalise and, it was hoped, to eradicate what were perceived as 'deviant and degenerate' sexual and sex-related practices.

Chapter 2 investigates the prosecution of 'Professor' Abraham Eastburn in 1919 as a means of exploring the interaction between the law and the moral panic surrounding venereal disease (VD) in early twentieth-century Scotland that reached its peak during and immediately after World War I. A detailed narrative of his background and practice, together with a content analysis of his posters and handbills, furnish valuable insights into the widespread and continuing recourse to unregistered healers and quack remedies. The failure of qualified practitioners and established therapies to meet the needs of those suffering from venereal infections is surveyed. Eastburn's prosecution is then contextualised within the social politics shaping the creation of a nationwide health system for the diagnosis, treatment and prevention of VD, and the outlawing, under growing pressure from the medical profession, of all venereal advice and treatment by unqualified practitioners under the Venereal Disease Act 1917.

VD also figures in Chapter 3 as a prism through which to examine child sexual abuse in early twentieth-century Scotland and the competing discourses surrounding its prosecution. At the heart of the study is a set of High Court cases of sexual assault upon children involving the aggravated offence of communicating VD, and the role played in such cases of the enduring superstition that 'having connection with a virgin' was a cure for the affliction. The chapter traces how this 'pernicious delusion' figured in medical testimony to legal proceedings and government enquiries throughout the period. Thereafter, it explores both the impulses and constraints shaping the response of the law to 'child outrage'. The impact of these cases on the campaign by feminists, rescue workers, and purity activists to amend the criminal law and the conduct of investigation and trial in respect to sexual offences against women is documented, as is the growing importance of forensic medicine in securing convictions. High Court proceedings also reveal continuing resistance within the medical profession and judiciary, as well as within the family and local community, to recognising child sexual abuse. The chapter illustrates the many layers of denial that operated to deny the child victims justice and the extent to which, once violated, the legal process stigmatised them as sexual dangers to be institutionalised.

Chapter 4 constitutes a pioneering study of the practice and prosecution of bestiality in twentieth-century Scotland. In turn, it examines the social status, background, lifestyle and possible motive of offenders, the nature and location of the crime committed, and the process by which it was brought to the attention of the law. The variety of roles undertaken by the police in investigating complaints and preparing evidence for the procurators fiscal is detailed. In addition, the significant contribution of forensic and veterinary medicine to building the prosecution case is illustrated, as is the limited use of psychiatric evidence after World War I. In addition, the chapter discusses the impact of the social taboo surrounding bestiality on the reluctance of procurators fiscal at times to initiate prosecutions and the secretive nature of many trial proceedings. Finally, sentencing practices in the period 1900–30 are examined and the degree of continuity and change in medico-legal perceptions of the offence identified.

Illegal abortion is another area of illicit sex-related activity in early twentieth-century Scotland that has hitherto been neglected by social historians. Based on a detailed analysis of every prosecution heard in the High Court in the period 1900–30 involving a charge of abortion or attempted abortion, Chapter 5 provides a comprehensive survey of the practice.[18] It examines the age, marital status, class, occupation, and motivation of the women seeking an abortion. Abortion is revealed not as a single event but part of an elaborate process of social networking and medical intervention. An initial phase of self-treatment is explored followed by a review of the variety of ways in which women gained access to abortionists, including the role of relatives, friends and neighbours, community or workplace gossip, advertisements, chemists, herbalists and fortune tellers. Thereafter, the study provides a breakdown of the social and occupational status of the abortionists indicted before the High Court along with an overview of the fees that they charged. A further section summarises the abortion procedure including a review of the drugs and instruments employed and the medical outcomes. The chapter then describes how the police were alerted to an offence, the legal framework and particular constraints operating under Scottish criminal law, and the process of assembling a prosecution case with particular reference to the role of forensic medicine. Finally, variations in convictions and sentencing are examined and conclusions drawn as to the implications of this study for the historiography of abortion.

The second group of studies (Chapters 6–9), based predominantly on newspaper coverage of court proceedings and departmental archives, covers the later decades of the twentieth century and early years of the new millennium, a period that arguably witnessed a dramatic shift in sexual attitudes and practices and in the relationship of the law to the moral domain of the private citizen. Public, professional and political debate on sexual issues was dominated in turn by the proceedings and aftermath of the Wolfenden Committee on Homosexual Offences and Prostitution (1954–57), by the emergence of a new moral authoritarianism in the 1970s dedicated to containing the spread of pornography, and by the legal and ethical issues raised after 1983 by the threat of AIDS.

Chapter 6 explores the life of Dora Noyce and her business enterprise at 17 and 17a Danube Street, Edinburgh, as a peg upon which to hang a broader review of how the law operated at the local level to regulate prostitution and brothel-keeping in late twentieth-century Scotland. Primarily based on oral history interviews and newspaper reports, the study reveals the social background and outlook of Dora Noyce before describing the operation of her brothel, including details of sexual transactions and the social status and motivation of the women employed as prostitutes. Thereafter, the history of the Danube Street brothel is located within a more general review of the law relating to brothel-keeping in Scotland and its previous implementation prior to World War II. The study then focuses on the possible reasons for the degree of tolerance shown to Dora Noyce by the police authorities in Edinburgh from the 1950s through to the 1970s, and the extent to which this signified a more complex and nuanced relationship between the law and the sexual underworld than is conventionally conveyed in police and court records.

Chapter 7 moves on to investigate the medical perception and treatment of homosexual offenders in Scotland in the period 1950–80 and, in particular, the role that medical evidence played in the prosecution and sentencing of such offenders in the Scottish High Court. Two main sources of evidence are explored. First, the evidence of Scottish witnesses before the Wolfenden Committee is examined in order to establish how homosexual offenders were medically treated within the legal process in the 1950s. Secondly, with the benefit of privileged access granted by the Lord Justice General, an analysis is undertaken of the medical reports on homosexual offenders submitted by psychiatrists and other doctors to High Court trials and appeals during the period 1950–80, and of their role in court proceedings. This throws important light on the degree to which medical views and practices pertaining to homosexual offenders in Scotland changed over the quarter of a century following Wolfenden and how far and in what ways they influenced the legal process.

In Chapter 8, an account of the prosecution and closure of Scotland's first sex shop, the *Anne Boleyn* at St George's Cross in Glasgow in 1971, forms a prelude to a review of the subsequent crusade of a powerful coalition of puritanical groups and moral vigilantes in Scotland's cities against the spread of pornography and sexual display. While the Scottish Office was initially content to rely on clauses relating to obscenity in local Corporation Acts to counter the proliferation of sex shops, it was increasingly forced to contemplate the need for new statutory powers. The study explores in depth the various policy options advanced by Whitehall and Scottish departments of state, and the growing tension between advocates in Westminster of a new system of licensing of sex shops and the preference of Scottish officials and law officers for a more modest extension of existing planning controls that would not appear to legitimise the activities of retailers, some of whom were in the process of being prosecuted under existing laws of obscenity and indecent display. The outcome of this contentious debate, culminating in the creation of a modified licensing scheme under the Civic Government (Scotland) Act 1982, is charted. Finally, with the benefit of access under the Freedom of Information Act, the chapter reviews the extent to which sex shops were licensed over the following decade and the findings of a Scottish Executive Task Force subgroup set up to review the workings of the scheme and its viability in the new millennium.

The final study examines the relationship between the law, sex and society in the age of AIDS by focusing on the criminalisation of HIV transmission after 1983. The first section provides an historical perspective by reviewing the series of largely abortive attempts by Scottish lawmakers to criminalise the transmission of VD since 1900. A second section addresses the response of Scottish governance to the rising demand between 1983 and 2001 for additional public order and public health powers to contain the spread of HIV, fuelled after 1997 by media coverage of cases in which it was alleged that innocent victims had been carelessly or knowingly infected. There follows a detailed narrative of the trial and sentencing of Stephen Kelly at the High Court in Glasgow in February 2001 for knowingly infecting his partner with HIV, the first case of its kind in the United Kingdom. A further section then reviews the protracted medical, ethical and legal debate arising out of the case. Finally, the main strands of policy-making on the issue of amending the law during the period up to 2015 are outlined, including proposals for mandatory testing. This is set against the backdrop of three additional High Court cases between 2005 and 2010 and the publication of guidelines by the Crown Office and Procurator Fiscal Service in 2012 for the prosecution of 'intentional or reckless' transmission of sexually transmitted infections.

A concluding chapter explores the more general implications of this volume for an understanding of the interplay between the law, sex and society in Scotland since 1900, highlighting the common themes that interweave throughout the various studies and addressing the issues raised in the introduction.

NOTES

1. See, for example, Anderson and Morse, 'High fertility, high emigration, low nuptiality', 5–25, 319–43; Anderson, 'The demographic factor', 30–61; Anderson, 'Population and family life', 12–47; Anderson, *Scotland's Populations*.
2. See, for example, Jamieson, 'Changing intimacy', 76–102. A number of purportedly 'British' studies accord only a fragmentary reference to the Scottish experience [see, for example, Collins, *Modern Love*].
3. See, for example, Mahood and Littlewood, 'The "vicious" girl and the "street-corner" boy', 549–78.
4. See, for example, O'Neill, 'Youth, sexuality and courtship in Scotland', PhD thesis, University of Edinburgh, 2015; Macaulay, 'Birth control knowledge in Scotland', MD thesis, University of Glasgow, 2015; Meek, *Queer Voices in Post-War Scotland*.
5. See, especially, Davidson and Davis, *The Sexual State*.
6. Exceptions include Louise Settle's use of Burgh Court papers in her study of prostitution in Edinburgh prior to 1939 [*Sex for Sale in Scotland*] and Jeffrey Meek's use of High Court precognition and trial papers surrounding the later prosecution of homosexual offenders [*Queer Voices in Post-War Scotland*].
7. According to Foucault [*The History of Sexuality*, vol. 1, 83], 'sex is placed by power in a binary system: licit and illicit, permitted and forbidden ... [P]ower prescribes an "order" for sex that operates at the same time as a form of intelligibility: sex is to be deciphered on the basis of its relation to the law'.
8. The Crown Agent is the principal legal adviser to the Lord Advocate on prosecution matters.
9. The Lord Advocate, who is the chief public prosecutor in Scotland, the Solicitor General who assists him, and the Advocates Depute are collectively known as Crown Counsel.
10. Advocate Deputes are experienced practising members of the Faculty of Advocates appointed to the Crown Office to make decisions about proceedings in serious cases, prosecute cases in the High Court, and appear for the Crown in criminal appeals.
11. Robertson, 'What's law got to do with it?', 162.
12. Cook, 'Law', 76; Abrams, *Oral History Theory*, 19.
13. See, for example, McLaren, 'Illegal operations', 799.
14. Crowther and White, *On Soul and Conscience*, 51.

15. Robertson, 'What's law got to do with it?', 161.
16. Cook, 'Law', 74.
17. McLaren, 'Illegal operations', 798; Usborne, *Cultures of Abortion*, 14.
18. Though not legally defined as a 'sexual offence', as in rape cases, Crown counsel typically presented the female complainant in abortion cases as a 'victim' who had been sexually violated. Similarly, the emphasis of the prosecution case usually rested on evidence of vaginal penetration. In addition, testimony in abortion cases regularly included explicit details of the complainant's sexual and reproductive history including extramarital liaisons.

2

'Venereal Trouble': The Case of 'Professor' Abraham Eastburn

THE CHARGE

In November 1919, self-styled 'Professor' Abraham Eastburn appeared before Glasgow Sheriff Court charged with contravening the Venereal Disease Act 1917 in that, 'not being a qualified practitioner', he had treated Richard Vincent Copley, a merchant seaman, for VD.[1] According to Copley,[2] he had contracted VD from a 'prostitute' in Montreal in 1918 and developed a 'pain in the penis' on the voyage home. On arriving in Glasgow in October 1918, he had sought treatment. Near Central Station he had been handed a handbill advertising Eastburn's practice and had gone to his premises in Berkeley Terrace. This appeared to be a 'good, respectable establishment' surrounded by other medical practices, and he assumed from the handbill and the location of the premises that Eastburn was a qualified doctor. He was duly ushered in by a caretaker and left in a waiting room that contained a book by Eastburn entitled *The Citadel of Life and How to Guard It*. It recounted the story of a man who had 'let his venereal trouble go very far'. Despite complications, Eastburn had succeeded in curing him and the patient was now the proud father of a healthy boy.

Copley was then taken to the consulting room, where he was required to put down one guinea as a fee for the examination. Eastburn took a urine sample and then put something in it that 'caused a feathery appearance'. He told Copley that he was suffering from 'hard chancre' and from 'Nervousness' and that '[his] nature was passing from [him] into [his] urine'. Eastburn then offered to put him through a six-months' course of treatment for syphilis for £22 adding that, as soon as the sore was better, he would put him on a 'combined course for Nervousness for a further £34' lasting eight to ten months which he would allow

Copley to pay by instalments. On his next visit, he was given a bottle with 'greenish tablets' together with a 'small bottle of yellowish liquid' and a 'small camel's hair brush'. The tablets were to be taken before the three principal meals of the day and the liquid painted on the venereal sore night and morning.

Copley was subsequently sent several months' supply of the medications through the post and sailed for Philadelphia but, by December 1918, he was feeling 'very tired and worn out'. Red, dry spots broke out on his forehead, his throat became very sore and he had extreme pain in his back passage. On disembarking at Liverpool, he went to Liverpool Medical Hall and was treated by Dr Edward Ball. According to Ball, there were clear clinical signs of secondary syphilis and no blood test was necessary. In late December 1918 and early January 1919, he gave Copley three injections of mercury for a fee of three guineas each, some mercury and chalk tablets, and mercurial ointment. Ball informed Copley that Eastburn's treatment was worthless and that he was 'a fraud'. He advised him to sue Eastburn for recovery of his fees. However, when Copley contacted Eastburn the latter rejected Ball's accusations and responded that he would be happy to meet the charge of fraud in court. Further, he stated that, if Copley renewed his course of treatment, Eastburn would 'guarantee to draw the syphilis out of [his] system in 6 months'. After another voyage, Copley unwisely agreed to do this and paid further sums in return for chocolate-coloured tablets designed, it was claimed, to address both his VD and nervousness. But, when his anal discomfort recurred, in desperation he contacted the National Council for Combating Venereal Disease (NCCVD), a voluntary organisation that had originated during the proceedings of the Royal Commission on Venereal Diseases and was dedicated to the pursuit of 'social hygiene'.[3] The Council advised Copley to obtain proper medical treatment and, in August 1919, referred him to Dr Baker-Young at the newly established VD centre at Liverpool Cancer and Skin Hospital. Baker-Young diagnosed late secondary syphilis, verified by a Wassermann test, and carried out a course of Salvarsan treatment. In his opinion, clear signs of secondary syphilis must have been evident during Copley's previous visits to Eastburn and he was adamant that, had Copley's condition been treated properly at the outset, 'the trouble would ere have been carried out of his system'. Baker-Young subsequently reported Eastburn's activities to the President of the NCCVD who referred the case to Dr A. K Chalmers, a member of the Council's Executive Committee and Medical Officer of Health for Glasgow. He, in turn, alerted the Procurator Fiscal who apprehended Eastburn and initiated legal proceedings against him.

THE DEFENDANT

Abraham States Eastburn was born in Pennsylvania in 1854, the twelfth of thirteen children.[4] Little is known of his early life but legal documents suggest that, by the late 1870s, he was acting as an assistant to an itinerant 'healer', a self-styled 'Professor' William Henry Hale, helping to distribute handbills and pamphlets and to operate the 'Limelight' (a light produced by a combination of incandescence and Cando luminescence using heated quicklime) employed by Hale to illustrate his lectures.[5] In 1890–91 he was engaged by Hale to accompany him on a lecture tour to Scotland but soon afterwards their relationship came to an acrimonious end. Eastburn accused Hale of reneging on an agreement to share the profits of his enterprise, while Hale alleged that Eastburn had threatened both him and his family. He testified that Eastburn carried 'on his person a revolver, and iron 'knucks [knuckle-dusters] for placing on his hands for the purposes of violence' and that he frequently carried a dagger. Thereafter, Eastburn set up his own practice, first in Stirling and then, from about 1885, in response to growing demand, in consulting rooms in Cambridge Street, Glasgow.

Eastburn described himself as a 'Surgeon Professor Eclectic Medical Specialist' and used the letters A.M.S. (American Medical Specialist) after his name.[6] He claimed to be an 'alumnus of the Great American Eclectic School' and compared his skills to those of the leading medical clinicians of the day. Eclectic Medicine had expanded during the 1840s as part of a large, populist alternative medical movement in North America. It used many of the principles of Samuel Thomson's herbal medication as well as those of Native American Medicine. Its central philosophy was to practise in 'alignment with nature' and it represented a direct reaction to the use of purges with calomel and other mercury-based remedies employed by regular medicine, especially with respect to venereal afflictions.[7] However, Eastburn's activities in Scotland attracted growing attention from the General Medical Council and, in 1898, he was prosecuted in Glasgow Sheriff Court for falsely implying that he was a registered practitioner in contravention of the Medical Act 1858. Though he was found guilty and fined the maximum penalty of £20, he subsequently successfully appealed his conviction in the High Court of Justiciary, in part because correspondence between the GMC and the sheriff was ruled incompetent and prejudicial to his case.[8]

Despite such legal obstacles, Eastburn's business flourished. The Census of 1891 records him as living in a cottage in East Kilbride with his wife and three children and one servant but, by 1911, he had moved to a large residence in Helensburgh with two servants.[9] Eastburn promoted his practice across Scotland by means of distributing many thousands of handbills and posters [see Figure 2.1].[10] Indeed, so widespread was his operation that, in 1892, he was prosecuted for illegal bill-posting across large areas of central Scotland and subsequently sued by a leading landowner for the same offence.[11]

The posters and handbills, the wording of which changed very little over the years, had many of the salient features that Roy Porter has identified in quack publicity in the long eighteenth century.[12] First and foremost, they were designed to exploit guilt, anxiety, and fear surrounding perceived sexual transgressions, including masturbation (referred to as the 'early violation of Nature's laws') and sexual promiscuity.[13] Thus, in barely disguised reference to venereal disease, he emphasised his expertise in treating 'all manner of troubles, whether arising from youthful INDIVIDUAL indiscretion, the folly of riper years, or hereditary complaints'. His literature continued the quack tradition of linking a wide range of nervous disorders to 'shameful' sexual habits. Secondly, Eastburn's literature made grandiose claims to cure VD, either by means of a personal consultation or by 'the medium of correspondence'. He claimed that:

> It matters not whether the disease is internal or external; nor is it of any consequence how severe the affliction may be, nor of how long standing; neither is it a consideration whether it is one which has been pronounced difficult of cure, or even incurable; Professor Eastburn's system makes all easy.

Again, in line with earlier quack advertisements relating to VD and other sexual afflictions, Eastburn's handbills placed special emphasis on the issue of confidentiality. His promise to diagnose and treat patients by correspondence was primarily designed to allay their fear of exposure and their reluctance to confide in any regular doctor. Similarly, he stressed that any correspondence was unmarked except for the patient's address to ensure that secrecy was 'strict, sure, and inviolate', and that, when required, medicine could be sent to any railway station or post office and marked 'To lie till called for'.

According to Porter, 'the claim to cure the pox without recourse to mercury', with all its toxic side effects, was central to all quack therapies in the eighteenth and early nineteenth centuries,[14] and Eastburn followed in this tradition. In his handbills, he particularly urged 'those ladies and gentleman who [had] become tired of trying to be cured by the use of Mercury and other Mineral Poisons' to seek his services. He duly promised that those who had 'been maltreated by the administration of

Mineral Poisons' could have 'the virus with which their system [had] become contaminated entirely eliminated'. Finally, like other unlicensed healers operating in Europe in the late nineteenth century,[15] Eastburn also deployed religious imagery in his posters and handbills to widen his appeal. He described his dedication to eradicating medical 'evils' as 'a sacred duty' and his treatment regime as 'the greatest boon ever laid at the altar of suffering'. Patients suffering from 'venereal trouble' were encouraged to 'call at his rooms to 'receive the blessing' of 'renewed vigour, of renovated bodily functions, and restoration to all the strength of robust manhood'.

Eastburn's popularity reflected the widespread recourse to unregistered healers and quack remedies in this period. Evidence would suggest that a significant proportion of patients seeking institutional treatment for VD in late nineteenth- and early twentieth-century Scotland did so only after consulting a chemist or herbalist, or trying some advertised cure.[16] The use of self-administered 'alternative' potions and washes for sexual problems and infections was extensive, especially within working-class communities. An official inquiry reported in 1910 that 'in many of the great towns the treatment of venereal diseases [was] in the hands of unqualified persons', and this view was subsequently endorsed by Scottish evidence before the Royal Commission on Venereal Diseases (1913–16).[17]

In part, the demand for quacks and patent medicines was due to the enduring moral stigma attached to VD and the inevitable desire to conceal infection from family and community. A 'conception of venereal diseases as the just retribution of sin', which continued to shape public and philanthropic opinion towards institutional provisions for venereal patients, served merely to reinforce this tendency.[18] As Dr Leslie Mackenzie, Medical Member of the Local Government Board for Scotland, observed in 1907, it was customary to place 'every difficulty in the way of treatment and every indignity on the patient'.[19] VD sufferers were not encouraged to attend voluntary hospitals and, even under the National Health Insurance Act of 1911, 'misconduct clauses' retained the traditional exclusion from friendly society benefits of those afflicted with the disease.[20] In part, recourse to quack treatment was also due to the widespread lack of interest and training of many medical practitioners in venereal cases. Thus, David Watson, Surgeon to the Glasgow Lock Hospital, blamed the apathy of the medical profession for the fact that quacks controlled 'the larger proportion of gonorrhoea practice'.[21]

In addition, avoidance of professional treatment stemmed from an understandable aversion to the prevailing therapies for syphilis and

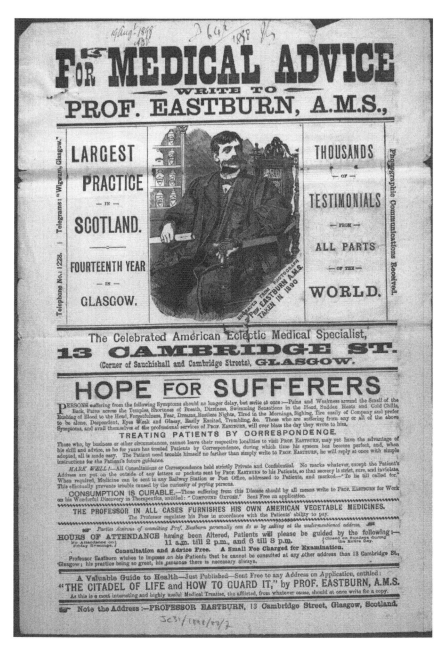

Figure 2.1 Billposter advertising the services of Abraham States Eastburn, 1898
[National Records of Scotland]

(Source: NRS, AD1898/27/7, Justiciary Appeals Processes)

gonorrhoea that were often painful, protracted and dangerous. Medical practices in Edwardian Scotland had not advanced significantly from those in the lock wards of the mid-nineteenth century. Though salivation had become discredited as a cure for syphilis, mercurial treatment, by pills, by inunction using strong ointments, by fumigation with vapour of calomel, or by intramuscular injection, remained the most common therapy for primary and secondary syphilis. Such treatment, commonly prescribed over a period of eighteen months or more, produced a range of symptoms of heavy metal poisoning. Moreover, even if a patient with primary syphilis subjected himself to the rigours of mercurial treatment, there was still a high probability of clinical relapse and/or the development of secondary syphilis.[22] For patients with gonorrhoea, the pills and salves dispensed by chemists and the 'rapid, painless, curative treatment' promised in quack advertisements must also have appeared an appealing alternative to the often brutal, invasive regime of the hospital wards. Thus, cases of acute gonorrhoea were treated in Glasgow Royal Infirmary either with a urethral injection of an antiseptic solution of silver salts every three to four hours or by gravity-fed irrigation of the urethral tract from a reservoir of potassium permanganate suspended up to five feet above the patient. Leeches were not infrequently applied to the scrota of patients with gonococcal epididymitis, while patients suffering from chronic gonococcal urethritis were subjected to an equally painful and hazardous course of dilatation with heated, steel sounds or bougies.[23]

THE SOCIAL POLITICS OF VD

The prosecution of Abraham Eastburn has to be seen against the backdrop of the moral panic surrounding VD in early twentieth-century Scotland that reached its peak during and immediately after World War I.[24] VD was widely perceived to be a 'racial poison' compromising the moral and physical health of the nation. It was increasingly viewed as a function of the breakdown in sexual conduct occasioned by the war and its erosion of traditional constraints upon promiscuity and 'dangerous sexualities'. Such concerns were both reflected in, and reinforced by, the proceedings and report of the Royal Commission on Venereal Diseases, with its startling conclusion that the 'number of persons . . . infected with syphilis, acquired or congenital, cannot fall below ten per cent of the whole population in the large cities, and the percentage affected by gonorrhoea must greatly exceed this proportion'.[25] As the editor of the *Edinburgh Review* observed, VD had been revealed as a 'scourge' that was 'chief among the Captains of Death and Disease'.[26]

Faced with a growing demand for action, the government used emergency powers under the Public Health Acts to introduce a wide-ranging set of regulations and administrative guidelines for the diagnosis, treatment, and prevention of VD.[27] The Public Health (Venereal Diseases) Regulations (Scotland) 1916, which were to form the basis of the Scottish VD Services until 1947, were circulated, along with an explanatory memorandum, on 31 October 1916.[28] Every local authority was required to prepare and submit for approval a 'scheme' for the diagnosis, treatment and prevention of the 'three great venereal diseases' (syphilis, gonorrhoea, and soft chancre). To ensure more effective diagnosis of VD, medical practitioners were to be provided 'without difficulty or delay', free access to the existing bacteriological and pathological laboratories of the medical schools, hospitals and local health authorities and, in particular, to the technical expertise required for the Wassermann test for syphilis. Provision had to be made by local authorities for the free and voluntary treatment of VD cases from 'all classes of the community' in hospitals or other institutions or in their homes. It was anticipated that the bulk of cases would be referred by medical practitioners to the hospitals and clinics but, where home treatment was more appropriate, 'skilled assistance by men trained in the technicalities of the modern methods of diagnosis and treatment of the venereal infections' was to be made available to the practitioner 'free of cost to him or his patient'. In addition, practitioners demonstrating proof of competence in the administration of new forms of chemotherapy were to be freely supplied with Salvarsan or its substitutes. To attract as many cases as possible, the regulations stressed the vital need for strict confidentiality and there was no provision for compulsory notification. The regulations were markedly reticent on the issue of preventive measures other than medical treatment and moral instruction. Mention of alternative strategies involving condoms, prophylactic self-disinfection packets, or the introduction of public ablution centres was significantly absent. Local authorities were merely empowered to provide for 'instructional lectures' and 'the diffusion of information' relating to VD, with priority to be given to its 'far-reaching and disastrous effects on the social efficiency of the family'.

Within the debate shaping these new regulations, the issue of 'quackery' loomed large. The report of the Royal Commission on Venereal Diseases in 1916 was unequivocal in condemning its impact upon public health, stating that:

The effects of unqualified practice are disastrous, and ... [its] continued existence constitutes one of the principal hindrances to the eradication of those diseases. It cannot be too strongly emphasised that the essential point in the control of VD is to secure for the patient the best treatment at the earliest possible moment. By the intervention of the unqualified person the stage at which the permanent eradication of the disease is possible was lost, and the many and terrible after-effects ... may supervene, for although the disease is difficult to cure, symptoms are readily made to disappear. In any case the treatment is rendered more difficult, protracted and expensive, and the risk of the disease being communicated to others is very largely increased.[29]

Accordingly, the Commission recommended that 'all advertisements of remedies for venereal diseases should be prohibited'.[30] Given that 'the direct and indirect effects of these diseases upon the race [were] so grave and the deception practised upon the public [was] so extensive', it also considered more 'repressive measures' that would have made the 'treatment of venereal diseases by unqualified persons a penal offence'. In the absence of an effective public health service for VD patients, this was felt to be premature. However, health administrators in both Whitehall and Edinburgh supported by the NCCVD, local authority associations and the Royal Medical Colleges, increasingly pressed for broader powers to curb the activities of quacks in the diagnosis and treatment of venereal cases and a Venereal Disease Bill was duly introduced in the spring of 1917.[31]

The proposal to grant a monopoly in venereal work to qualified practitioners received a mixed reception in the House of Commons. Opponents argued that medicine was a 'progressive science' that benefited from a range of insights and that the notion of professional infallibility should not be enshrined in legislation. Thus, Sir William Collins, surgeon and Liberal politician, maintained that:

[I]nfallibility in medicine is the monopoly only of the charlatan ... I should be prepared to see the practice of scientific medicine and surgery ... stand upon its own merits without these illegitimate rivals being suppressed under penalty of hard labour or fine. The profession suffers rather than gains by association with the policeman and the gaoler in enforcing its prescriptions ...[32]

Moreover, it was contended that a significant proportion of general practitioners lacked either the expertise and/or motivation to deal with venereal cases and that many so-called 'quacks' were better equipped to deal with them.[33]

Additional concerns were expressed at the undue focus of public health policy on the use of laboratory tests for diagnosis, and on Salvarsan – a patented 'German medicine' – for treatment. It was feared that this reliance would devalue clinical observation and endorse a chemotherapy whose efficacy was still uncertain and whose adverse side effects, sometimes fatal, were widely known.[34] However, the bill was vigorously defended on a number of counts.[35] First and foremost, it was argued that 'specious, fallacious, and pernicious remedies' had to be outlawed in the interests of public health and social hygiene. While it was recognised that the bill challenged the traditional liberty of the subject to choose where he or she sought treatment, VD was presented as a special case given its impact upon national efficiency in peace and war and its devastating effects upon the family and community. It was also stressed that, while the lack of adequate state provisions might previously have excused the use of alternative therapies, the creation of a new nationwide system of free VD clinics rendered such a justification invalid. Furthermore, with the advent of new diagnostic techniques and chemotherapies, such as Salvarsan and Neosalvarsan, health officials insisted that VD had to be treated, and infectivity contained, by the use of 'scientific methods'. In particular, it was contended that Salvarsan treatment required surgical expertise that could be safely administered only by a qualified practitioner. In fact, despite its very considerable benefits in the treatment of syphilis, the emphasis placed on Salvarsan in the debates surrounding the Venereal Disease Bill had as much to do with medical politics as its curative properties.[36] In a period when venereology was emerging as a medical specialty, it furnished a powerful excuse for the suppression of quackery, a long-standing wish of the medical profession. Certainly, the fact that the Venereal Disease Bill effectively gave the profession a monopoly in the handling of venereal cases undoubtedly allayed many of its concerns about the likely impact of the new state-funded VD service upon the independence and livelihood of general practitioners.[37]

In the event, the views of the government prevailed, and under the Venereal Disease Act 1917, only qualified medical practitioners were permitted to treat VD or to prescribe or advise in connection with venereal infections. In an effort to discourage recourse to 'quack' remedies, commonly obtained at chemists, and to strengthen the position of the clinics, it was also enacted that only drugs or other preparations prescribed by a qualified practitioner might be dispensed for the treatment of VD. Heavy penalties were also imposed on those advertising unauthorised consultations or remedies.[38]

THE PROSECUTION CASE

In 1919, in response to mounting pressure from a range of political, medical, and religious pressure groups advancing the cause of social hygiene, the newly created Scottish Board of Health was anxious to promote the system of public health VD clinics that had slowly been established since 1916. A range of constraints operated to frustrate the aims of the Board. There was an acute shortage of medical staff. Despite a Treasury subsidy, many local authorities were reluctant to provide facilities for the treatment of a disease that was widely stigmatised as the outcome of wilful promiscuity. In addition, many voluntary hospitals were resistant to co-operating with the Board's proposals. Some argued that the admission of venereal patients would contravene their constitutions and otherwise 'contaminate' their wards. Others feared that municipal VD schemes might threaten the autonomy of the voluntary hospitals and the status of their medical staff.[39] A further significant constraint, however, was the continuing extent of unqualified treatment persisting in interwar Scotland, in spite of the fact that, by 1919, the 1917 Act had been applied by order of the Scottish Board of Health to all the major Scottish towns and cities in which VD schemes had been established.[40]

When complaints against Abraham Eastburn first surfaced, Scottish public health authorities and law officers were therefore predisposed to pursue the case as a deterrent to others. It is clear from evidence previously submitted by a Scottish law officer to a parliamentary inquiry in 1918 that Eastburn's activities had been under scrutiny for some years. The wording of Eastburn's handbills had been quoted verbatim as an example of the type of practice that merited prosecution.[41] The police were also aware that, on a number of occasions, accusations of blackmail had been levelled at him by patients suffering from VD, and that only their overriding desire to remain anonymous had prevented charges being brought.[42] Once J. Drummond Strathern, Procurator Fiscal in Glasgow, had been alerted by the Medical Officer of Health to Copley's case, Eastburn was arrested and his premises searched, and Copley questioned at length.[43] From the record slips found in Eastburn's consulting rooms, it was immediately evident that he was operating a highly lucrative business based on the supposed prevention and treatment of VD in patients across Scotland and the north of England. Strathern advised the Crown Office that, in addition to the treatment of Copley, many more charges could be brought. As, in his view, the case might be the 'most important prosecution to date', he recommended that it should be heard before a higher court where the penalties for conviction would be greater. In view of the difficulty of obtaining evidence from other victims who might be loath to reveal their condition to local doctors, Strathern secured permission to precognosce them in Glasgow. On his recommendation, all were medically examined by John Glaister, Regius Professor of Forensic Medicine and Public Health at the University of Glasgow, and by Dr John Anderson of the Victoria Infirmary, and a single report produced for the court proceedings. In addition, they were required to comment on the report of the City Analyst on the 'various tablets, powders and liquids' seized from Eastburn's premises, and to examine his patient record slips for references to VD.

In the process of assembling a prosecution case, the Fiscal's office was focused on obtaining evidence on a specific set of issues. It sought to establish, first, that Eastburn was knowingly, and for financial reward, advising and treating patients with venereal afflictions; secondly, that his 'remedies' were largely worthless, ignoring modern forms of diagnosis and chemotherapy and leaving his patients in a deteriorating and infective state; and finally that his whole operation was designed to defraud the public at the expense of the nation's health.

Witness statements and medical reports duly addressed all these issues. Evidence clearly indicated that Eastburn (known throughout the city of Glasgow as 'Professor Eastburn') was operating a highly lucrative business from Berkeley Terrace, with an income of many thousands of pounds per annum. His premises included twelve to fifteen waiting rooms, a consulting room, an office and caretaker's accommodation. He attracted patients by means of handbills that were 'extensively delivered in the public street, by small posters in public lavatories, and in special handbills for country districts'. Specific venues such as shipyard gates or race meetings at Ayr were especially targeted. His case records clearly indicated that a large proportion of his patients consulted him on venereal infections. Medical reports indicated that some 50 per cent of the record slips found in Eastburn's premises bore words or notations relating to VD.

After charging an initial consultation fee of £1, reduced to 10 shillings for 'working men', Eastburn contrived to furnish a diagnosis that would justify lengthy and expensive courses of treatment. Typically, he would add a few drops of liquid to a sample of the patient's urine that created a 'whitish substance' variously described as having a 'feathery appearance' or the appearance of 'the white of an egg'. On the basis of this he would declare that the patient's 'nature or vitality was passing into his water' and that he needed an extended period of treatment not only for syphilis but also 'nervousness' and 'constitutional weakness'. Charges for this combined course, which were usually paid in instalments over a period of six to twelve months, varied from around £40 to as much as £265 in the case of Natale Battilana, a 29-year-old Glaswegian, (equivalent to around £1,658 and £10,880 respectively in 2017 prices, calculated using the retail price index).

For these very considerable sums, Eastburn's patients normally received, either in person or by post, a mixture of coloured tablets – some 'yellowish', some 'greenish' and some 'chocolate coloured'. In some cases a liquid wash was also dispensed for the treatment of syphilitic sores. According to one patient, Eastburn was adamantly opposed to injections, claiming that they 'were not so successful' and often led to 'blood poisoning supervening'. According to the testimony of Glasgow's City Analyst and medical witnesses for the prosecution, there was clear evidence from a sample of medications seized by the police that Eastburn had been treating VD. His potions included a solution of potassium permanganate, commonly known as Condy's fluid and employed in cases of gonorrhoea by means of a syringe as an injection into the urethra. A 'dilute solution' of acid nitrate of mercury, traditionally used in the treatment of venereal sores, was also found, as were bottles labelled Liq. Cop (the resin from the Copaiba tree of South America) and Liq. Santal Co. (an oil distilled from the wood of *Santalum album*, an Indian tree), often prescribed for use internally for gonorrhoea.[44]

It was equally evident, however, that Eastburn was not employing effective remedies that properly addressed the medical needs of his patients. He did not use Salvarsan or its derivatives, and the mercurial preparations that he did possess were not recognised by medical experts as having any curative value.[45] Other remedies found in his premises contained tannic acid, phosphorus, lead acetate, and atropine, a naturally occurring alkaloid extracted from deadly nightshade. The tablets, from which Eastburn derived the bulk of his income, were found merely to contain 'vegetable matter of an unrecognised kind'.

Not only did the evidence suggest that Eastburn was failing to provide safe and effective treatment, it was also apparent from witness statements that, after an expensive and protracted course of his medication, patients were often diagnosed as 'cured' when, in fact, they were still highly infectious. Thus, after two courses of treatment (coloured tablets) for syphilis costing £60, William Laurie, a 29-year-old patient from Scotstown, was told by Eastburn that 'it [was] all right'. Within weeks, however, Glaister and Anderson found him to be still positive for syphilis on the Wassermann test. Similarly, although James Higginson, a 45-year-old riveter from Whiteinch, had been declared cured by Eastburn in late 1919, Dr David Watson, head of the VD Centre at Glasgow Royal Infirmary, subsequently testified that the patient was still visibly suffering from a primary syphilitic sore that was not a fresh infection. Watson affirmed that, although his diagnosis was duly confirmed by a Wassermann test, the syphilis 'was clearly apparent on clinical grounds'. One witness, Natale Batillana, had recently married having been assured by Eastburn that he was 'quite free of the disease'. Yet, medical evidence showed him also to be positive on the Wassermann test and to be suffering from syphilis.

THE OUTCOME

In the event, Eastburn was indicted before the High Court in Glasgow in February 1920 on twelve charges of contravening the Venereal Disease Act 1917. At a preliminary pleading diet, objections to six of the charges were sustained on grounds of 'irrelevancy'.[46] These were cases where Eastburn had merely examined patients and/or offered to treat them. In the view of the presiding judge, Lord Salvesen, 'willingness to commit a contravention of the Act [did] not constitute a contravention. There was nothing in the Act which [made] it illegal for an unqualified medical practitioner to examine a person and to tell him what was wrong with him'. A contravention could be 'relevantly alleged' only if he 'healed him or prescribed any remedy or gave advice as to how the man should treat himself'. At the second diet on 24 February 1920, after hearing evidence for some six hours, the jury found Eastburn guilty on four of the six remaining counts. In passing sentence of six months' imprisonment, Lord Salvesen observed that 'he was afraid he would not be doing his duty to society if he did not impose a sentence which was at all events a deterrent'. Eastburn also incurred a substantial financial penalty. Having found irregularities in his financial accounts, the Crown Office reported him to the tax authorities and facilitated their access to the records that the police had seized from his consulting rooms. However, after Eastburn had served four months' imprisonment, the Secretary of State for Scotland recommended in June 1920 that the remainder of his sentence be remitted. There is no record of his subsequent activities. He died in 1937, at the age of eighty-two in Helensburgh of 'cerebral degeneration' and 'asthenia', the death certificate duly recording his profession as 'Medical Specialist (retired)'.

There is no evidence in High Court records of any further prosecutions in Scotland under the 1917 Act. It is possible that some cases were heard in sheriff or magistrates' courts but their records are not available and no press reports relating to such cases have been identified. In part, this may be explained by the gradual decline in public and political interest in VD after 1922. As S. M. Tomkins has concluded:

> No doubt sheer ennui was a factor, as was growing concern with Britain's other social and economic ills in the interwar period. Following the anticipated post-war high, rates of new infections began to drop, and although venereal diseases remained a major source of death and misery the sense of crisis which had characterized the late 1910s and early 1920s began to diminish.[47]

Thus, though in Scotland the interwar years saw a sustained campaign by local health authorities and venereologists to introduce compulsory notification and/or treatment for VD, a good deal of the moral panic that had impelled the prosecution of Eastburn began to dissipate.

It is possible that a decline in prosecutions of unqualified practitioners under the 1917 Act may also have been a function of the increasing provision of VD clinics across Scotland providing free, less judgemental, specialist advice and treatment. However, scattered evidence suggests that this is not the case. Despite the vigilance of the police and health authorities, a significant amount of unqualified treatment persisted in Scotland throughout the interwar period, and adverts for 'alternative' therapies continued to appear in the popular press.[48] Such practice was encouraged by the continuing policy of many Approved Societies of withholding health insurance benefits from VD patients on the grounds that their incapacity was due to misconduct. David Lees, venereologist in charge of Edinburgh Corporation's VD Scheme, considered that in the mid-1920s there were still more people obtaining unqualified and illicit treatment than having recourse to the clinics; a view he reiterated in his annual report for 1930.[49] Evidently, the trial and conviction of Abraham States Eastburn had not proved the deterrent hoped for by the Scottish Board of Heath and Crown Office. Many 'quacks', albeit operating on a more modest scale than Eastburn, continued to exploit the social stigma and not infrequent medical negligence surrounding venereal disease.

NOTES

1. *Glasgow Herald*, 17 November 1919.
2. Unless otherwise stated, the following account is based on National Records of Scotland [hereafter NRS], AD15/20/62, Crown Office precognitions in the case against Abraham States Eastburn.

3. For a discussion of the activities and ideology of the NCCVD, see especially, Tomkins, 'Palmitate or permanganate', 382–98.
4. Walton and Reeder, *The Eastburn Family*, 179, 185.
5. NRS, CS275/44/36, Court of Session, Abraham S. Eastburn: Suspension: Respondent William H. Hale, 1882.
6. NRS, JC31/1898/27, papers relating to Bill of Suspension by Abraham S. Eastburn, 1898.
7. http://en.wikipedia.org/wiki/Eclectic medicine (last accessed 11 January 2018); Porter, *Quacks: Fakers and Charlatans*, 203–4.
8. NRS, JC31/1898/27, papers relating to Bill of Suspension by Abraham S. Eastburn, 1898; *British Medical Journal* [hereafter *BMJ*], 23 July 1898, 277; 26 November 1898, 1657.
9. Census Records for 1891, Return 643/00 006/00 004; Census Records for 1911, Return 503/00 002/00 030.
10. Legal evidence in 1898 in Glasgow Sheriff Court referred to the printing of 20,000 large bills in the course of a year and '100,000 of the small handbills . . . ordered at a time, though the delivery was spread over a long period' [*BMJ*, 23 July 1898, 277].
11. NRS, JC31/1892/26, Justiciary Appeal by Abraham States Eastburn, medical specialist, and Thomas Jones, bill poster, 1892; CS46/1899/10/41, Decree of suspension and interdict and for payment of expenses, *Sir Michael Robert Shaw Stewart of Greenock and Blackhall, Baronet* v. *Abraham States Eastburn* [1899].
12. Porter, *Quacks: Fakers and Charlatans*, Ch. 6.
13. Unless otherwise stated, the following is based on the posters and handbills in NRS, JC31/1898/27.
14. Porter, *Quacks: Fakers and Charlatans*, 136.
15. de Blécourt, 'Prosecution and popularity', 83–6.
16. In giving evidence to the High Court in 1915, Charles Alder, a herbalist operating in both Edinburgh and Glasgow, testified that there was a constant demand for his services in treating VD and that he had '50 cases regularly'. Such was the publicity surrounding his activities and the growing public disquiet at the presence of his billboards on Edinburgh's city centre streets that, in 1916, the Royal College of Physicians of Edinburgh initiated legal proceedings against him for fraudulently claiming to be a medical doctor in contravention of the Medical Act 1858 [RCPE Archives, RCP/FEL/3/7, trial transcript in the case of *Lord Advocate* v. *Alder*, 115–17; papers relating to the case of *RCPE* v. *Dr Temple Co. Ltd*].
17. *Report on the Practice of Medicine and Surgery by Unqualified Persons*, 15–16; *Royal Commission on Venereal Diseases* [hereafter *RCVD*], *Minutes of Evidence*, 351; *Final Report*, 75–6.
18. *Local Government Board, Report on Venereal Diseases*, 26.
19. *Royal Commission on the Poor Laws and Relief of Distress, Oral and Written Evidence from Scottish Witnesses*, 185.

20. Newman (Surgeon to the Glasgow Royal Infirmary), 'The history and prevention of venereal disease', 167–8.

21. Watson, *Gonorrhoea and its Complications*, vi.

22. Wheeler and Jack (Assistant Physician to Glasgow Western Infirmary), *Handbook of Medicine and Therapeutics*, 91–2; Munro (Physician to Glasgow Royal Infirmary), *Manual of Medicine*, 138–9.

23. Watson, *Gonorrhoea and its Complications*, Chs 5, 7.

24. See especially, Davidson, *Dangerous Liaisons*, Ch. 2.

25. *Final Report of RCVD*, 23.

26. *Edinburgh Review*, vol. 223 (1916), 363.

27. On the social politics surrounding these initiatives, see especially Davidson, *Dangerous Liaisons*, Ch. 2; Evans, 'Tackling the "Hideous Scourge"', 413–33.

28. *Local Government Board for Scotland, Venereal Diseases: Circulars issued on 31st October 1916.*

29. *Final Report of RCVD*, 75–6.

30. Ibid., 75–6.

31. Evans, 'Tackling the "Hideous Scourge"', 438.

32. *Hansard (HC)*, vol. 92, 23 April 1917, col. 2100.

33. Ibid., col. 2086.

34. Ibid., cols 2085, 2121, 2123–4.

35. Ibid., cols 2071–80, speech by the Parliamentary Secretary to the Local Government Board.

36. Ross and Tomkins, 'The British reception of Salvarsan', 411–12, 418–21.

37. Evans, 'Tackling the "Hideous Scourge"', 422–3.

38. *Venereal Disease Act 1917 (7 & 8 Geo. 5, c.21).*

39. Davidson, *Dangerous Liaisons*, 49–51.

40. Ibid., 83–4.

41. *Joint Select Committee on the Criminal Law Amendment Bill, Minutes of Evidence*, q. 3046.

42. NRS, AD15/20/62, note by J. D. Strathern, Procurator Fiscal, 20 January 1920.

43. Unless otherwise stated, the following account is based on NRS, AD15/20/62, Crown Office precognitions in the case against Abraham States Eastburn.

44. This product had been the subject of prosecution and seizure in the United States in 1919 under the Food and Drug Act for fraudulent misbranding and misrepresentation.

45. In fairness to Eastburn, evidence at his trial revealed that many family doctors were also ignorant of the latest diagnostic and therapeutic techniques. In the case of William Laurie, despite suffering from syphilis, his 'own doctor did not tell him what was wrong and merely gave him a bottle'. Similarly, Thomas Hutchinson, a 30-year-old electrician, stated that his family doctor had merely 'prescribed carbolic acid for spots on

his penis' that were subsequently diagnosed by John Glaister and John Anderson as syphilitic. Even where institutional treatment was sought, outdated methods of treatment might still prevail. At Liverpool Medical Hall, having been diagnosed with secondary syphilis, Richard Copley was given a box of 'yellowish ointment for his back passage', a series of mercury injections, some mercury and chalk tablets, and Lambkins Cream, yet another mercurial preparation. A Wassermann test was not conducted and Salvarsan or its derivatives were not used.

46. The following account is based upon *Glasgow Herald*, 25 February 1920; *The Scotsman*, 16 and 25 February 1920; NRS, AD15/20/62, Crown Office precognitions in the case against Abraham States Eastburn; JC15/31, Books of Adjournal; JC13/132, Minute Book of West Circuit Court of Justiciary; 1937, Statutory Deaths 503/00 00031.

47. Tomkins, 'Palmitate or permanganate', 397.

48. Edinburgh Public Health Department [hereinafter EPHD], *Annual Report for 1922*, 43; T. F. Dewar, 'On the incidence of venereal disease', 330; Scottish Board of Health, *Eighth Annual Report*, PP 1927 (Cmd. 2881) X, 82.

49. Dewar, 'On the incidence of venereal disease', 330; EPHD, *Annual Report for 1930*, 74.

3

'This Pernicious Delusion': Law, Medicine and Child Sexual Abuse[1]

THE 'ABOMINABLE SUPERSTITION'

In January 1913, Robert James Corbett, a 37-year-old coalminer, was indicted in the High Court, Glasgow, on a charge of raping his nine-year-old niece and of the aggravated offence of communicating to her 'gonorrhoea and other venereal disease with which his private parts were at the time affected'. In preparation for the trial, Crown Counsel specifically requested the Procurator Fiscal to question prosecution witnesses as to 'whether there exists a common superstition . . . that intercourse with a virgin is a cure for venereal disease'.[2] The enquiry elicited a revealing consensus among medical witnesses. Dr J. M. Thompson of Aidrie responded: 'It is a common belief among the lower classes that connection with a virgin will cure a venereal disease.' Similarly, Dr Elizabeth Smith, Physician to Glasgow Lock Hospital, considered it to be 'a widespread idea . . . in all the lower classes that contact with an untouched virgin [would] cure the disease'. The evidence of Dr James Devon, HM Prison Surgeon, was even more sweeping:

> There is a curiously persistent and widespread belief that a man who suffers from venereal disease can get rid of it by having connection with a virgin. I have been surprised at discovering the existence of this belief in people generally well informed as well as among the comparatively illiterate . . . I have tried to find evidence for the theory that it is a belief traceable to certain districts but I have discovered it among people of different places and of different occupations – so different that now I should scarcely be surprised to come across it anywhere.[3]

There is, of course, in Britain and elsewhere in Europe and North America, a wealth of historical evidence for the earlier persistence of such a belief, both in medical folklore[4] and legal discourse, normally portrayed as a superstition of the 'lower orders', but also frequently associated with xenophobic, if not racial, stereotyping.[5] In twentieth-century Scotland, a range of contemporary sources echoed the testimony of the High Court prosecution witnesses that belief in the curative powers of sexual congress with a virgin as a medical strategy remained potent within medical folklore.

As Carol Smart has vividly documented, evidence before the Royal Commission on Venereal Diseases (1913–16), especially from rescue workers and from surgeons working in the lock hospitals, testified to the extent of child infection contracted as a result of sexual assault and the continuing role of 'the abominable superstition that intercourse with a virgin cures venereal disease in a man'.[6] The Medical Women's Federation presented similar testimony in evidence to the Joint Select Committee on the Criminal Law Amendment and Sexual Offences Bills in 1920.[7]

More immediately, the prevalence of 'this appalling idea', 'this strange belief, widespread and of old origin' is a common theme in the evidence presented to the Departmental Committee on Sexual Offences against Children and Young Persons in Scotland (1924–25). Psychologist, J. J. Murray, identified this belief, along with feeblemindedness and a general predisposition to 'viciousness', as a major factor in motivating sexual offenders, and a range of police witnesses echoed this view.[8] Indeed, one of the committee's recommendations insisted: 'It should be made known publicly that this is an ignorant superstition, which has no foundation in fact',[9] a task that was devolved to the Scottish Committee of the British Social Hygiene Council.

Significantly, this 'ignorant superstition' also figured in leading contemporary texts on forensic medicine. Thus, in the first five editions of his *Textbook on Forensic Medicine* (1902–31), John Glaister, Professor of Forensic Medicine and Public Health at the University of Glasgow maintained that:

> It is a fact beyond dispute, owing to the prevalence of a widespread belief amongst persons of the lowest classes, that coitus with a healthy young person of the opposite sex will cure them of gonorrhoea, that gonorrhoeal infection is conveyed to young children – especially females – and hence it is that rape upon young female children under twelve years of age is so prevalent.[10]

Such views were all the more influential, given the prominent role played by men such as Glaister in court proceedings involving the communication of VD.

CONFRONTING 'CHILD ABUSE': THE IMPULSES

The question arises as to why this so-called 'pernicious delusion' involving sexual offences against children should have figured so markedly within legal and medical discourses in early twentieth-century Scotland. Its widespread invocation was, of course, part of a more general crisis of confidence in public order and public morality. As in many other countries at the turn of the century, VD had become a metaphor for physical and moral decay, for the forces of pollution and contamination that appeared to threaten the institutions of social order and racial progress. Alarm over the issue of VD, especially its more repugnant forms of transmission, therefore offered an opportunity to express concern about changing standards of conduct and the moral values of society. Given the supposedly wilful nature of its spread and its threat to social hygiene, it also provided a powerful justification for the social construction and proscription of 'dangerous sexualities'.

A key issue, addressed by the new medico-moral agenda at the level of both the central and local state, was the need to penalise the wilful transmission of VD, which not only offended against conventional rules of moral conduct but also abrogated the health responsibilities of citizenship as defined by the social hygiene movement. At the centre of the discourse surrounding such initiatives was the concern to reduce the level of child sexual exploitation.[11] It was 'child outrage' that, to a significant extent, fuelled the campaign of feminists, rescue workers and purity activists after 1916 to amend the criminal law in respect to sexual offences and which informed a succession of private members' bills through to the mid-1920s.[12]

Such proposals resonated with regional and local concerns and initiatives. Significantly, it had been public outrage at the number of young girls in the Glasgow Lock Hospital who had been infected through sexual assault that had triggered the establishment of the National Vigilance Association in Scotland in 1909. Similarly, it was after a child assault case in Edinburgh in January 1920, in which a young girl had been infected with VD, that a Child Outrage Committee was established. In its subsequent submission to the Lord Advocate, the committee's central recommendation was that the communication of VD in such cases should be an aggravating offence under statute law so that the severity of the crime should be fully recognised and adequately reflected in sentencing. With support from the Medical Women's Federation and the Scottish Society for the Prevention of Cruelty to Children, the Child Outrage Committee also continued to campaign for the use of women doctors, police officers, and court officials to support children through the medical and legal ordeal of criminal prosecution proceedings. Such views clearly informed the evidence presented to the Departmental Committee on Sexual Offences against Children and Young Persons in Scotland in 1924–25. Though eschewing the more draconian measures advocated by police witnesses, such as the more liberal use of the 'Cat' [whipping], castration, or 'exposure to the "X" rays', women's organisations and social hygiene activists pressed for stiffer statutory penalties in respect to the aggravated offence of communicating VD, and for the compulsory notification to the police by medical authorities of all cases of VD in girls under the age of sixteen.[13] The Committee recommended action on both counts.[14]

Yet, perhaps the most revealing reflection of contemporary concerns surrounding sexual offences against children was in the new vigour with which Scottish law officers after 1910 deployed Scots common law to penalise offenders who communicated VD to young girls as a consequence of rape, attempt to ravish, or lewd or libidinous practices.[15] There was clear precedent in Scots common law, dating back to the mid-nineteenth century, for the transmission of venereal disease to constitute an aggravated offence in cases of sexual offences against children,[16] and a handful of such cases had been prosecuted within the sheriff courts. However, it was only after 1910 that the law officers, perhaps in response to the moral panic that was sweeping the Scottish cities, fully utilised their authority and instructed the procurators fiscal to ensure that such crimes were heard before the High Court rather than in the Sheriff Courts. In the words of Lord Dundee in the case of William Armstrong, tried at Glasgow High Court in February 1912 for using lewd, indecent and libidinous practices towards three young girls and infecting them with VD, this was 'one of the most foul crimes upon the calendar'.[17] Thereafter, a steady succession of such cases (some thirty-four in all) appeared before the Scottish High Courts up to the late 1930s.[18]

Unfortunately, there are no surviving transcripts of these cases. Moreover, as the court invariably directed that evidence be heard in camera, only the plea, verdict and sentence were routinely reported in the press. However, we do have restricted access to the precognitions (statements of prosecution witnesses), justiciary processes (case papers) and minutes (record of court proceedings). They reveal important shifts in the use of medical evidence and expertise in the prosecution of child sexual assault. First, the power of medical evidence in securing convictions was directly related to the growing sophistication of diagnostic techniques for VD, including the Wassermann reaction blood test for syphilis, and, more important, the use of microscopic examination of gram-stained smears and culture tests in the detection of gonorrhoea.[19] What one sees in the case papers is a shift over time to increasingly systematic medical procedures for obtaining forensic evidence from the sexual organs both of the victim and the offender. Prosecutors also increasingly relied on the evidence presented by a small pool of scientific and medical specialists rather than the clinical observations of general practitioners. The expert witnesses included John Anderson, patholo-gist at Glasgow Victoria Infirmary, Joseph Hume Patterson, pathologist to the Venereal Disease Scheme for the County of Lanark, William Tulloch, Professor of Bacteriology at the University of St Andrews, Harvey Littlejohn, Professor of Forensic Medicine at the University of Edinburgh, John Glaister, Littlejohn's counterpart in Glasgow, and Andrew Allison, University Assistant to Glaister and latterly a police surgeon lecturing in medical jurisprudence at St Mungo's College. After 1916, these specialists were increasingly reliant on the laboratories des-ignated for each VD Scheme under the Public Health (Venereal Diseases) Regulations (Scotland) 1916; in particular, the Glasgow Corporation Public Health Laboratory and the laboratory of the Royal College of Physicians of Edinburgh which serviced the Edinburgh Corporation VD Scheme.

This appears to be part of a broader process by which medical exper-tise, armed with new technologies of microscopy and bacteriology, was accorded an authoritative role within the legal process.[20] In Scotland, the long-standing association between forensic medicine and public health, stemming from continental ideologies of 'medical police', possibly rein-forced this role.[21] Certainly, the process of accommodation between medical knowledge and legal evidence is clearly visible, with both an increasing use by the courts in such cases of the technical language of diagnosis and a clear focusing of medical reports on key issues surround-ing the timing, duration and communicability of venereal infection.[22]

The archives also suggest that, within the Scottish legal system, there were significant, albeit slow and limited, advances in the recognition of the need to 'feminise' the criminal justice system in the interests of child victims of sexual assault.[23] Under pressure from purity groups, such as the National Vigilance Association, and women's organisations, such as the Medical Women's Federation and Women Citizens' Association, police authorities appointed policewomen in Glasgow and Edinburgh with a specific remit to investigate and oversee cases of child sexual assault. By the mid-1920s, in such cases, female officers would frequently (but by no means invariably) interview the child, attend any medical examination, take charge of collating the forensic evidence and other witness statements, and give 'moral' support to the victim and other female witnesses in court.[24] An analysis of the High Court cases involving the communication of VD indicates that these procedures increasingly became the norm after their validation by the Departmental Committee on Sexual Offences in Scotland in 1926.

CONFRONTING 'CHILD ABUSE': THE CONTINUING CONSTRAINTS'

High Court proceedings involving the communication of VD, however, along with public health archives, also reveal enduring resistance within the medical profession and judiciary to recognising child sexual 'abuse'. Two main levels of denial persisted:[25] first, that the symptoms displayed by the girls were indications of venereal disease; and secondly, that, if the disease *was* venereal, that it had been transmitted through sexual contact.[26] In many cases, local medical practitioners, who frequently played a decisive role in determining whether the police became involved, can be found uncritically echoing the warning of nineteenth- and early twentieth-century medical jurists that vaginal discharges in young girls were likely to be the result of 'worms or uncleanly habits' or a range of other non-venereal factors relating to poor hygiene and social deprivation.[27] As Louise Jackson has argued, medical interpretations of bodily signs in cases of sexual assault 'were coloured by class as well as gender prejudices' and possible signs of abuse were read 'within a wider symbolic framework' based on the cultural meanings of disease, dirt and pollution.[28]

Thus, in many of the High Court cases, the initial treatment prescribed was merely 'a wash' for the child's privates. In the case of Jessie B., sexually assaulted by her father in 1913 in their Glasgow tenement flat, the GP's assistant found the discharge 'leucorrheal' in character, and 'judged it to be due to general uncleanliness of the house' and 'lack of personal cleanliness' and 'fingering of the parts' rather than 'criminal interference'.[29] His views were shared by the School Board Medical Officer who testified that 'the infection could certainly [have been] conveyed from one child to another by means of towels, clothes etc.', given that they shared a bed. Similarly, in the case of several girls abused by William Barclay at his confectioner's in Aberdeen over a period of years from 1913, while examination of their sores and blood at Aberdeen Royal Infirmary eventually established that they were all suffering from secondary syphilis, initial diagnoses by local GPs included 'piles' and 'rupture'.[30]

Hospital doctors could also be dismissive. Catherine S., a nine-year-old who had been raped and infected by a neighbour's eighteen-year-old son in 1910, was seen three times at Glasgow Royal Infirmary without a venereal disease being acknowledged.[31] According to the child's mother, on the first occasion, the doctor merely 'told [her] to bathe her but did not tell [her] what was wrong'. On the following day, she was again told to 'bathe her and keep her clean', advice that was repeated a fortnight later, despite the child continuing to suffer from swollen labia and a persistent vaginal discharge. Similarly, according to the mother's evidence in the case of Lizzie Jane Mc., a nine-year-old who had been sexually assaulted by her uncle in 1912, the doctor at Glasgow Eastern General Hospital:

> said she must have had worms, and he gave me a powder with which to bathe her. He did not examine her. I do not know why he did not do so. I explained to him about the matter going on to her drawers, but still he did not examine her.[32]

Instead, the mother was given some powder to apply with a pad of cotton wadding. Likewise, in a case in Bo'ness in 1921, a mother reported that a lady doctor had initially 'said that it arose from the child getting dirt about her parts, and she gave me some lotion'.[33] Medical witnesses for the defence were particularly prone to advance non-venereal explanations. Thus, in the prosecution of Donald Noble at the High Court in Aberdeen in 1917, Dr Nicolson testified that, although he had not microscopically tested the discharges from the two girls involved, in his opinion it was a simple case of vaginitis. 'I have', he argued, 'many a time seen it in other children – it arises from filth, strumous [scrofulous] children get it and it often follows measles'.[34] Although the increasing reliance on microscopy in the preparation of prosecution evidence eroded the power of such assumptions, it is likely that they continued to inhibit the access of young girls who had been infected as a result of sexual assault to appropriate medical treatment and recourse to the law.

The second level of denial, which refused to believe that VD in children had been sexually transmitted, was also much in evidence within contemporary legal and public health discourse. As Karen Taylor has revealed, there was powerful precedent for the refusal of medical practitioners to make an explicit connection between child VD and sexual contact with adults, even when immediate family members were infected. According to Taylor, a growing stress in the later nineteenth century on 'innocent' (fomitic) infections from contaminated objects in the house-hold, such as soiled clothing, bedding or personal utensils, enabled the medical profession to appear environmentally active while still denying a 'sexual abuse' aetiology.[35]

As Carol Smart has noted, fomitic explanations continued to inform the medical approach to VD (especially gonorrhoea) in young children well into the second half of the twentieth century.[36] Certainly, they dominate the explanations advanced by Scottish health authorities throughout the interwar period, even where the child's disease was clearly linked to infection in adults. A scatter of quotations from the annual reports of Edinburgh's Public Health Department is revealing:

> 1924: A small percentage of these cases was due to criminal assault; the large number resulted from contamination from clothing, towels, etc. in the home.[37]

> 1925: [the increase in cases of vulvo vaginitis] proves the need of bringing home to adult patients suffering from gonorrhoea the importance of personal cleanliness in their homes and the danger of infecting young girls by contaminated towels, clothing, baths, sponges etc.[38]

> 1936: [the reduction in incidence of vulvo vaginitis] indicates that adults infected with gonorrhoea are seeking advice earlier and profiting from the warnings about infectivity of discharges and how to avoid spread of infection. Improved housing conditions, with the steady lessening of overcrowding, and better sanitary facilities must also exert an influence in preventing the contiguity which favours accidental infection.[39]

Such views were also strongly articulated both in textbooks and university lectures on forensic medicine and venereology.[40] In addition, they recurred in the medical witness statements in High Court proceedings. Thus, in the case of Jessie B., previously cited, the School Board Medical Officer was adamant that she had 'no means of knowing how the child became infected' but that 'the infection could certainly be conveyed from one child to another by means of towels, clothing etc. especially as this child and her sister shared one bed'.[41] Similarly, in the case of Jane McLaren P., heard before the High Court in Perth in 1913, the prosecution case had to be constructed regardless of the family doctor's view that the girl might have contracted the disease 'from infected clothing, without there having been penetration'.[42] In 1929, Dr Robert Black was equally committed to a fomitic explanation of events when giving evidence as a defence witness in the trial of Henry Thompson at the High Court in Glasgow on charges of attempting to ravish a young girl in his home and of communicating VD to her. Despite clear evidence from laboratory tests that both the victim and defendant were suffering from gonorrhoea, Black was insistent that:

> The disease the child is suffering from could be contracted in other ways than by contact with a male organ. In my own experience I have had cases of children having contracted the disease when there was no possibility of any assault. One way it can be contracted is by the child coming in contact with soiled linen. It is very easy for a child to contract the disease quite apart from being interfered with by a male person.[43]

Finally, this form of denial was perhaps at its most evident in the absence of any reference to sexual assault in the VD legislation proposed in Scotland during the campaign for compulsory VD controls.[44] During the 1920s, nearly 20 per cent of female cases but only 3 per cent of male cases attending Scottish VD clinics were under the age of fifteen, and this sixfold difference continued into the 1930s.[45] However, the implications of these statistics for revealing possible levels of sexual assault were not addressed. Even when draft legislation, such as the Venereal Disease (Children) Scotland Bill 1923 and the Edinburgh Corporation Venereal Disease Bill 1928, would have compelled parents of infected children to undergo medical examination and treatment, the issue of congenital or fomitic transmission was discussed, but not sexual transmission.

Additional constraints operated on the use of medical evidence in establishing sexual assault. While the application of new diagnostic techniques provided powerful clues for identifying an assailant, the medical evidence remained contentious and often problematic from a legal standpoint.[46] A common problem for the prosecution was establishing the date on which the venereal disease had been transmitted and 'the latitude in libelling the time of an indictment' was not infrequently the subject of legal objection.[47] Other complications included the lag between alleged sexual assault and the onset of venereal symptoms; the problem of obtaining clear-cut, uncontested forensic evidence, especially if there had been a delay in initiating legal proceedings; and the difficulty of establishing the infectiousness of the offender at a particular juncture, especially when the defendant had sought treatment immediately after the offence when the acute clinical symptoms had disappeared (as with tertiary syphilis and secondary gonorrhoea),[48] or when the defendant/ victim had a previous history of infection. Thus, in the sad case of Isabella Gibson C., heard before the High Court in Glasgow in 1921, the prosecution's case against her uncle was greatly complicated by the fact that she had previously been infected by her grandfather and the medical experts could not state absolutely 'whether it was a recurrence or fresh infection'.[49] The absence of VD in a wife could also be cited in a man's defence. In addition, where sexual penetration was difficult to prove, additional medical testimony had to be employed to convince the court that VD could be transmitted purely by contact with the 'private parts'.[50]

In some cases the issue of confidentiality threatened to impair the presentation of medical evidence. A central feature in the promotion of the state-funded system of VD clinics after 1916 was a commitment to medical confidentiality, without which it was feared that those who suspected that they might be infected might be deterred from seeking early diagnosis and treatment. The judiciary was of the view, however, 'that the doctor's duty to inform the law trumped any duty of confidentiality to the patient'. As a result, the early interwar years proved to be a period of particularly intense debate over how far medical professionals might appropriately be compelled to participate in legal proceedings.[51] Thus, in the case of David Smith, sentenced at the High Court in Edinburgh in 1924 for sexual assault, incest and the communication of VD, Dr Walter Brown, the superintendent of Heathfield Hospital declined to have his medical report on the defendant's venereal status used as a production in court, arguing that it might 'undermine the usefulness of the hospital in healing VD' and 'make him liable for damages'.[52] In the event, Smith pleaded guilty at Ayr Sheriff Court and was referred for sentencing without trial but not before the Procurator Fiscal had responded to Brown that 'communications made by a person to his medical attendant were not privileged, and that while there was no desire to force a medical man to disclose communications of a confidential nature, the interests of justice sometimes made that necessary'.

The prosecution of Henry Thompson in 1929 exposed similar tensions between law officers and clinicians over the use of laboratory reports for trial purposes. Both Dr Mary Liston, venereologist at the Royal Infirmary of Edinburgh, and her father, Colonel W. G. Liston, Director of the laboratory of the Royal College of Physicians of Edinburgh, had submitted medical reports identifying gonorrhoea in both the defendant and victim but were strongly opposed to giving evidence in court. As Colonel Liston pointed out, the rules of the Royal College's laboratory explicitly stated that reports were only 'issued on condition that they [might] not be used for legal proceedings'. Dr R. C. Batchelor, Acting Clinical Officer at the Royal Infirmary of Edinburgh wrote a strongly worded protest to the Procurator Fiscal for Falkirk. Citing the emphasis on confidentiality in the Public Health (Venereal Diseases) Regulations (Scotland) 1916 and in memoranda issued by the Local Government

Board for Scotland in association with the establishment of the system of public health VD clinics, he sought reassurance that no doctor attached to the Edinburgh Corporation VD Scheme would be required to appear in the witness box. In response, the Procurator Fiscal informed the Crown Agent that the punishment of offenders who communicated VD should always have priority over the protection of medical confidentiality and that the Listons should be precognosced and forced to give evidence, a view shared by the Procurator Fiscal in Edinburgh. Initially they were cited to appear but subsequently the Crown Agent opted for a less confrontational approach and arranged for alternative medical reports to be obtained that did not involve doctors associated with the VD services.[53]

Finally, not only did diagnostic practices vary (typically, family practitioners and Prison Medical Officers relied primarily on clinical examinations) but standards of microscopy, both in the collection and interpretation of specimens, also differed. As a result, despite the best efforts of Crown Counsel and the procurators fiscal, medical evidence could vary markedly, thus endangering the prosecution case. Though High Court cases involving the communication of VD enjoyed a high conviction rate (around 96 per cent),[54] it is clear that many more such cases were never proceeded with or were subject to significantly reduced charges within the lower courts as a result of insecure medical evidence.

Moreover, although in some respects legal processes within Scotland became more receptive to evidence from the victims of child sexual assault, it is arguable that, as in nineteenth- and early twentieth-century England, such victims were still viewed as a sexual danger once their innocence had been violated.[55] Therefore, they were seen as being in need not only of protection but also control, including institutionalisation.[56] Evidence from the police and social workers before the Departmental Committee on Sexual Offences clearly reflected 'this discursive trick', as Carol Smart has aptly termed it.[57] Thus, Katherine Scott, a Police Court Sister in Edinburgh, while pressing for a feminisation of legal processes, stressed the need to regulate the demoralised victim on the grounds that such assaults led 'in many cases to undesirable habits, which they all too readily teach to others, and in some cases eventually to prostitution'.[58] Dr Isabel Venters, working with VD patients at the Edinburgh Women and Children's Hospital, also identified the innate potential for sexual precocity and prostitution in the young victims of sexual assault. In her view, victims were 'unfitted by this too early stimulation to live among other girls or even to go to the same schools'.[59] Though the departmental committee did not wholly endorse such a view, it noted a strong consensus of opinion that 'victims of indecent assault should be segregated as being potential disseminators of depravity'.[60]

As a result of this belief, shared not only by many within the medical profession and the police force but also by rescue workers and women's organisations, many girls who were victims of sexual assault that resulted in their being infected with venereal disease were transferred after medical treatment in the lock wards and hospitals to industrial schools, children's homes, or Magdalene asylums.[61] As Linda Mahood has argued, given the perceived threat that early sexual experience, whether through abuse or seduction, would lead to prostitution, 'the solution to the problem was to catch girls at risk and to channel them into an appropriate regime of moral rehabilitation'. The object, once a girl had become initiated sexually, was to contain the danger of 'contamination' by isolating her from her friends.[62] Significantly, of the fifty-seven female cases of criminal assault sent under the Children Act to Maryhill Industrial School, Glasgow, over the period 1910–25, 35 per cent had contracted VD.[63]

The failure of attempts by social hygienists, purity activists and some women's organisations to criminalise the transmission of VD in child sexual offence cases under statute as well as common law also reveals a continuing inability or unwillingness within the legal and medical establishments fully to comprehend the social dynamics of 'abuse'. Part of their reluctance stemmed from the difficulties that had been encountered in the administration of Defence of the Realm Act, regulation 40D, during World War I, which had prosecuted women having or soliciting sexual intercourse with troops while infected.[64] According to Scottish law officers, the task of establishing the timing, locus, type, and transmission of infection had proved insuperable in most cases. In addition, there were fears that compulsory medical inspection in cases of child sexual assault, viewed by campaigners as vital to securing an aggravated charge of the communication of VD, would infringe civil liberties.

Moreover, despite widespread evidence that many cases of aggravated sexual assault were going unreported and frequently untreated, the Scottish Board of Health firmly resisted the recommendation of the Departmental Committee on Sexual Offences that 'all persons, authorities and institutions having knowledge that a girl under sixteen is infected with venereal disease . . . should be required to notify the fact to the police authorities with a view to investigation'.[65] In the board's view, such a proposal would breach the fundamental principles of medical confidentiality and deter people from seeking treatment at the clinics.

The responsibility for reporting such infections should, it submitted, be left solely with parents and guardians.[66]

'THIS STUPID AND BRUTAL IDEA' REVISITED

In many respects, the discourse surrounding the belief in a 'virgin cure' both reflected and reinforced such constraints. Interestingly, none of the accused in the Scottish High Court cases that concerned the communication of VD to minors in the period 1910–37 cited this notion in justification of their behaviour. Indeed, in the case of Alfred McCormack, indicted before the High Court in Edinburgh in 1928 for ravishing and infecting two young girls, the defendant vehemently denied such a motive for his actions. In a handwritten note, he confessed that:

> I can think of no excuse for misconducting myself. It must have just been lust. The venereal disease from which I was suffering may have excited me unduly . . . It is entirely untrue to say that I was trying to get rid of the disease by having intercourse with these girls.[67]

Similarly, Frank Pitt, indicted before the High Court in Glasgow in 1926, was alleged to have said to the complainant's mother: 'I couldn't interfere with anyone. You know I'm suffering from a runner! [gonorrhoea].'[68] In every case in which the belief was mentioned, it was at the instigation of the investigating officers or prosecution counsel.[69]

In fact, it was the judiciary, medical experts and health policy-makers who deployed the myth most powerfully. It was a means by which they might comprehend the crime of sexual assault against children without challenging prevailing ideals of male sexuality and the family. For example, in the case of John Fearn in 1912, the Procurator Fiscal in Glasgow suggested to the Crown Agent that a charge of attempting to 'ravish' be dropped in favour of 'using lewd and libidinous practices towards the girl' on the grounds that:

> It is possible that accused did not mean to attempt to have connection with the child but merely to endeavour to get quit of the disease by contact with rubbing against her person. This is not uncommon among some of the lower classes.[70]

As Carol Smart has demonstrated, by representing child sexual assault as a 'damaging medical strategy' rather than sexual gratification, the 'virgin cure' was deployed by the medical and legal professions as a way of deflecting the moral thrust of contemporary purity and feminist campaigns directed at male sexuality.[71] In addition, by desexualising the sexual transmission of VD, the focus was shifted almost exclusively to the physical rather than emotional damage done to the (female) child, except insofar as she had been sexualised by the assault and hence constituted a threat.

Above all, the alleged role of infectionist beliefs in sexual offences against children helped reinforce a view of 'abusers' as lower-class moral degenerates, 'marginal characters' who had no place in the family. Sentencing Joseph Cook, an eighteen-year-old fireman in an engineering firm in 1915 for sexually assaulting and infecting a six-year-old girl, Lord Anderson pledged to 'do all in his power' to suppress this 'disgusting offence' as 'the daughters of respectable people must be protected from lustful ruffians such as the accused'.[72] Hence, as Lynn Abrams argues:

> Child abuse was removed from the home and placed on the street, in the park, in the cinema, and . . . the ice-cream parlour. Sexual assault was something that happened to girls when they wandered to a dangerous place and encountered a strange man. Men in general were largely absolved from this crime. The family remained intact.[73]

Such social constructions of 'abuse' ignored the medical and legal evidence. Thus, of the child sexual assaults involving VD reported to the police in the Glasgow Western Division during the period 1921–24, over one-third were committed by relatives of the victim in the home.[74] Similarly, of the victims of criminal assault admitted with venereal disease to Maryhill Girls' Industrial School in the years 1910–25, 40 per cent had been assaulted by relatives (15 per cent by fathers, 15 per cent by step-fathers, and 10 per cent by brothers).[75] Likewise, the High Court cases involving sexual assault and the communication of VD over the period 1910–37 clearly reveal the family and close neighbourhood[76] locus of abuse (See Table 3.1).[77]

Yet, it is noteworthy that, even where there was a history of venereal infection in the home and circumstantial evidence of family abuse, the police were reluctant to arrest family members when an alternative suspect outwith the family was identified. Thus, in the case of Robert Fisher, an eighteen-year-old apprentice packer, indicted before Glasgow High Court in 1910, there was corroborated evidence that, when playing with her friends, the complainant had 'told them every time she gave her father his hole he gave her a halfpenny' and that the mother had previously rowed with her husband about interfering with his daughter and called him a 'rotten poxy bastard'. Nonetheless, despite the evidence that might have exonerated Fisher, the police did not pursue this line of inquiry.[78]

Table 3.1 Relationship of accused to child victim in Scottish High Court cases involving the aggravated charge of communicating VD, 1910–37

Relationship	Number of victims	Percentage
Blood relative	9	22
Boyfriend of mother/sister	3	7
Local shopkeeper	4	10
Known neighbour	17	40
Lodger/Lodger's son	2	5
Father's work colleague	1	2
Stranger	6	14

Source: NRS, AD15, Crown Office precognitions.

It is also noteworthy that the most rigorous and widely publicised prosecution and punishment were reserved for 'alien' offenders, invoking contemporary fears of racial degeneration, and again reinforcing the image that such assaults represented the loathsome behaviour of marginal social groups who lacked family and community roots. Thus, in the cases of Carmine Paravana, a manager of an ice cream shop, and Umberto Pinocci, the proprietor of a chip shop, heard in Glasgow High Court in 1910 and 1917, sentences of seven years penal servitude were meted out, in addition to Expulsion Orders under the Aliens Act 1905.[79] These punishments compared very unfavourably with the average sentence of four years and four months for all defendants found guilty of offences involving the communication of VD in the High Courts between 1910 and 1937.

As with all forms of sexual abuse, this was clearly a crime 'constructed through time in relation to notions of gender, ethnicity and class'.[80] Thus, whether or not the belief in a 'virgin cure' was genuinely held, it certainly operated discursively to contain the extent to which early twentieth-century Scottish society could and would address the issue of child sexual 'abuse'. Above all, as deployed within the Scottish High Courts, this notion served to reinforce a legal and medical mindset that desexualised child sexual assault and located it within a model of urban or racial 'degeneracy' often far removed from the reality of the crime.

NOTES

1. This chapter is a revised and extended version of an article originally published in the *Journal of the History of Sexuality*, Volume 10, Number

1, January 2001, 62–77. (Copyright 2001, The University of Texas Press. All rights reserved).

2. NRS, AD15/13/70, Crown Agent to Procurator Fiscal, 11 December 1912.

3. Ibid. Similar views were expressed by the Medical Officer of HM Prison, Edinburgh and as late as 1927 by John Glaister, Professor of Forensic Medicine and Public Health, when furnishing a medical report to Crown Counsel [NRS, AD15/28/48, precognition of J. Glaister, 5 December 1927].

4. 'In folk medicine the law of contact, and of contagion, almost invariably has to do with the magical divestment of disease' [Hand, *Magical Medicine*, 309]. For the role of such beliefs in sexual offences against children, see ibid., 18, 26; Rorie, *Folk Tradition and Folk Medicine in Scotland*, 101.

5. See, Smith, *The People's Health*, 303; Simpson, 'Vulnerability and the age of female consent', 193–6; Merians, 'The London Lock Hospital and the Lock Asylum for Women', 134; Spongberg, *Feminizing Venereal* Disease, 110; Taylor, 'Venereal Disease in nineteenth century children', 431–64; Sacco, *Unspeakable: Father–Daughter Incest*, 109–19.

6. Smart, 'A history of ambivalence and conflict', 396–7. See also, *Reports and Minutes of Evidence of the Royal Commission on Venereal Diseases*, 1914 (Cd. 7475) XLIX, q. 2822; 1916 (Cd. 8189) XVI, 28; 1916 (Cd. 8190) XVI, qq. 13,874–80.

7. PP, 1920 (222) VI, 524.

8. NRS, ED11/447, papers and transcripts of evidence.

9. *Report of Departmental Committee on Sexual Offences Against Children*, 54. The committee was especially impressed by the views of Dr Samuel Cameron [Professor of Gynaecology at the University of Glasgow] in his *Manual of Gynaecology*, third edition (London, Edward Arnold, 1925, 128) that: 'The disgusting superstition, surviving amongst ignorant and vicious men, that contact with an immature vulva will ensure a cure of venereal disease, is still responsible in many cases.'

10. See, for example, Glaister, *A Textbook of Medical Jurisprudence*, 1902 edition, 329; Glaister and Glaister Jr, *A Textbook of Medical Jurisprudence*, 1931 edition, 530. For details of Glaister's medical ideology and career as a 'medical detective', see Crowther and White, *On Soul and Conscience*, Ch. 3.

11. Unless otherwise stated, the following narrative is based on Innes, 'Love and work', PhD thesis, University of Edinburgh, 1998; Abrams, *The Orphan Country*; Smart, 'Reconsidering the recent history of child sexual abuse, 1910–1960', 55–71; Smart, 'A history of ambivalence and conflict', 391–409; Mahood, *Policing Gender, Class and Family*.

12. See especially, *Minutes of Evidence to the Joint Select Committee on the Criminal Law Amendment Bill, Criminal Law (no. 2) Bill and the Sexual Offences Bill*.

13. NRS, ED11/446, 447, Departmental Committee, transcripts of evidence.

14. *Report of Departmental Committee*, 29–30, 32.

15. Under the common law of Scotland, sexual intercourse with a girl under twelve constituted rape, while an attempt to have sexual intercourse, though unsuccessful, constituted the crime of attempt to ravish. An act of indecency short of intercourse or attempted intercourse could be indicted as indecent assault and/or lewd and libidinous practices. Previous convictions for offences of a similar nature, the communication of venereal disease, and the relation in which the offender stood to the victim, could be libelled as an aggravation. In addition, in Scotland, the practical effect of Section 4 of the Criminal Law Amendment Act 1885 was to render unlawful carnal knowledge of a girl between the ages of 12 and 13 an offence equivalent to rape, punishable by penal servitude [NAS, ED11/447, notes by Advocate Depute on Existing Law and Practice in Scotland, 1925].

16. *Justiciary Reports, Irvine, Vol. 3 1858–60*, 310, Case of James Mack.

17. *Glasgow Herald*, 28 February 1912.

18. Forty-two victims were involved, all girls, varying in age from three to thirteen, with an average age of about eight years at the time of the offence.

19. Medical testimony to the communication of VD was often crucial in sexual assault cases, in which corroborative evidence was frequently lacking or withheld. The Crown Agent urged that 'everything should be done to make the scientific testimony as complete as possible' [NRS, AD15/14/109, note by Crown Agent, 29 November 1913].

20. Crowther and White, *On Soul and Conscience*, 2–3, 44. For a comparative perspective, see Robertson, 'Signs, marks, and private parts', 345–88.

21. Crowther and White, *On Soul and Conscience*, 3–4, 7–8, 26.

22. For a general discussion of these issues, see Smith and Wynne (eds), *Expert Evidence: Interpreting Science in the Law*.

23. Sexual offences against children were primarily perceived and debated in terms of abuse against 'young girls'. According to Louise Jackson, '[T]he reason for the invisibility of boys . . . lies in the emergence of the issue from the social purity and rescue societies' preoccupation with "fallen" women and young female prostitutes.' [Jackson, *Child Sexual Abuse in Victorian England*, 5]. All the High Court cases researched for this study involved adult male assaults on young girls. There *were* instances of women being indicted for communicating VD to young boys as a consequence of lewd, indecent and libidinous practices but they were extremely rare [Glaister and Glaister Jr, *Medical Jurisprudence and Toxicology*, 1931 edition, 530].

24. See especially, NRS, ED11/447, Departmental Committee on Sexual Offences against Children and Young Persons in Scotland, evidence of P. Duncan, policewoman, City of Glasgow Police, and Detective Lt A. J. Sangster, Edinburgh City Police, 20 and 28 April 1925.

25. Using evidence from cases heard in mid-level English courts, Victoria Bates has contested the use of the term 'denial' in this context. She argues that a major factor in inhibiting a diagnosis of sexual abuse and infection was the continuing diagnostic confusion surrounding gonorrhoea. In her view,

this was compounded by the dependence of many general practitioners on purely clinical observation and it was this 'diagnostic uncertainty' that 'created a space in legal testimony for questions of class and cleanliness to be raised' [Bates, ' "So far as I can define without a microscopical examination" ', 38–55].

26. For an exhaustive analysis of such denial prior to 1900, see Taylor, 'Venereal Disease in nineteenth-century children', 431–64.

27. See, for example, Swaine Taylor, *Medical Jurisprudence*, 692–6; Ogston, *Lectures on Medical Jurisprudence*, 91; Brend, *A Handbook of Medical Jurisprudence and Toxicology*, 99; Burridge, *An Introduction to Forensic Medicine*, 262. John Glaister's texts also highlighted the role of 'natural' causes in producing such discharges (uncleanliness, scratching with dirty fingers, local irritation such as threadworms in rectum, cold, etc.) and the dangers of misdiagnosis 'by a careless examiner for gonorrhoea'. See Glaister, *Textbook of Medical Jurisprudence*, 1902 edition, 329; Glaister and Glaister Jr, *Medical Jurisprudence and Toxicology*, 1931 edition, 530–1. For similar views in English texts, see Jackson, *Child Sexual Abuse*, 75–6; Bates, 'Venereal disease diagnosis', 51.

28. Jackson, *Child Sexual Abuse*, 73, 87. On the impact of cultural factors in shaping diagnoses, see also Bates, 'Venereal disease diagnosis', 47–54.

29. NRS, AD15/13/100, precognition of Dr A. E. Clayton, June 1913.

30. NRS, AD15/21/8, precognitions in the case against William Barclay, 1921.

31. This was all the more surprising given that a neighbour had previously examined the girl and diagnosed a 'runner' (gonorrhoea).

32. NRS, AD15/13/70, precognition of Agnes Jane C., 9 December 1912. School doctors were also prone to treating venereal symptoms as cases of worms. See, for example, NRS, AD15/21/76, precognition of Jane McCalister, 10 May 1921.

33. NRS, AD15/21/71, precognition of Isabella C., 26 May 1921.

34. NRS, AD15/17/92, precognition of Dr S. Nicolson, 30 May 1917. Dr George Duncan, Lecturer in Bacteriology at the University of Aberdeen, concurred that 'it was only a discharge which many children have when they are not kept clean and that it was also when they have any infectious fever or when they are scrofulous'. Scrofula was a constitutional disease characterised by chronic enlargement and degeneration of the lymphatic glands. It was commonly viewed as a symptom of moral corruption.

35. Taylor, 'Venereal Disease in nineteenth-century children', 442, 447, 450–3. For similar patterns of 'denial' in the United States, see Sacco, *Unspeakable*, 7–8, 75–8. 88–95.

36. Smart, 'Child sexual abuse', 57–60.

37. Edinburgh Public Health Department, *Annual Report for 1924*, 56.

38. Ibid., *Annual Report for 1925*, 55.

39. Ibid., *Annual Report for 1936*, 84. Almost identical views were voiced in

the interwar reports of public health authorities and social hygiene activists in the USA. See Sacco, *Unspeakable*, Chs 4–5.

40. Burridge, *Forensic Medicine*, 262; NRS, ED11/447, Departmental Committee on Sexual Offences against Children and Young Persons in Scotland, precis of evidence of David Watson, Lecturer in Venereology, University of Glasgow and Surgeon to Glasgow Lock Hospital.

41. NRS, AD15/13/100, precognition of Dr L. M. Jones, 9 June 1913.

42. NRS, AD15/14/109, precognition of Dr Brooke Young, 2 December 1913.

43. NRS, AD15/29/62, precognition of Dr Robert Black, 13 October 1929.

44. For details, see Davidson, ' "A scourge to be firmly gripped"', 213–35.

45. Davidson, *Dangerous Liaisons*, Ch. 3.

46. For earlier examples of such problems, see Robertson, 'Signs, marks, and private parts', 383; Spongberg, *Feminizing Venereal Disease*, 111. For similar problems in English courts, see especially Bates 'Venereal disease diagnosis', 47–8.

47. This problem was often compounded by the delay in a child reporting a sexual assault for fear of being blamed and punished. Thus, in the case of Catherine S. in 1910, the mother had 'previously strapped her daughter having found her with inflamed private parts' [NRS, AD15/10/126, Crown Office precognitions]. See also, AD15/13/70.

48. See, for example, NRS, AD15/12/81, Crown Office precognitions in the case against William Armstrong. Symptoms could often vary dramatically between medical examinations, depending on the incubation period or stage of the venereal infection.

49. NRS, AD15/21/71, Crown Office precognitions.

50. NRS, AD15/28/48, Crown Office precognitions in the case against Allan Ferguson.

51. On the interprofessional rivalry over confidentiality in early twentieth-century Britain, see especially, Ferguson, 'Speaking out about staying silent', 99–124.

52. NRS, AD15/24/24, Procurator Fiscal to Crown Agent, 12 September 1924.

53. NRS, AD15/29/62, correspondence in case against Henry Thompson.

54. A plea of 'not guilty' was recorded in 54 per cent of these cases.

55. See especially Jackson, *Child Sexual Abuse*, 6–7, 58.

56. Jackson attributes the problematic position of the sexually abused girl in late nineteenth- and early twentieth-century society to 'a Christian moral economy, promoted by the middle classes' that constituted her as both 'victim' and 'threat' in need not only of protection but also retraining and reform [*Child Sexual Abuse*, 6–7, 53–4]. As in English child assault cases [Jackson, *Child Sexual Abuse*, Ch. 5; Jackson, 'The child's word in court', 222–37; D'Cruze, *Crimes of Outrage*, 148], a good deal of the medical evidence submitted in early twentieth-century Scottish cases involving VD focused on details (for example, the degree of 'defloration') pertinent not only to the severity of the charge but also to the sexual reputation of the

complainant. In addition, precognition statements by the victims of assault were invariably structured by investigating officers so as to address issues of previous sexual experience.

57. Smart, 'A history of ambivalence and conflict', 404. Different readings of court evidence could reinforce this 'trick'. Thus, while some 60 per cent of High Court cases involving the communication of VD revealed some form of bribery (sums of money, ice cream, chips etc.), this evidence was often used to legitimate contemporary fears of young girls abusing their sexuality by 'offering themselves to men for pennies'. See, for example, NRS, ED11/447, Departmental Committee on Sexual Offences against Children and Young Persons in Scotland, precis of evidence of J. J. Hunter, Secretary of the National Vigilance Association of Scotland.

58. Ibid., precis of evidence.

59. Ibid., precis of evidence.

60. *Report of Departmental Committee on Sexual Offences against Children and Young Persons in Scotland*, 35, 50. Such evidence resonates with anthropological accounts of 'pollution behaviour' as a 'reaction which condemns any object or idea [in this instance either the sexually abused child or more specifically her symptoms of sexual violation and disease including precocious discharges] likely to confuse or contradict cherished classifications' [Douglas, *Purity and Danger*, 36]. See also, D'Cruze, *Crimes of Outrage*, 43, 141. For similar views in England in the mid-1920s, see Jackson, *Child Sexual Abuse*, 64–5.

61. For a general discussion of the sexual ideologies underpinning these strategies and of the powers invested in the police and local authorities under the Criminal Law Amendment Act 1885, the Industrial Schools Acts 1866 and 1880 and the Children Act 1908, see especially, Mahood, *Policing Gender, Class and Family*, Ch. 3; Abrams, *The Orphan Country*, Ch. 6; Jackson, *Child Sexual Abuse*, Ch. 7.

62. Mahood, *Policing Class, Gender and Family*, 136; Abrams, *The Orphan Country*, 228.

63. NRS, ED11/447, Departmental Committee on Sexual Offences against Children and Young Persons in Scotland, transcripts of evidence.

64. *Minutes of Evidence to Joint Select Committee on Criminal Law Amendment Bill and Sexual Offences Bill*, qq, 2660, 2781–4.

65. *Report of Departmental Committee on Sexual Offences against Children and Young Persons in Scotland*, 54.

66. NRS, ED11/447, Departmental Committee on Sexual Offences against Children and Young Persons in Scotland, submission of Scottish Board of Health, 25 May 1925.

67. NRS, JC26/1627, HCJ processes, note from accused.

68. NRS, AD 15/332, precognition of Agnes Mcleish, 21 July 1926.

69. Thus, in the case against William Carr, heard in Inverness High Court in 1918, the statement of the victim's sister that 'I am quite sure that Carr did

not say anything to me about getting rid of his disease by having connection with my sister' is clearly a response to targeted questioning [AD15/18/64, precognition of Mary Sutherland, 15 February 1918].

70. NRS, AD15/12/98, J. N. Hart to Crown Agent, 3 June 1912.

71. Smart, 'Child sexual abuse', 68.

72. *Glasgow Herald*, 25 August 1915.

73. Abrams, *The Orphan Country*, 226–7. See also Jackson, *Child Sexual Abuse*, 32; Jackson, 'Family, community and child sexual abuse', 136.

74. NRS, ED11/447, Departmental Committee on Sexual Offences against Children and Young Persons in Scotland, evidence from Helen Blair, policewoman, 25 May 1925.

75. Ibid., transcripts of evidence.

76. In eight of the cases involving known neighbours, the girls either ran messages for the accused, or baby-sat for him, or delivered his newspaper. In seven of these cases, the neighbour was a relative of a playmate.

77. In comparison, Jackson found a much lower proportion of cases involving family offenders in her sample of child sexual assault cases in Middlesex and Yorkshire for the period 1830–1910: 12 per cent and 16 per cent respectively. Table 1 more closely resembles estimates of the proportion of late twentieth-century child sexual abuse perpetrated within the family. See Jackson, *Child Sexual Abuse*, 43–5, 167.

78. NRS, AD15/10/126, Crown Office precognitions.

79. NRS, AD15/10/125, AD15/17/70, Crown Office precognitions, For the racial aspects of social politics surrounding VD in early twentieth-century Scotland, see Davidson, *Dangerous Liaisons*, Ch. 2.

80. Jackson, *Child Sexual Abuse*, 10.

4

'Unnatural Carnal Connection': Bestiality and the Law in Early Twentieth-century Scotland

INTRODUCTION

On several occasions in November 1914, Alexander Ashwood, a carting contractor with premises in Park Street, Motherwell, discovered that the padlock on his stable door had been forced and that a barrel had been placed behind the mare that was housed there.[1] He reported these incidents to the police but, before they could investigate, he witnessed Owen Gunnery, an unmarried labourer who lodged in an adjoining house, standing at the rear of the mare 'with his trousers unbuttoned and his member inserted into the mare's parts'. According to Ashwood, the mare's tail was up and she was discharging as if she was being served. A struggle ensued and Gunnery escaped but, when he was later apprehended at his lodgings, the police noticed discharge on his trousers and shirt.

Meanwhile, the police had collected forensic evidence from the scene of the crime including a sample of the hairs and discharge from the mare's hindquarters as well as precise measurements of the height of the barrel and the animal's private parts. The evidence was duly examined by Dr Joseph Hume Patterson, Bacteriologist for the County of Lanark, along with the clothes worn by the accused. On Gunnery's shirt Patterson found coarse hairs that matched those of the mare, fragments of hay and particles of 'foreign faeces'. He also found matching hairs on Gunnery's trousers and drawers along with 'recent seminal fluid' although he could not detect any spermatozoa from specimens taken from the mare. Despite having admitted to the police that he had had 'connection' with the mare on three separate occasions, blaming his behaviour on drink, Gunnery initially pleaded not guilty at Hamilton Sheriff Court to a charge of bestiality. However, when the case was remitted to the High Court in Glasgow in February 1915, he changed his plea to guilty and was sentenced to six months imprisonment.

Some fifteen years later, on 3 February 1929, two police constables on patrol in New Cumnock, Ayrshire, entered the steading of Broadfoot Farm and noticed the reflection of a flickering light on the skylight window of the byre.[2] According to the report of the Procurator Fiscal, summarising their precognitions:

> They cautiously approached the byre door which was ajar. Fifteen yards off they saw the accused [Patrick McCourt] standing on top of something, and immediately behind the hindquarters of a cow. He was holding a lighted match in his left hand and a penis in his right. His trousers being open. The accused's penis, which was erect, was directly opposite the cow's vagina. The accused was seen to make connection with the cow, and to be over her back. The match was extinguished ... One of the constables shone his electric torch on the accused who was so startled that he fell on the floor at the foot of the cow ... The accused had been standing on a milking stool, a potato basket, and four canvas sacks.

The police collected hair and dandruff from the cow along with McCourt's clothes for forensic examination and a vet was summoned to corroborate that the animal had been interfered with. On being apprehended, McCourt, a 36-year-old widower, sought to explain his behaviour by reference to his heavy drinking the previous day and a head wound sustained in World War I. Nonetheless, he pleaded guilty at Ayr Sheriff Court to a charge of 'unlawful carnal connection with a cow' and was subsequently sentenced on 25 February 1929 to six months imprisonment at Glasgow High Court.

These were but two of the twenty-three Scottish High Court cases involving the charge of bestiality or attempted bestiality in the period 1900–30 for which records survive.

Exploring the socio-legal context and implications of these cases, and the cultural resonance of bestiality in this period, is problematic. First, unlike 'child outrage', prostitution, sodomy, or the wilful transmission of venereal disease, bestiality was not the focus of contemporary moral panic. Though bestiality may have featured in the work on sexual perversion of the early sexologists,[3] as an offence it did not preoccupy the policy-makers within the Scottish Office nor did it feature in the counsels and publications of the Scottish medical and legal establishments. Bestiality was not on the agenda of the Scottish church assemblies and synods nor of the social hygiene and purity movements. This lack of contemporary public exposure has subsequently been compounded by the reluctance of historians of early twentieth-century British society to investigate how this sexual crime was perceived and prosecuted.[4]

A second major constraint lies in the limitations of the primary source materials. As with other sexual offences, there are no verbatim transcripts of the trial proceedings in cases of bestiality, nor of the judges' summing up prior to sentencing. As a result, the historian is heavily dependent on evidence contained in the precognitions and miscellaneous trial papers or processes held by the prosecution. As discussed in the introductory chapter, however, the precognitions do not capture the defence case and witness statements. They are purely reports, usually gathered by a procurator fiscal, for forwarding to the Crown Office in Edinburgh for a decision on whether or not to proceed to trial. They are not, therefore, verbatim witness statements but are more accurately seen as official and somewhat formulaic reconstructions of responses to a limited repertoire of questions designed to support a prosecution. Moreover, newspaper reports of these cases are either non-existent or extremely brief and evasive.[5] The term 'bestiality' never appeared in the court reports. Only the verdict was recorded, and no details of the court proceedings were published. As in so many societies in the past, bestiality remained 'the unmentionable vice'.[6]

More broadly, it is perhaps questionable how far one can draw general conclusions about the social response to bestiality from a small cluster of High Court prosecutions. It is possible that other cases, especially where the charge was attempted bestiality, may have been dealt with by Sheriff Courts, whose records have either not survived or not been catalogued. Moreover, even where records are accessible to the historian, they may represent only a fraction of all reported incidents of bestiality as they are confined only to those cases regarded as trial-worthy by the criminal justice system. Nor do the legal files capture the extent to which bestiality was policed by informal mechanisms of social control within the local community, such as the intimidation, ridiculing and ostracising of offenders. Finally, the closure of legal records in accordance with the Data Protection Act 1998 renders it impossible to locate this study within a longer chronological perspective from which patterns of continuity and change in the response to bestiality in early twentieth-century Scotland might more readily be discerned.

Nonetheless, the surviving High Court precognitions and processes do provide a valuable source of information on the practice and prosecution of bestiality in this period. They enable the historian to gain considerable insight into the social status, background and lifestyle of defendants, the nature and geography of the crime committed, and the process by which it was officially acknowledged and investigated by the criminal justice system. Important light is thrown on the role of the police and procurators fiscal as well as on the contributions of forensic and veterinary medicine and psychiatry. In addition, information on the conduct of trials, on the verdicts delivered and sentences imposed, and on the degree of public exposure accorded to the more salacious and unsavoury aspects of the offence, can be seen to reflect contemporary attitudes towards bestiality in the wider community. Above all, these case papers enable the first tentative exploration of a crime so far hidden from twentieth-century Scottish history that, it is to be hoped, will be more thoroughly charted in future years as the records become more fully available.

THE ACCUSED

Age profile

Of the twenty-one defendants involved in this study,[7] all of whom were men,[8] the oldest was sixty-five and the youngest was seventeen years of age. The average age was around forty and, insofar as these cases can be taken as representative, bestiality appears to have been a crime most often committed by the middle aged and elderly. Over 60 per cent of cases involved men over the age of thirty-five and men under the age of thirty accounted for only around 13 per cent of cases.[9]

Marital status

Some 75 per cent of the defendants in bestiality cases were unmarried at the time the crime was committed, including two widowers. Of those

Table 4.1 Age distribution of defendants in Scottish High Court cases involving bestiality, 1900–39

Age range	Percentage of cases
15–20	6
20–25	6
25–30	1
30–35	25
35–40	31
40–45	6
45–50	6
Over 50	19

Source: NRS, AD/15, Crown Office precognitions.

few who *were* married, one was recorded as of no fixed abode, while another's wife 'kept house and resided with' another workman. Such evidence would seem to support the theory that, in some instances, bestiality may have been related to the lack of an alternative sexual outlet.[10]

Occupation

Of the twenty-one defendants, the occupation of eleven was recorded as 'labourer'. Their specific duties were only rarely specified but evidence from precognitions would suggest that most were employed on the land with a small number associated with heavy manual work in and around pitheads. Of the others, four were associated with coalmining or the iron and steel industry – a colliery boiler fireman, a furnace builder, a shot firer and a smelter. In addition, those indicted for the crime of bestiality included a baker, a carter, a naval seaman, 'a motor wagon attendant', a sawyer, and a tinker. None of the accused was from the professional or managerial classes and most were in unskilled occupations or social class V as defined in contemporary census classifications.[11]

Residence

The low social status of offenders was clearly reflected in their housing arrangements. Of those for whom details are available, three were lodgers, five stayed with relatives, while four were recorded as residing in common lodging houses (including the so-called Model Lodging House at Wishaw) frequented by the destitute and homeless. Four were 'of no fixed abode', typically sleeping rough around sources of heat such as pithead boilers, or dossing down in a stable or farm shed at night. Frequently, the accused were housed adjacent to the field or stable in which the crime of bestiality was alleged to have been committed.[12]

Criminal record

Nearly a quarter of defendants had one or more previous convictions for bestiality or attempted bestiality,[13] evidence that would suggest that, in some cases, there might have been a fetishistic element to their behaviour. Thus, William Simpson, accused in August 1912 of attempting to 'have carnal connection' with a mare in a stable in Perth occupied by a coal merchant and a carting contractor, had three previous convictions in 1901, 1905, and 1909 along with an acquittal on a similar charge in January 1912.[14] Such convictions were often common knowledge and the basis of persistent rumour and unease within the local community.[15]

Moreover, the precognitions indicate that, in many bestiality cases, the specific act that led to arrest was the culmination of a series of offences that had gone undetected or unreported. Thus, in 1915, in the case of Thomas Peacock, prior to his arrest for assaulting a calf at a farm in Shotts, the farmer had noticed that the 'door of the hay shed had been forced', and that an Ayrshire cow in an adjoining byre showed evidence of having been 'tampered with'.[16] Again, in 1921, in the case of James McEwen, charged with 'unnatural carnal connection' with domestic fowls, it is clear from the succession of dead hens found every Sunday morning from July through to mid-September that he had committed a series of sexual offences before the police were alerted.[17]

THE CRIME

The victim

In the twenty-three bestiality cases examined, the most commonly chosen victim was a mare (in ten cases). A cow figured in seven cases while the remainder involved a male donkey, two donkey mares, a lamb and a ewe, a young bull and a henhouse of domestic fowls. Apart from the case involving the bull – where the accused had initially tried to insert his penis in its nostrils before attempting to insert it in its rectum – all the orifices penetrated were vaginas. It has been argued that, contrary to conventional representations enshrined in Scottish legal writing, such a pattern of sexual behaviour locates bestiality with heterosexual sex rather than with sodomy.[18]

Although the physical damage to animals involved in cases of bestiality was not part of the formal charge brought by the Crown Office, it was viewed as an aggravating feature of the crime, albeit primarily as an infringement of property rights rather than an issue of animal welfare. Over and above the victim's sexual arousal that commonly accompanied the offence, a range of injuries, some deliberate and sometimes fatal, were sustained. Frequently their sexual organs were left 'inflamed' and 'distended'.[19] In the case of Thomas Peacock, cited above, considerable violence had been employed. Peacock had wedged the calf's head up against the side of the loose box to 'get purchase on the rear of the animal' and left it with a 'bloody discharge coming from the vagina' and a bladder that was 'lacerated and torn'.[20] Evidence suggests that, a year later, the same offender may have used a broken bottle in an assault on a mare in Dalziel, Lanarkshire.[21] In 1921, James McEwen left a trail of dead fowls in and around a henhouse near Kirkudbright as a result of his sexual predations. In addition to rupturing their vents, it appeared that he was possibly throttling the birds in order to enjoy the sexual frisson of their dying contractions.[22] Finally, in 1924, in Lude Park, Blair Atholl, Perthshire, Duncan Townsley suffocated a ewe by forcing it on to its back and smothering it in order to 'obtain carnal knowledge of the animal'.[23]

The location

Of the twenty-three incidents of bestiality or attempted bestiality, eight were recorded as having taken place in a field, park or common, eight in a stable, six in a byre and one in a poultry house. Clearly, ready access to animals and a concern for secrecy dictated many of the locations, while the high proportion of al fresco offences may largely reflect their greater risk of exposure to the gaze of the public and police. However, the majority of offences did not take place in isolated rural locations. Many of the fields were adjacent to major road or rail connections or coalmining operations.[24] Moreover, many of the stables identified in the High Court cases were attached to commercial and industrial enterprises, such as coalmines and coal merchants, timber merchants, and carting contractors, reflecting the continuing reliance of the urban economy on horses for haulage in early twentieth-century Scotland.[25]

Early indications of an offence

In many cases, the first indication that a crime had taken place was damage to the door of a farm building – most commonly a stable.[26] The displacement of objects such as barrels, corn bins, and milking stools also served to raise suspicions. Thus, in the case of Peter Roy in 1910, the wife of the horse dealer first raised the alarm when she went to the byre to milk the cow and 'saw the boiler which [her] husband used for making food for his animals standing immediately behind the cow, upside down'.[27] However, it was the condition of the animal that most often alerted its minders to the fact that an act of bestiality had been committed. Typically, its posture was akin to that of an animal that had just been served. Thus, in the case of William Simpson in 1912, the police sergeant testified that, on entering the byre, he noticed that the mare's 'tail was up and she was spending as if she had just been served by a horse' and her discharge was 'like what comes from a mare which has been newly covered'.[28]

Reporting the crime

A significant proportion of the offences, especially those committed in byres and stables, were first reported to the police by the owners of the animals involved, usually on information supplied by employees in daily contact with the livestock.[29] In contrast, offences committed in the open were more likely to be reported by local residents accidentally witnessing events. In a few cases, offenders were discovered by policemen on routine patrol of areas known to harbour undesirables or men with previous convictions. For example, in 1912, on encountering William Simpson 'worse for drink' in South Street, Perth, and knowing his proclivity for bestiality, Sergeant Motion and PC Paterson of the City Police followed him back to a nearby stable and detained him when he exited the premises.[30] The following year, two constables patrolling the old railway line from Inverkeithing to North Queensferry, allegedly 'frequented by drunks', spotted Ernest Johnson, regarded by the police as a 'sexual pervert', 'standing behind a donkey' and arrested him after a short period of surveillance.[31]

In some instances, delay in alerting the authorities, especially on the part of co-workers, appears to have stemmed from a feeling of shame that the crime reflected on the whole community and that, by acting as a witness, they had in some way been morally implicated in the offence. Thus, in the case of Robert Reed, indicted in 1909 for having 'unnatural carnal connection' with a mare in Kirkmabreck, Kirkudbrightshire, the Procurator Fiscal reported that Reed had been suspected of 'bestial practices' ever since his release from prison for a previous conviction but witnesses, whether women or men, were unwilling to speak 'in such cases'.[32] Similarly, witnesses in the case of Charles Dougan, charged with sexually assaulting a mare in Govan in 1913, delayed reporting his behaviour because they were 'ashamed to do so' and to be associated in any way with the 'goings on' in the stable.[33] This pattern of evasion would accord with the established view of sociologists and social anthropologists that bestiality, by breaching 'social or symbolic boundaries' that underpinned the moral framework of society, was perceived not just as a problem of a single person, the animal and its owner, but a 'violation of the whole community', and hence a taboo subject.[34] In addition, where a product such as milk or eggs was being sold, there was an understandable reluctance to associate it in the public mind with the sexual contamination of bestiality.

THE POLICE INVESTIGATION

The police played a variety of roles in investigating complaints of bestiality and preparing the evidence upon which a procurator fiscal might initiate legal proceedings. First, they routinely corroborated witness evidence about the condition of the animal and suspected assailant. In the case of Robert Reed, the police sergeant at Creetown testified that, on arriving at the stable, he had examined the wet marks on the mare's hindquarters: 'It was "slimy". I said at once it was discharge from a man's private member ... The accused smelt strongly of horses and the appearance of his private member indicated that it had recently had connection.'[35] Similarly, in the case of Peter Roy, accused in 1910 of bestiality in Invergordon, the first action of the police constable attending the scene was to examine the 'hindparts of the cow'. It appeared to him 'that she had been abused'.[36] Again, in the case of James McEwen in 1921, the police corroborated the evidence of the farm tenant who owned the hens that, when they shone an electric flashlight into the hen-house, the 'accused had his hands at the open fly of his trousers' and a slate-coloured hen was 'falling to the floor', apparently dying.[37]

Secondly, in view of the fact that the offence of bestiality often involved animals, especially mares, of considerable stature, the police collected circumstantial evidence indicating that sexual connection had been physically possible. In both cases involving William Simpson in 1911–12 and that of Owen Gunnery in 1915, the police carefully measured the height of the mare's vagina and of the barrel the accused was presumed to have stood on.[38] Similarly, as we have seen, in the case of Patrick McCourt in 1929, the police evidence placed particular emphasis on the fact that the penis of the accused was erect, and that the step he had assembled from a variety of paraphernalia lying around in the stable was directly in line with the cow's vagina.[39]

Thirdly, in several of the cases, after reports of suspicious behaviour around livestock, the police initiated surveillance of farm buildings or fields, leading directly to an arrest. In the case of Harry Embrow, the police followed up on rumours that a sailor was 'misconducting himself with a female donkey', kept the field in question under observation and testified to having clearly witnessed him 'covering' the animal.[40] In the case of John Gordon, having been alerted to his activities, the police kept watch on the stable at Bogie Mains Farm and personally witnessed Gordon 'put his private member in the mare's vagina', the police constable emphasising in his statement that 'he had a good view of the connection'.[41] In 1921, near Kirkudbright, a similar vigil enabled the police to observe at close quarters James McEwen sexually assaulting a hen and to testify that his trousers were open and 'private member exposed and nearly erect'.[42] In November of the same year, having received reports of various incidents in a stable in Fife, the police arranged for a straw hide to be built within the stable to facilitate surveillance, resulting in a speedy arrest with compelling evidence of bestiality.[43]

Finally, and perhaps most importantly, the police gathered forensic evidence from the crime scene for examination by medical and some-times veterinary experts. Typically, this would include hairs taken from the animal and from the suspect's clothes, together with swabs of any discharge from the animal's vagina and of any foreign matter on the sus-pect's trousers, shirt, vest, and drawers.[44] In addition, occasionally, burnt matches, used by the accused to enable him to see what he was doing during the sexual assault, were collected along with unused matches in his pockets.[45]

PREPARING THE PROSECUTION CASE

In preparing the case for prosecution, the police and procurators fiscal were mindful that to secure a conviction under Scots law required evi-dence from at least two witnesses to the offence or the corroboration of one witness by other irrefutable evidence. In addition, to prove that 'unnatural carnal connection' with an animal had taken place, as with cases of sodomy, firm evidence was required of the completion of the offence by 'penetration'.[46] Evidence of 'emission' was not indispensable but was regarded as providing valuable support for the prosecution case.

The process of precognoscing witnesses followed a clearly defined path, reflecting the agenda of the prosecution. When the offence had been directly witnessed, the emphasis was on securing a detailed account of the scene: in particular, the position of the accused in relation to the animal and his bodily movements; the state of his clothing and 'private parts'; the condition and behaviour of the victim; and evidence of the positioning of any object designed to facilitate the sexual act. In a period when electricity was rare in most areas of Scotland and many farm buildings were without any form of lighting, the ability of witnesses clearly to discern what had been going on when the crime was commit-ted after dark was also routinely explored in the precognitions.[47]

Forensic evidence

In the fifth edition of his textbook on medical jurisprudence and toxicology, John Glaister senior observed that:

> Of bestiality little need be said, since in most of the cases the culprit is caught in the act, and therefore there is no need for medical opinion. Any evidence of a medical kind must either be supplementary to that of eye-witnesses or be purely circumstantial.[48]

Nonetheless, as with cases of child sexual abuse and illegal abortion in this period (see Chapters 3 and 5), High Court cases involving bestiality reflected the extent to which medical expertise, armed with new technologies of microscopy and bacteriology, was increasingly accorded an authoritative role within the legal process.[49] A small group of forensic experts applying laboratory techniques was routinely employed by the procurators fiscal to examine evidence from the scene of the crime in order to establish that some form of sexual connection had taken place. For example, in the case of Robert Reed in 1909, John Glaister, Regius Professor of Forensic Medicine and Public Health in the University of Glasgow, established that the hairs on the clothing of the accused matched those taken from the hindquarters of the mare although he could not detect any evidence of spermatozoa in the 'substance coagulating them'.[50] Likewise, in a range of cases, J. Hume Patterson, Bacteriologist for the County of Lanark, was asked to examine clothing for animal hairs and 'washing' from the animal's private parts for traces of 'human seminal fluid' that might indicate that penetration and emission had taken place. Typical of his findings were those he reported to the Procurator Fiscal in 1915 in the case of Thomas Peacock:

> I visited the farm to obtain hairs from the hind quarters of the calf and a swab from the liquid issuing from the vagina . . . Shirt had evidence of calf hairs and bovine faeces and stain matching calf's discharge; vest – evidence of bovine faeces and litter from floor of calf shed; drawers and cap – evidence of coarse hairs similar to calf's. No evidence of seminal fluid in calf's discharge.[51]

In a small number of cases, a medical inspection of the genital organs of the accused was also undertaken at the request of the police immediately after an arrest, and evidence of abrasions, semen, or foreign matter duly noted and reported.[52]

Veterinary evidence

In addition, in a few cases, veterinary reports were requested either by the owner or by the procurator fiscal when an animal had been seriously injured or some form of sexual sadism was suspected.[53] The procurator fiscal might also authorise a report in order to corroborate other witness statements as to the likelihood of sexual penetration having taken place. In the case of John Macdonald, accused in 1921 of having 'unnatural carnal connection' with two mares in a tent at Biddall's Travelling Circus on Cannon Common in Arbroath, two schoolboys testified to having seen Macdonald 'shoving it (his member) into the mare' that was 'groaning' and emitting 'discharge'. Though he had not been present at the scene, a vet subsequently reported that one would 'not see the vagina readily discharging unless the animal was "in use" or "seeking the horse"'.[54] Similarly, in the case of Alexander McKenzie in 1921, because of a delay in inspecting the animal involved, the vet could not confirm that sexual connection had taken place but he listed the symptoms he would have expected to have found had he undertaken an immediate inspection and confirmed that this fully 'tallied with the evidence of other witnesses'.[55]

Psychiatric evidence

The use of psychiatric evidence was notably absent from the cases of bestiality brought before the High Court during the period 1900–30. The mental health of the accused was investigated in only three instances, all three of which took place after World War I. In the case of John Gordon, accused in 1921 of 'unnatural carnal connection' with two mares in Kirkcaldy and Kingussie,[56] the Procurator Fiscal at Cupar, Fife, requested medical reports from the staff of HM Prison, Perth as well as from HM Prison, Dundee, where Gordon had been imprisoned for a similar offence in 1919. Dr A. M. Stalker, Medical Officer to HM Prison, Dundee, described Gordon as 'a pallid, ill-nourished looking man with a stupid somewhat cunning and shifty expression'. In his opinion, 'his appearance and bearing taken together with his offences '[made] it clear that he [was] a moral pervert overmastered frequently by libidinous impulses and thus a danger to the community and of unsound mind'. Drs H. Ferguson Watson and J. Edwards of HM Prison, Perth, did not regard him as dangerous but considered that he was a 'congenital imbecile' who showed all the 'stigmata of degeneration' and consequent 'arrest of mental and physical development'. In their opinion, his was not a suitable case for guardianship and required 'institutional treatment'.

Subsequently, at the High Court in Perth, the jury found Gordon guilty of bestiality but a defective within the meaning of the Mental Deficiency and Lunacy (Scotland) Act 1913. The court ordered that the Procurator Fiscal should present a petition to the Sheriff Substitute for a judicial order under the Act. However, although the Sheriff Substitute was in full agreement with the process, on being informed by the General Board of Control for Scotland that all existing certified institutions for adult mental defectives were fully occupied, he was forced to refuse the petition.[57] Consequently, Gordon was detained for 'due process of law' and the case was remitted to the High Court in Edinburgh for resolution. In delivering his judgment, the Advocate Depute, Lord Sands, regretted that institutional provision had not kept pace with the reform of the law on mental deficiency but he regarded any access to 'a more beneficent form of treatment' by the legislature to be 'a privilege rather than a right'. He also regretted that the accused had not pleaded 'insanity in bar of the trial' or 'insanity or imbecility' when the alleged offence had been committed. However, in his view, in the circumstances, Gordon had to be regarded as a man who, 'though not mentally normal, [was] not so abnormal' as to be relieved from criminal responsibility and therefore liable to be sentenced for any crime he had committed. In line with the jury's verdict at Perth High Court, he therefore moved the High Court in Edinburgh to convict the panel and proceeded to sentence Gordon to twelve months imprisonment.[58]

Unsurprisingly, mental health issues also figured in the case of James McEwen, indicted in 1921 for his sexual predations in a poultry house on the outskirts of Kirkudbright.[59] His mother had been insane and died in an asylum. He, himself, had been invalided out of the army owing to sunstroke and sent to Crichton Royal Institution for a period in 1914–15. In view of his history and the bizarre nature of his alleged offences, the Procurator Fiscal arranged for him to be medically examined in the prison cells. Dr Murray Stewart duly reported that he 'could detect no sign of insanity whatever'. Given the unsavoury nature of the case, however, the Crown Office was keen, if possible, to deal with the accused under the Mental Deficiency Act 1913 rather than by means of criminal proceedings, and additional reports were called for. In the event, Dr Joseph Hunter, Prison Surgeon at HM Prison, Dumfries, confirmed that the accused was fit to plead. He stated that McEwen had 'displayed no signs of mental abnormality of any kind' and that he could not 'be said to come under any of the four categories set out in the Mental Deficiency Act'. Though a 'special defence of insanity' was submitted at the subsequent High Court trial in Dumfries, a jury came to a unanimous verdict of guilty and McEwen was sentenced to three years penal servitude.

In the final case of James Peters, a 16-year-old labourer from Perthshire, accused in 1927 of having 'unnatural carnal connection' with a cow, it appears that the judicial system made every effort to take account of his mental state and to spare him from a prison sentence.[60] Having initially pleaded guilty at Perth Sheriff Court, his case was remitted to the High Court in Edinburgh for sentence. However, the Medical Officer of HM Prison, Edinburgh, Dr J. B. Cunningham cautioned that Peters' mental condition warranted further investigation. Cunningham suspected that Peters was suffering from the sequelae of *Encephalitis Lethargica*, a form of sleeping sickness that, he claimed, often included 'moral perversions'. Accordingly, the defence counsel argued at the High Court that Peters was unfit to plead and 'moved the Court to allow the previous plea of guilty to be withdrawn'. The Advocate Depute readily agreed with the motion but instructed that the panel be further examined by two 'alienists', Dr John Keay, Superintendent of Bangour Village District Asylum and Dr James Skeen, Medical Superintendent of New Saughton Hall. Keay confirmed Cunningham's view that Peters' behaviour was probably affected by the sequelae of *Encephalitis lethargica* which he described as a 'progressive disease . . . frequently accompanied by mental and moral deterioration with aberration of conduct, uncontrollable impulses and lapses of a criminal nature'. In his view, the accused was not certifiably insane but he was 'enfeebled', 'mentally deficient' and 'unfit to plead to a criminal charge'. Skeen broadly agreed with Keay's assessment. He found Peters to be 'a degenerate' and a 'feeble-minded person' with 'abnormal instincts', and recommended that the most appropriate outcome would be probation under careful guardianship as a 'certified weak-minded person'.

On the basis of these reports, the diet was deserted and the Crown Office instructed that 'endeavours [should] be made to get the accused admitted to an institution and failing that to be kept under supervision'. The first option proved problematic. As the Procurator Fiscal at Perth noted, in that the medical reports did not indicate that Peters was a lunatic or in a 'mental state threatening damage to the lieges', he could not be sent to an asylum under the terms of the Lunacy (Scotland) Act 1862. He could be sent to a private asylum as a voluntary patient but there was no public funding available. The parents could not afford it and, in any case, they did not consider their son to be 'mentally defective' and requiring detention in an institution. Instead, the High Court decided that Peters be 'liberated' and 'handed over to his parents at Perth prison with a strong message of the need for constant supervision' and for the police to continue to keep him under observation.

THE TRIAL

The hesitancy of witnesses to report their suspicions to the police and to become involved in criminal proceedings associated with acts of bestiality was sometimes echoed in the reluctance of procurators fiscal to indict suspected offenders.[61] For example, in the case of Ernest Johnson, in an effort to minimise public involvement in the more revolting aspects of the evidence, the Procurator Fiscal suggested that a summary trial might suffice, thus dispensing with the need for a jury.[62] In the case of Harry Embrow, a naval seaman charged in 1918 with having 'unnatural carnal connection' with a donkey mare in a field adjacent to Shore Road, Granton, the Procurator Fiscal for Edinburgh argued that the 'facts [were] not suitable for trial before a jury' and that the most desirable solution would be 'for the naval authorities to remove him and for him to be set at liberty elsewhere on the understanding that he [did] not return to the district'.[63] Similarly, in the extraordinary case of James McEwen, the Procurator Fiscal for Kirkudbright questioned whether a possible option was to adopt a process authorised in some cases by Crown Counsel whereby proceedings would be dropped 'if the accused undertook to and did leave the country'.[64] In all three cases, given the severity of the charge, the Crown Office instructed the Procurator Fiscal that the case should proceed to trial at the High Court.

However, the feelings of revulsion surrounding the crime of bestiality also shaped the nature of trial proceedings. In the majority of cases that went to trial, the judge ordered that 'evidence be taken behind closed doors' and, in a third of cases (mainly those involving some element of sexual sadism or serious damage to the animal's sexual organs), the Crown Office ordered that a 'men only jury' should be appointed.

Plea and verdict

In eight out of the twenty-three cases examined, the accused pleaded guilty in a Sheriff Court and the case was then remitted to the High Court for sentencing under section 31 of the Criminal Procedure (Scotland Act) 1887.[65] In a further four cases, though initially pleading not guilty, after being 're-interrogated' at the High Court, the panel changed his plea to guilty. Thus, nearly half the defendants charged with bestiality or attempted bestiality opted for trial by jury in the High Court, of whom four received a verdict of not guilty or not proven.

In the absence of court transcripts, one can only infer the reasons for the four acquittals from the precognitions and correspondence between the procurators fiscal and the Crown Office. In the case of Ernest Johnson, there were doubts as to how far the police had actually witnessed the sexual act. In addition, in their rush to get the accused to the police station so that the sergeant could witness his condition, the officers failed to carry out an immediate inspection of the donkey involved.[66] In the case of Harry Embrow, the lack of corroborative evidence seems to have been the major factor in failing to secure a conviction. As the Procurator Fiscal warned the Crown Agent, the 'evidence of connection' was narrow. Witnesses testified that they had seen the accused near the 'hindquarters of a mare' but could not corroborate the claim of the police constable that Embrow was actually 'covering the animal'.[67] Lack of corroboration also weakened the prosecution in the case of Isaac Flavell. Though the police constable claimed he had clearly seen the accused having connection with a cow and 'his erect private member come out of the cow's vagina', the initial medical examination of Flavell in the cells at Hamilton had revealed 'no animal hairs'. More seriously, the farmer could not identify the cow that had been interfered with, with a consequent lack of forensic evidence.[68]

Perhaps the most baffling outcome was in the case of William Simpson in 1911. Despite the accused having three previous convictions for bestiality, and compelling evidence from the farm grieve and police of the mare's abuse, the jury delivered a verdict of not guilty. The fact that neither the actual moment of connection nor overt signs of Simpson's sexual arousal had been witnessed, may have been decisive. In addition, the medical evidence was inconclusive, 'no evidence of sperm or hair' being found on the accused, a finding that was duly exploited by the defence. It was no doubt with considerable satisfaction that Scottish Law Officers observed Simpson being sentenced to five years penal servitude in 1912 for the self-same crime.[69]

The defence

There is little direct evidence of the type of argument used by defendants in these cases. Having been apprehended, none of the men accused of bestiality chose to make a Judicial Declaration explaining their actions, and the High Court minutes do not detail the closing arguments of the defence counsel prior to sentencing. Here also, one has to rely on a process of inference from the trial papers of the prosecution and from the manner in which precognitions were structured by the police and procurators fiscal in preparation for court proceedings. Those pleading not guilty to the charge of bestiality claimed that 'carnal connection' had not been attempted or effected. Typically, their need to sleep off the effects of alcohol and/or to urinate/defecate were advanced as an explanation of their presence in a field or stable, as well as their state of undress.[70] Forensic evidence was frequently challenged, with the defence in one case that the semen stains on the accused had been the product of a subsequent bout of masturbation in his own bed.[71]

Undoubtedly, for those pleading guilty, the most common argument in mitigation of their offence was that they had acted irrationally due to 'drink'. In virtually every case, the precognitions referred to the inebriated state of the accused and, where the defence case was explicitly mentioned in the trial papers, the impact of alcohol in producing the disinhibited and transgressive behaviour of the panel was foremost. Interestingly, despite the fact that so many of the offenders were single and unlikely to have ready access to commercial sex, the role of sexual frustration in the offence was rarely alluded to, although at least one precognition suggests that it may have been an important factor.[72] Very occasionally, the mental and emotional effects of war service were referred to as a possible explanation.[73]

Sentencing

The crime of bestiality had ceased to be a capital offence under the Criminal Procedure (Scotland) Act 1887. In practice, as with convictions for sodomy, it had already been well established that the prosecutor would normally press instead for a heavy sentence of penal servitude: that is, imprisonment with hard labour.[74] Evidence suggests, however, that, by the early twentieth century, a broader range of penalties was being adopted by the High Court in cases involving 'unnatural offences'. Of the seventeen offenders convicted of bestiality or attempted bestiality in the period 1900–30, five were sentenced to penal servitude for between three and five years while the remainder received normal prison sentences ranging from three to twelve months and averaging around 7½ months. Most of the harsher sentences of penal servitude preceded World War I and were imposed on offenders with a substantial record of previous convictions. The lowest sentences of from three to six months imprisonment were reserved for those convicted of the lesser charge of attempted bestiality, often as a result of some form of plea-bargaining. There does not appear to have been any clear relationship between the level of the sentence imposed and the severity of the injuries sustained by the animal involved. For example, in the case of Duncan Townsley, despite veterinary evidence that his sexual assault had been responsible for the ewe's death, his conviction by a majority verdict of the jury at the High Court in Perth only resulted in a six months prison sentence.[75]

CONCLUSION

While it would be unwise to draw from so few cases any firm conclusions with respect to shifts in the discourse surrounding the prosecution of bestiality in the period 1900–30, certain features may perhaps usefully be highlighted. Certainly, by 1900 the more familiar biblical references to the act and the retribution to be exacted by society had been replaced by a more purely secular, legalistic approach to the offence.[76] The historical conflation of bestiality with sodomy had also been eroded, permitting a more nuanced attitude to the crime. Even by 1930, however, a more medicalised/psychologised discursive approach was still muted in court proceedings and forensic reports, and the moral assumptions and rhetoric of *fin de siècle* degenerationism were still prevalent.[77] The mental capacity and fitness to plead of the defendant rather than his sexual orientation and motivation dominated psychiatric evidence and there is little evidence of engagement with the work and insights of the early sexologists in the field of sexual deviation. As in the treatment of homosexual crimes during the interwar period in Scotland,[78] the police and judiciary remained focused on bestiality as a criminal act demanding strict legal process rather than as a sexual pathology. As late as 1937, David Henderson, Physician Superintendent of the Royal Edinburgh Hospital and Professor of Psychiatry at the University of Edinburgh, criticised the legal system in the Scottish press for continuing to treat offenders as 'outcasts and degenerates' and 'as vicious sinners . . . acting with malice aforethought' rather than as 'unevenly immature persons whose psychopathy [had] taken a particular bias' which '[might] be loathsome but [was] nonetheless real' and which required medical treatment rather than imprisonment.[79] It would appear that, despite gradual advances in the understanding of the psychological forces shaping sexual behaviour, bestiality remained the object of primitive fears and loathing in interwar Scottish civil society.

NOTES

1. The following account is based on NRS, AD15/15/46, JC26/1915/16, JC14/33, Crown Office precognitions, High Court of Justiciary [hereafter HCJ] processes and minute books.
2. The following account is based on NRS, AD15/29/47, JC26/1929/62, JC14/40, Crown Office precognitions, HCJ processes and minute books.
3. See, for example, Krafft-Ebing, *Psychopathia Sexualis*, 404–7; Ellis, *Studies in the Psychology of Sex*, vol. 5, 67–74.
4. This contrasts with the literature available for the early modern period. See especially, Maxwell-Stuart, 'Wilde, filthe, execrabill, detestabill and unnatural sin', 82–93; Thomas, 'Not having God before his eyes', 149–73.
5. The cryptic mention of Patrick McCourt's trial and conviction for bestiality in 1929 as a 'case of an unsavoury nature' was typical of contemporary newspaper coverage [*Glasgow Herald*, 26 February 1929].
6. Parker, 'Is a duck an animal?', 96.
7. Two of the accused appeared before the High Court on more than one occasion in this period.
8. While in England a woman might be prosecuted for bestiality, it does not appear to have been so in Scotland. Archibald Alison, in his standard reference work on *The Principles of the Criminal Law in Scotland* (Edinburgh: Blackwood, 1833), described bestiality as 'the connection of a man with an animal'. According to G. H. Gordon 'there are no reported cases of bestiality by a woman in Scotland' [*The Criminal Law of Scotland*, 837].
9. This contrasts with the evidence for Queensland for a similar period where it was typically 'a young man's sexual offence' [Collins, 'Woman or beast?', 37]. It also contrasts with the Swedish experience, where: 'Young men and boys were grossly overrepresented among those who were prosecuted for bestiality' [Rydström, *Sinners and Citizens*, 195].
10. Certainly, Krafft-Ebing considered that 'lack of opportunity of natural indulgence' was one of the principal motives for 'this unnatural means of sexual satisfaction' [Krafft-Ebing, *Psychopathia Sexualis*, 405].
11. Swedish evidence suggests a similar class profile in adult offenders accused of bestiality [Rydström, 'Sodomitical sins', 250].
12. See, for example, NRS, AD15/15/46, AD15/22/87, Crown Office precognitions in cases against Owen Gunnery and Alexander McKenzie.
13. In addition, one defendant had previously been convicted of indecent exposure and another of lewd and libidinous practices. A further defendant had previously been prosecuted for contravention of the Cruelty to Animals Act 1850.
14. NRS, AD15/12/56, Crown Office precognitions in case against William Simpson.
15. See, for example, NRS, AD15/09/68, AD15/21/155, Crown Office precognitions in cases against Robert Reed and John Gordon.

16. NRS, AD15/15/58, precognition of Thomas Marshall, 30 March 1915.

17. NRS, AD15/21/193, Crown Office precognitions in case against James McEwan.

18. Collins, 'Woman or beast?', 36, 41. From a feminist perspective, she argues that this association furnishes 'insights into the interchangeable and coercive character of male sexuality'. For a discussion of the traditional conceptualisation of bestiality as a 'sodomitical sin', see Thomas, 'Not having God before his eyes', 152–4. This association of bestiality with homosexual offences lingered in Scottish legal textbooks. As late as 1987, in the ninth edition of Gloag and Henderson, *Introduction to the Law of Scotland*, 910, the editors coupled 'Sodomy and Bestiality' together as a separate category of sexual offence.

19. See, for example, NRS, AD15/10/58, Crown Office precognitions in the case against Peter Roy, statement of David Calder, horse dealer.

20. NRS, JC26/1915/34, HCJ processes, report by John Jarvie, veterinary surgeon, 28 March 1915.

21. NRS, AD15/16/80, Crown Office precognitions in case against Thomas Peacock.

22. NRS, AD15/21/193, Crown Office precognitions in case against James McEwen. Krafft-Ebing had referred to similar cases [*Psychopathia Sexualis*, 85].

23. NRS, AD15/24/82, precognition of W. S. Lornie, veterinary surgeon, 2 June 1924.

24. Thus, in the case of Michael Cannon, accused of 'unnatural carnal connection' with a cow in a field in Bonhill, West Dunbartonshire, the police were alerted by a tramway conductor en route from Balloch to Dumbarton [NRS, AD15/13/60, Crown Office precognitions]. Other fields were located adjacent to the Caledonian Railway, to the Fife Coal Company, and to Bellahouston Park, Ibrox [NRS, JC26/1915/50, AD15/26/9, AD15/19/27, HCJ processes and Crown Office precognitions].

25. See, for example, NRS, AD15/12/56, AD15/13/129, AD15/16/80, Crown Office precognitions.

26. See, for example, NRS, AD15/15/46, AD15/15/58, AD15/22/87, Crown Office precognitions.

27. NRS, AD15/10/58, precognition of Joan Calder, horse-dealer's wife, 1 November 1910. See also, AD15/09/68, AD15/12/14, AD15/12/56, AD15/15/46, AD15/15/58, Crown Office precognitions.

28. NRS, AD15/12/56, 'Statement of facts' by Deputy Procurator Fiscal, Perth, 4 September 1912.

29. In no case was the offender the owner of the animal involved.

30. NRS, AD15/12/56, 'Statement of facts' by Deputy Procurator Fiscal, Perth, 4 September 1912.

31. NRS, AD15/13/143, Procurator Fiscal, Dunfermline, to Crown Agent, 23 September 1913.

32. NRS, AD15/09/68, Procurator Fiscal, Kirkudbright, to Crown Agent, 7 January 1909. The police sergeant at Creetown testified that 'people hesitate to make a complaint on account of the nasty nature of the crime'.

33. NRS, AD15/13/129, precognitions of James Furay and Edward McNally, firewood company workers, 22 November 1913.

34. See, for example, Brown, 'A comparative study of deviations from sexual mores', 140–2; C. Davies, 'Sexual taboos and social boundaries', 1032–3. For an historical perspective on the 'powerful cultural resonance' of bestiality, alongside other sexual behaviour 'viewed as lewd or subversive of the natural order', see Thomas, 'Not having God before his eyes', 150, 154.

35. NRS, AD15/09/68, precognition of Sergeant Isaac Thomson, 4 January 1909.

36. NRS, AD15/10/58, precognition of PC William Campbell, 1 November 1910.

37. NRS, AD15/21/193, precognition of Gordon Anderson, 27 September 1921.

38. NRS, AD15/12/56, AD15/12/133, AD15/15/46, Crown Office precognitions. See also, AD15/16/80. For similar methods of investigation in cases of bestiality in Sweden, see Rydström, 'Sodomitical sins are threefold', 241–2.

39. NRS, AD15/29/47, Crown Office precognitions.

40. NRS, AD15/18/24, precognition of PC Alexander Souter, 26 July 1918.

41. NRS, AD15/21/155, precognition of PC Blyth Adams, 11 November 1920.

42. NRS, AD15/21/193, precognition of Gordon Anderson, 27 September 1921.

43. NRS, AD15/22/87, Crown Office precognitions.

44. See, for example, NRS, AD15/09/68, AD15/12/14, AD15/21/176A, JC26/1915/34, Crown Office precognitions and HCJ processes.

45. See, for example, NRS, AD15/12/56, Crown Office precognitions in case against William Simpson.

46. Proof of penetration had long played a vital role in the prosecution of bestiality. See, for example, Fudge, 'Monstrous acts', 25.

47. Thus, in the case of Michael Cannon, police statements repeatedly emphasised the visibility afforded by the electric light from the tramcar [NRS, AD15/13/60]. In the case of Owen Gunnery, the carting contractor emphasised in his precognition that he had been able to 'witness the connection' as 'the glare from the Dalziel Steelworks lights up the stable when the door is open' [NRS, AD15/15/46].

48. Glaister and Glaister Jnr, *A Textbook of Medical Jurisprudence and Toxicology*, 1931 edition, 551.

49. For an excellent overview of the use of medical forensic experts in Scottish legal cases during this period, and the analytical techniques employed by them, see Duvall, 'Forensic Medicine in Scotland, 1914–39', PhD thesis.

50. NRS, AD15/09/68, Reports from John Glaister, 20 and 27 January 1909.

During this period there was little advance in the techniques employed to identify semen on material evidence. The sole criterion for the positive identification of semen remained the microscopic discovery of spermatozoa [Duvall, 'Forensic Medicine in Scotland', PhD thesis, 82].

51. NRS, JC26/1915/34, medical report by Dr J. H. Patterson, 30 March 1915. See also JC26/1916/35, medical report by Dr J. Anderson, Pathological Department, Victoria Infirmary, Glasgow, 20 November 1916.

52. See, for example, NRS, AD15/12/14, AD15/12/133, AD15/15/75, JC26/1915/34, Crown Office precognitions and HCJ processes in cases against William Smillie, William Simpson and James Maley.

53. See, for example, NRS, AD15/15/58, AD15/16/80, AD15/24/82, Crown Office precognitions.

54. NRS, AD15/21/176A, report by veterinary surgeon, 21 May 1921.

55. NRS, AD15/22/87, report by veterinary surgeon, 8 November 1921.

56. The following account is based on NRS, AD15/21/155, JC26/1921/57, JC9/17, Crown Office precognitions, HCJ processes and minute books.

57. In this case, the nature of the offence may also have been a consideration in the response of the General Board of Control. Their communication stressed that 'while, in the past, institutions have made every effort to improvise accommodation for the less objectionable cases of persons guilty of offences, they have strongly expressed their unwillingness to admit cases of the type of John Gordon' [NRS, AD15/21/155, General Board of Control to Crown Agent, 3 February 1921].

58. The panel refers to any person or persons charged with a crime or offence in Scots law.

59. The following account is based on NRS, AD15/21/193, JC12/55, Crown Office precognitions and HCJ processes.

60. The following account is based on AD15/27/43, JC26/1927/67, JC9/21, Crown Office precognitions, HCJ processes and minute books.

61. The reluctance of the legal system to investigate acts of bestiality, and the possible motives behind the offence, owing to 'the social taboo' surrounding it, appears to have survived into the late twentieth century [Bollinger and Goetschel, 'Sexual relations with animals', 36].

62. NRS, AD15/13/143, Procurator Fiscal, Dunfermline, to Crown Agent, 2 October 1913.

63. NRS, AD15/18/24, Procurator Fiscal, Edinburgh, to Crown Agent, 1 August 1915.

64. NRS, AD15/21/193, Procurator Fiscal, Kirkudbright, to Crown Agent, 30 September 1921.

65. This enabled the defence to plead guilty and have its case immediately processed for sentencing without trial and the need to name witnesses.

66. NRS, AD15/13/143, Crown Office precognitions.

67. NRS, AD15/18/24, Crown Office precognitions.

68. NRS, AD15/19/73, Crown Office precognitions.

69. NRS, AD15/12/56, AD15/12/133, JC26/1912/132, Crown Office precognitions and HCJ processes.

70. See, for example, NRS, AD15/12/133, AD15/13/143, AD15/21/176A, AD15/18/24, Crown Office precognitions in cases against William Simpson, Ernest Johnson, Harry Embrow and John Macdonald.

71. NRS, AD15/13/143, precognitions of PCs J. Peebles and R. Falconer, 29 September 1913.

72. Thus, in the case of Alexander McKenzie in 1922, the police constable claimed to have overheard the accused mutter 'something about "having a lot of stuff to get rid of tonight"' and ' "by Christ there's a good fuck for me here tonight" ' [NRS, AD15/22/87, Crown Office precognitions].

73. See especially, NRS, AD15/29/47, report to High Court by Procurator Fiscal, Ayr, 1 February 1929.

74. Macdonald and Macdonald, *A Practical Treatise on the Criminal Law of Scotland*, 204; Green's, *Encyclopaedia of the Laws of Scotland*, Vol. 5, 136–7. As bestiality was a common law charge brought in the High Court of Justiciary, or remitted there for sentence, any term of imprisonment might be imposed.

75. NRS, AD15/15/24/82, JC26/1924/46, Crown Office precognitions and HCJ processes.

76. All biblical references to bestiality prescribe a penalty of death [*Exodus* 22:19–20; *Leviticus* 18:22–23; *Deuteronomy* 27:21–22].

77. This 'vacillation' between medical and moral discourses was also a feature of early twentieth-century Swedish legal proceedings [Rydström, 'Sodomitical sins', 253–4]. On the longer-term shift from the 'outmoded theological rhetoric of demonic influences to the deterministic straightjacket of mental abnormalities', see Beirne, 'On the sexual assault on animals', 206–7.

78. Merrilees, *The Short Arm of the Law*, 121–2.

79. *The Scotsman*, 23 February 1937, 5 April 1937. See also, Henderson, *Psychopathic States*, 75–7.

5

'There's the Man who Shifts the Babies': Abortion in the Scottish High Court 1900–30

INTRODUCTION

In contrast to other countries in the United Kingdom, Europe and North America,[1] little is known about the abortion practices and prosecutions in early twentieth-century Scotland. Where the Scottish legal history surrounding the crime of procuring abortion has been explored, it has primarily been as a cursory preamble to a discussion of the 1967 Abortion Act and the implications for its subsequent interpretation of disparities between Scottish common law and English statute law.[2] This detailed analysis of High Court cases seeks for the first time to reveal the process of abortion and its interface with the law in Scotland over the period 1900–30.

In drawing conclusions from these court proceedings, the social historian is subject to a range of limitations. First, it is uncertain how far the abortion narrative captured in the High Court records was representative of the many illegal abortions that were neither reported nor prosecuted, and that according to contemporary commentators resulted in the termination of as many as one in eight of all pregnancies and accounted for a similar proportion of maternal mortality.[3] Secondly, the gender bias of the legal process has to be recognised. As Usborne has observed, women's testimonies in abortion cases were 'often shaped by the specific questions asked by male interrogators who followed a set pattern of enquiry' and by the recasting of their answers in legal and medical language.[4] As a result, their experiences and perspectives could often be subordinated to the more limited (quintessentially male) agendas of policing and prosecution. Thirdly, the absence of trial transcripts limits the degree to which the competing legal, medical and popular narratives within courtroom proceedings can be examined. In addition, as with other offences, without access to the judge's closing remarks, it is difficult to capture the views of the judiciary on illegal abortion and the social ideology that informed them. Such constraints are compounded by the scarcity of substantive newspaper reports of High Court abortion cases. Apart from a very few trials where a prominent member of the community, such as a leading medical practitioner, was involved or an exhumation required, court proceedings were rarely reported in any detail. As Lesley Hall has commented, prior to 1930 abortion was 'not a subject publicly discussed: it was debated by doctors and lawyers under discreet veils of professional privilege, or in whispers and hints between unwillingly pregnant women, their partners and their associates'.[5] Consequently, there is limited evidence with which to gauge how the crime was perceived in the public domain beyond the immediate social milieu of the abortionists and their clients and how far, in passing sentence, the courts validated such views.

Nonetheless, an in-depth study of the precognitions and processes for all High Court cases over the period can provide some valuable insights into the social and sexual relationships prevailing in the Scottish cities in the early twentieth century, and their relationship with the law. While the process of abortion was usually veiled in secrecy owing to a combination of medical confidentiality and fear of criminal prosecution, as McLaren argues, court records spotlight 'the fact that abortions were not carried out in isolation; they were social acts the investigations of which reveal the particular nature of the relationships of women ... with their male partners, their friends, their doctors, and ultimately the judiciary'.[6] In addition, as Usborne observes, criminal depositions afford a unique opportunity to reconstruct 'the organisation and experience of abortion from below'.[7] The historian can explore the socio-economic profile and motives of women undergoing illegal abortions and of their abortionists; the extent and cultural acceptance of self-treatment; the often complex social networking and negotiation that underpinned the operation and the nature and outcome of the procedure. Meanwhile, the same sources can document the factors shaping the prosecution and sentencing of offenders; the means by which illegal abortions came to the notice of the police and procurators fiscal; the methods of investigation and evidence collection, especially the use of forensic medical expertise; and, above all, the legal framework in Scotland within which the Crown prosecution operated and how it was interpreted by the Crown Office and judiciary.

THE WOMEN SEEKING ABORTIONS

What do the High Court records reveal about the women who sought an abortion in early twentieth-century Scotland? The ages of the seventy-eight women who were cited in the indictments in the period 1900–30 ranged from sixteen to forty-six. Their average age was twenty-six with a marked continuity between the pre-war and interwar years. A breakdown of their age distribution [see Table 5.1] reveals that just under a fifth of the women were in the fifteen to twenty age range with well over half in their twenties. Around a quarter were aged over thirty but, after 1918, they clustered predominantly in the thirty-one to thirty-five age group with a marked drop in the oldest cohort.

The overwhelming majority of the women cited in High Court cases as having been the subject of illegal abortion were from the lower social classes within the major cities,[8] often with a history of low-paid and/or insecure employment, poor housing, and limited financial reserves. Because they did not have the influence and resources of their social superiors to secure discreet medical terminations, but were usually dependent on the more dangerous and publicised practices of lay abortionists, they inevitably dominated criminal proceedings. The court records confirm previous evidence that abortion was primarily an urban experience. Eighty-six per cent of the women resided in the four main cities, with Glasgow the predominant location (51%) followed by Edinburgh (16%), Aberdeen (12%) and Dundee (7%). A scatter of more rural locations accounted for only 9% of addresses. Of the women cited in the High Court indictments 52% were single, 28% were married, 5% were married but separated, and 10% were widowed. The marital status of the remaining 5% is not recorded.

Over 60 per cent of the women involved in High Court proceedings were recorded as in paid employment at the time their case came to trial.

Table 5.1 Age distribution of women seeking abortions cited in Scottish High Court cases, 1900–30.

age	% 1900–30	% 1900–18	% 1918–30
15–20	18	19	18
21–25	36	33	35
26–30	22	24	21
31–35	15	10	23
Over 35	9	14	3

Source: NRS, AD15, Crown Office precognitions.

Table 5.2 Occupational distribution of women seeking abortions cited in Scottish High Court cases, 1900–30

Occupation	number
Cleaner	6
Domestic servant	11
Factory/workshop worker	7
Farm worker	2
Landlady	2
Office worker	7
Shop assistant	6
Theatre attendant	1
Transport worker	2
Waitress/Barmaid	5
Unrecorded	29

Source: NRS, AD15, Crown Office precognitions.

They were engaged in a wide spectrum of occupations [See Table 5.2]. Certain of these, such as domestic service, often exposed young women in particular to sexual exploitation often resulting in pregnancy and recourse to abortion. Those for whom no occupation was identified in the court papers tended to fall into two main groups: those in the very youngest age group and the more mature married and widowed women with more than one child.

Establishing what motivated these women to seek an abortion is problematic. It has to be remembered that precognitions and court evidence were tailored to the agenda of law officers who, as we shall see, were primarily focused on the motives of abortionists rather than their clients.[9] In addition, it is likely that the degree of pressure from partners, parents and siblings on women to seek a termination is greatly understated given their concern to avoid being prosecuted as accessories to a crime. Nevertheless, the legal records for the period do provide the basis for some broad conclusions about motivation. Often a range of interrelated reasons are advanced encompassing a mix of financial, emotional, and moral considerations.

A main justification for approaching abortionists, advanced especially by the younger age groups, was the lack of an ability to marry and legitimise the process of childbirth with the attendant fear of social stigma and of disgracing the family.[10] Often relationships broke down or their 'sweethearts' failed to fulfil their promises to marry once the pregnancy was confirmed. In some instances, it transpired that they were already married and leading a double life. Objections (either real or anticipated) from parents to a young woman's boyfriend on grounds of age, class or religious affiliation could also rule out marriage. Where the pregnancy was the result of a single episode of casual sex or sustained promiscuity, where an affair with a married man had been conducted, or where sexual assault was involved, recourse to abortionists was even more likely.

A desire to limit family size formed another major reason for seeking termination and was more typical of the older married women, aged over thirty, who had already several children. Such women were already frequently suffering from financial hardship and could ill afford an addition to the family. The incentive to avoid having further children was compounded by other factors, such as the death of a husband, marital separation, unemployment within the family, or the lack of adequate accommodation. It was not uncommon for witnesses who had been the subject of abortions to share a two-roomed apartment with another family, with the kitchen recess acting as a bedroom.

THE PROCESS OF OBTAINING AN ABORTION

Self-treatment

The High Court precognitions reveal that abortion was not a single event but often part of an elaborate process of social networking and medical intervention. The initial phase of the process was commonly a period of self-treatment,[11] often facilitated by friends, neighbours and relatives, in which many women tended to blur the boundaries between menstruation and pregnancy and to view the issue primarily as one of restoring their menses rather than abortion, and not as an illegal act.[12] They frequently ingested abortifacients as soon as a period was late or even when a period was due to ensure that it came on time. The milder treatments included the consumption of Epsom salts or Kruschen salts together with hot mustard baths.[13] More commonly, however, as Henry Littlejohn, Professor of Medical Jurisprudence at the University of Edinburgh, observed, Scottish women used more 'drastic purgatives' in an attempt to miscarry. Thus, in 1909, Elizabeth Ettles, a 22-year-old laundry worker in Aberdeen, persuaded her mother to take her to a local herbalist to 'see if [she] could get something to put her right'.[14] Over the next six weeks she paid out as much as £2 for a range of pills. Thereafter, she spotted a newspaper advert for medicine that would 'ensure menstruation' and sent away to a Glasgow address for more pills 'and a mixture' costing 19/6d, all to no effect.[15] In 1911, Willamina

Snowden testified that she made her own 'corrective pills' composed of pennyroyal,[16] bitter aloes,[17] diachylon,[18] and bitter apple,[19] which she also dispensed to friends whose periods had failed to materialise.[20] The following year, Margaret Gemmel admitted to a neighbour that she had taken 7/6d worth of pills 'she had got from England, with a view to inducing a miscarriage' and that 'when in the family way on several occasions she had succeeded in effecting a miscarriage by means of powders that she had obtained from a herbalist in Greenock'.[21] In 1918, it was alleged that Elizabeth Gordon, a 35-year-old former munitions worker from Dumbarton, who had died following an illegal abortion, had previously possessed her own douche and 'talked about aborting herself' and purchasing pearl ashes and isinglass.[22] Again in 1923, it was reported that Naomi McPhee, a 27-year-old stewardess, had taken 'Hickory-Pickory' prior to approaching an abortionist.[23] The same year, Margaret McGill, the victim of rape, sent away to a 'Medical Specialist' in Leeds offering the so-called 'Challenge Remedy' consisting of five bottles of medicine containing liquid essence of ergot and tincture of steel, to be taken along with a hot water douche or hot baths.[24] In 1927, Nellie Belbin, a 36-year-old tramcar conductress testified to having taken 'pills and quinine powder on different occasions' as well as using a douche prior to making contact with the accused, Catherine Craig.[25] Finally, in 1929, Agnes Logan, finding herself pregnant, sent her daughter to the chemist to shop for saltpetre, and on the recommendation of a local barmaid friend took a 'mixture of syrup of squills, pennyroyal and steel drops'.[26]

Interestingly, apart from the occasional use of douches, there is virtually no reference in the precognitions to the use of instruments, such as catheters, speculums, bougies or crochet hooks, by women seeking to self-induce an abortion. As in England, use of these instruments 'was more likely to require assistance from abortionists and therefore to be more expensive, and the results were likely to be more traumatic and painful'.[27] It was also in the interests of the prosecution to play down a practice that could very easily weaken the case against the professional abortionist who might subsequently have been employed. However, within the High Court records there is evidence of violent 'physical exercise' being used in an attempt to procure abortion. In 1915, Littlejohn observed that it was a 'public belief' and that 'many women try that as a first means' and 'will bicycle before they confide in anyone' in an attempt to bring on their menses, albeit to no effect.[28] In 1928, Mary Anne Moss, a 28-year-old barmaid in Trinity, Edinburgh, testified that her abortion was 'the result of what I did myself. I had the idea that physical exercise and severe jerks and jumping would cause abortion and I often during the period after Christmas jumped violently on and over the counter . . . for this purpose.'[29]

Contacting an abortionist

Women obtained information on, and access to, abortionists in a wide variety of ways. In many instances, abortionists were recommended by a relative, friend, lodger or neighbour, some of whom had previously used their services or heard about their reputation for 'relieving women' on the local rumour mill.[30] Often the information conveyed was at second or third hand and contact with the abortionist made through a circuitous series of social encounters. For example, in 1909, Helen McKendrick made contact through her boyfriend's mother with William Hay, the Glasgow herbalist who operated on her. She had previously heard about him when she had worked at a restaurant in the Gallowgate. Hay had come into the restaurant and another girl had said : 'There's the man who shifts the babies'.[31] In the case against George Bell Todd in 1912, the witness Mary Orman, a 22-year-old domestic servant in Edinburgh, had been told about him by a friend 'who had heard his name mentioned by a butcher in Dalry Road, whose wife had used him'.[32] Again, in 1928, Mary McKan, a 20-year-old waitress in the Waldorf Palais de Danse, Sauchiehall Street, accessed the accused, Jane Hudson, through a network of contacts. An acquaintance, Lily Reposo, who worked in the Picture House Cafe resided with a woman, Elizabeth Christie, who in turn confided in Esther De Marco who knew of Hudson's reputation for procuring abortions and agreed to take McKan to Hudson's rooms in Crow Road.[33]

In some cases, women responded to advertisements in newspapers and shop windows or learnt of abortionists through publicity surrounding criminal proceedings. Thus, in 1911, two farm servants, Annie and Christina McDougall both contacted Mary Russell after they saw her advert as a 'midwife' offering 'private rooms for accouchement' and having 'heard from other women' that she 'did away with unborn children'.[34] Two of the women involved in the prosecution of George Bell Todd in 1912 had been made aware of his reputation for performing abortions by the newspaper coverage of his trial in the previous year.[35] Similarly, in 1925, Margaret McGill, a 25-year-old housekeeper, testified that she had 'heard that maternity nurses sometimes assisted girls like [her] to be rid of their pregnancy': 'I read advertisements of nurses in the paper and decided to approach the accused'.[36] Again, in 1929, in the prosecution of Annie Lawrie and Agnes Wilson, the process of accessing their services was initiated by an advert in the *Evening News* for 'Nurse Wilson's pills for irregularities'.[37] Suggestive window displays could also feature in the story. In the widely publicised case against Charles Alder in 1915, the boyfriend of Margaret Anderson, his deceased client, had approached Alder in his shop in West Register Street, Edinburgh to 'get some medicine to bring on the periods' having seen its display board advertising 'Cure for female irregularities'.[38] A similar display in Argyle Street, Glasgow in 1929, led Agnes Thompson, a 58-year-old widow, to make contact with the salesman, James Crichton, who was subsequently found guilty of attempting to procure her abortion.[39]

Chemists, herbalists, and sometimes fortune tellers also played a role, referring women on to abortionists after self-treatment had failed, apart from causing severe pain and sickness. In the case against Benjamin Jepson in 1911, two of the witnesses had been introduced to him by Margaret Leitch, a self-styled palmist and clairvoyant in Aberdeen, who, it was alleged, regularly supplied him with women 'who wanted to talk about their courses'.[40] Anne Borland, also from Aberdeen, testified the same year to having been given the address of her abortionist by Jean Chalmers, a fortune teller.[41] In the case against Constance McCurdie in 1918, Mary McMillan, a 28-year-old former munitions worker, had been introduced by her boyfriend to a fortune teller who had directed her to Sarah Wright, a chemist, who in turn had referred her to McCurdie after her prescription of quinine and whisky had proved ineffectual.[42] Again, in 1926, Christina Gerry located her abortionist, Catherine Clark, through Jeannie Milligan, a local chemist, who furnished her with a letter of introduction and who clearly acted as a procurer for Clark on a regular basis.[43]

Women seeking to find an abortionist 'to put them right' or restore their 'monthly illness' also gleaned information from current or former workmates or just general workplace rumour and gossip. In the case against Jane Anderson in 1911, two of the witnesses had formerly worked with her in the Dundee Calendar (cloth finishing) Works and had heard of her reputation for assisting girls requiring a termination.[44] The following year, in Aberdeen, Mary Johnston learnt of James Brongo's (real name James Leslie Harper) reputation for performing abortions from a colleague working at the Railway Station Refreshment Rooms.[45] Similarly, in 1919, Joan Miller accessed her abortionist, Jane Hudson, partly on the basis of rumours at her workplace, Langs Restaurant in Partick, that 'she would douche out girls in the condition and make them alright'.[46]

Meanwhile, High Court records would appear to indicate that, while husbands might be aware of their wives' intentions to try to terminate their pregnancy, and on occasions tried to dissuade them from undergoing dangerous procedures, they played a relatively minor role in initiating the process of abortion. This may be partly due to the tendency of women to understate the part performed by their partners in order to protect them from prosecution. In addition, as in Canada,[47] when an abortion involved a married woman, courts in Scotland tended to play down the husband's participation, especially when the termination had proved fatal. Evidence suggests, however, that, as elsewhere in Europe, husbands in Scotland 'were largely absent from the abortion market' with the final decision to abort within marriage being viewed primarily as the 'woman's province'.[48] Husbands not infrequently denied all knowledge of events, only being alerted by the intervention of qualified medical practitioners and the police, following an abortion. Thus, in the prosecution of Jane Anderson in 1911, William Murray stated that, while he had known that his deceased wife was 'getting pills from Anderson to get rid of the child', he had been unaware that she was subsequently undergoing invasive procedures. He claimed that: 'They never talked about it again . . . During the remaining fortnight of my wife's life I said no more about the matter, and I do not know that I troubled myself about the matter'.[49] Similarly, in the trial of George Todd in 1912, John Gemmell and Mungo Borthwick both claimed that they had not been involved in their wives' decisions to obtain an abortion or in their subsequent terminations.[50] The following year, in his summing up in the trial of Thomas Campbell, the judge expressed his astonishment that, although the fatal abortion of Barbara Murray in Parkhead had taken place 'within a few weeks of marriage of this woman', 'not a word was communicated to her husband of what had happened or what was happening'.[51] In the case against Catherine Clark in 1926, the lead witnesses claimed that her husband had not suggested an abortion, had not been involved in the process, and 'had been told nothing until after the foetus had been disposed of'.[52]

In contrast, where pregnancy was the outcome of an adulterous affair or just casual sex, men might play a more active role, either to protect their reputation or to evade any marital obligations. For example, when, in 1912, Maggie Cameron, a 25-year-old assistant hairdresser in Aberdeen got pregnant by her married employer, he used information he had picked up from a 'traveller' to secure an abortionist in Glasgow, fearing that any approach to a local doctor might lead to gossip and 'not be good for business'.[53] In 1915, in the case against Charles Alder, the boyfriend of Margaret Anderson claimed that he had not been convinced she was pregnant and thought she 'was tricking him into marriage'. He had procured permanganate of potash pills for her and then paid £5 to Alder to 'bring on the girl's courses' in order to escape from the relationship.[54] Finally, in the case against Margaret and William Purves in 1930, Helen Lyons testified that she had had an affair with her friend's husband, Robert Anderson. He was anxious for her to terminate the pregnancy before it became common knowledge, supplying her with 'capsules and white pills' and then arranging for her to go to a herbalist for more invasive treatment.[55] It is worth noting that, to a significant extent, the process of contacting an abortionist was gendered; while women primarily accessed female abortionists through a network of female friends and contacts, male lovers, when they were prepared to become involved, primarily sought a male abortionist through male networks.

Payment

High Court records suggest that, over the period 1900–30, the average cost of an abortion was in the region of £5, with the average for the pre-war period being nearer £3.[56] However, the fees charged could vary significantly. In a very few cases, where the abortionist viewed his/her practice as primarily a social service to the community, a minimal charge might be made.[57] In other cases the fee was determined more by the social and economic status of the client. For poorer women desperately seeking an abortion, payment might be discounted or deferred. For example, in the case against George Todd in 1912, while his normal fee for procuring an abortion was £5, 'being a working man's wife', Margaret Gemmel 'had got it done for £2'.[58] Similarly, in 1928, Margaret Shaw reduced her normal fee of £4 to £5 to two guineas for her client, Euthemia Henderson, in view of the fact that she was unemployed and two guineas was all she had left in her Penny Savings Account.[59] Likewise, in 1930, Mary Shannon was allowed to pay her abortionist in instalments after she had recovered and returned to work.[60] At the same time, however, where, as was customary, the man responsible for the pregnancy was paying for the abortion, and appeared to be comfortably off, the fee might be calibrated accordingly. For example, in 1916, the manager of a coal merchants paid as much as £25 for a termination for one of his employees whom he had sexually exploited.[61] Higher fees were also incurred where several procedures were needed, including the administration of pills and mixtures, repeated douching and the use of invasive instruments.[62] In addition, abortionists charged more the further a pregnancy was advanced, given the higher risk of medical complications and detection, quite apart from the ethical considerations involved in dealing with a more developed foetus.[63] The highest fees, in the region of £10 to £15, tended to occur where midwives and doctors (qualified as well as 'quack') were involved, clients assuming that their medical expertise would ensure a safer and more hygienic procedure.[64] Abortionists commonly shared a portion of their earnings with women in the community who procured business for them or permitted their property to be used for the procedure, although such women were keen to deny any financial relationship for fear of being prosecuted as an accomplice to the crime.[65]

THE ABORTIONISTS

Some fifty-three people were indicted in the Scottish High Court for the crime of procuring or attempting to procure abortion during the period 1900–30. Of these, twenty-four (45 per cent) were men and twenty-nine (55 per cent) were women. However, the gender distribution of defendants varied significantly over time. In the period 1900–14 some 80 per cent were men as compared with 35 per cent for the period 1915–30. Seven women and two men were prosecuted more than once. The average age of the men indicted, for whom information is available, was forty-six; the comparable figure for women was forty-nine, on average some twenty-three years older than their female clients.[66]

The majority of the women indicted were, or claimed to be, either 'midwives' or 'nurses', and typically enjoyed a reputation in their local communities for terminating unwanted pregnancies.[67] While some of what might be termed 'paramedical abortionists' were registered midwives, the status of many others was open to doubt. For example, although, in 1911, Mary Hall advertised herself as a midwife taking in 'confinement cases', the prosecution could find no evidence of her registration by the Central Midwives Board for Scotland.[68] Nan Main, indicted for murder by performing an illegal abortion on a young woman in 1919, claimed she had 'been studying midwifery for two years' but was, in fact, unemployed, having previously worked as a photographic assistant and munitions worker.[69] Similarly, Jane Robertson, tried on charges of culpable homicide and of procuring abortion in 1916 and 1927, had falsely claimed to clients that she had practised as a midwife in order to secure their confidence, much to the disgust of the National

Vigilance Association for Scotland, who had been closely monitoring her activities.[70] How experienced some of the self-styled 'nurses' were who were indicted before the High Court is also open to question. Certainly, law officers and medical experts believed that a rogue element within the nursing profession was heavily involved in the practice of illegal abortion. In 1916, the Procurator Fiscal for Glasgow reported that there was believed to be 'a systematic procuring of abortion in various nursing homes in Glasgow', a view later confirmed by the staff of the Royal Maternity Hospital in Rottenrow.[71]

The remaining female 'lay' abortionists prosecuted in the Scottish High Court were typically 'middle-aged', married women, with children, who operated on a more ad hoc basis. Rather than advertising, they attracted clients through their local network of friends and neighbours. Often, these 'wise women' had acquired over the years a degree of 'expertise' (along with a range of drugs, douches and medical instruments) based on their own efforts to abort or on their participation in procedures carried out by midwives and nurses, an expertise that was widely recognised or, in the common parlance, 'known' within the community.

In a very few instances, altruistic motives were pleaded by female defendants. For example, in the trial of Jane Anderson, a 39-year-old sick nurse, charged in 1911 with seven offences of procuring and attempting to procure abortions in Glasgow and Dundee, defence witnesses argued that she was 'no criminal trading on the sins of her fellows'. According to Canon John Shepherd, Rector of St Mary Magdalene's, Dundee:

> She seems not to have ever realised that what she did was more than a good turn to some of her neighbours. She was led into something probably out of a desire to get someone out of what seemed to her 'a trouble' . . . As to the sin and criminality of her action she seems to have only a slight idea. She has made no money out of it and has been pestered by girls coming to her as the result of the first wrong step.[72]

In the case against Margaret Shaw in 1928, the arresting officer claimed she had protested that she 'did it for sheer charity's sake'.[73] Similarly, in the trial of Gladys Peadon, the 33-year-old wife of a Glasgow police constable, charged with seven offences of procuring abortion in 1929, evidence suggested that she had charged a minimal fee of between 2/6d and 10 shillings and 'was apparently quite willing to conduct the practices upon anyone who approached her'.[74] Defence counsel argued that 'the acts were committed as an obligement and not for reward'.[75] Such cases were exceptional, however, and generally female 'lay' abortionists viewed the fees derived from their abortion work as providing a welcome supplement to an otherwise meagre family income.[76]

Meanwhile, of the twenty-four men prosecuted in the Scottish High Court for offences relating to abortion, five were either qualified medical practitioners or had previously undertaken some form of formal medical training. They included James Brander, arrested in 1909 in Aberdeen. At one time a successful physician and surgeon, he had 'taken to drink' and become increasingly involved in performing illegal abortions while reduced to living in a corporation lodging house. In 1898 he had been tried in the High Court for performing an abortion in Aberdeen but found not guilty. In 1906 the General Medical Council had debarred him from practising for 'drunkenness and riotous behaviour'. At his trial in 1909, he was found guilty and sentenced to three years penal servitude.[77] George Bell Todd MD, CM was also prosecuted twice in the High Court. He operated from upmarket consulting rooms in Glasgow's West End. He had acquired extensive experience as a general practitioner and medical officer, specialising in gynaecology. He was a Professor of Zoology in Anderson's Medical School and had for many years been an assistant physician in the Royal Samaritan Hospital for Women. In 1911, he was indicted on two counts of procuring abortions in his consulting rooms in Landsdowne Terrace but acquitted. However, the following year he faced nineteen similar charges. Though he only pleaded guilty to four of the charges, he was duly sentenced at the High Court in Edinburgh to seven years penal servitude. According to the judge, it was the first case of a licensed medical practitioner being sentenced for this offence in Scotland.[78]

Chemists also featured in the list of defendants, being ideally placed to oversee the prescription and consumption of abortifacients under the guise of innocent medications for 'blocked menses' and 'female irregularities', sometimes in collusion with a midwife or nurse.[79] A further group of offenders described themselves as herbalists, frequently posing as medical doctors when advertising their services and when dealing with female clients. Perhaps the most notorious of this group was James Lesley Brongo. Described by the Procurator Fiscal for Aberdeen as a 'man of colour' who was 'by habit and repute a most skilled abortionist', Brongo was a native of the West Indies brought up in Aberdeen who had previously been a member of a touring theatre company in England. Subsequently, he had travelled to fairs and markets all over the country where 'he sold pills, medicines, and corn cures' and extracted teeth while his wife acted as a 'Character Reader'. He moved back to Aberdeen in 1910 where he extracted teeth in Castle Street and also began to sell 'quack herbal medicines' styling himself a doctor on his business cards [See Figure 5.1]. In 1912, Brongo was narrowly acquitted at the High Court in Aberdeen of a charge of procuring an abortion but, eventually, in 1922, the police were able to secure a conviction against him, attracting a sentence of four years penal servitude.[80]

Finally, a small but discernible group of men prosecuted in the High Court were employed in the sale of a range of marital, menstrual and reproductive aids.[81] Charles Alder was a prime example. In his youth, he had contemplated a medical career and frequented the medical practice run by his elder brother. Instead, he had run a succession of businesses south of the Border in gentleman's outfitting, dry cleaning, and dentistry, before establishing himself as a herbalist and masseur in Allison Street, Glasgow in 1910. Significantly, in the same year, a barmaid with whom he had cohabited was prosecuted at Newcastle Assizes for procuring an illegal abortion. 1n 1914 he took over the management of premises in West Campbell Street, Glasgow, and West Register Street, Edinburgh, operating under the name of 'Dr Temple and Co.' that sold 'rubber goods', contraceptive devices, along with quack/homeopathic cures for VD and 'female irregularities'. Alder rapidly assumed the title 'Dr Temple' in dealing with customers. In 1915 he was indicted on a charge of murder following the death of one of his clients after his alleged use of an instrument to procure her abortion, but the jury returned a not-proven verdict.[82]

THE ABORTION

Procedures

Rather than one illicit act, most of the abortions documented in the High Court records involved a series of procedures, often repeated over several weeks. Initially, every effort was made to induce a miscarriage by the use of drugs either in the form of pills or liquid preparations. The most common drugs prescribed and/or administered were aloes, ergot, pennyroyal, quinine, and steel drops.[83] Often very large and repeated doses were dispensed without regard for the acute discomfort of the client and the danger posed to her health. For example, in the case against Louie Brady and John Archibald in 1921, Mary Rennie, a 23-year-old shop assistant, was administered a wide range of drugs over a two-week period including aloes, ergot, iron, penny royal, quinine, and salts. She was also instructed to take violent exercise to 'hasten the effect'. She was constantly and violently sick. When the preparations

Figure 5.1 Business card of the Aberdeen abortionist, 'Dr' Brongo, 1922
[National Records of Scotland]
(Source: NRS, AD15/22/83/2, Crown Office precognitions)

failed to induce an abortion, the accused merely doubled the dose for the next three weeks, leaving the complainant 'retching for hours'.[84]

In the majority of cases, drugs alone proved ineffective as a means of procuring an abortion, at which point more invasive procedures were employed. As a first step, douching with solutions of Lysol, pearl ashes, or quinine, using a wide variety of enema syringes and catheters was commonly administered.[85] If douching failed to trigger an abortion, a range of metal instruments was used, often a number of times, in an effort to puncture the foetal membrane and induce the womb to contract and evacuate its contents. These included crochet hooks and pins, dilators, vulsellum or curette forceps, stylettes and uterine sounds, along with many unspecified pieces of wire.[86] In a few instances, a sea-tangle uterine tent, originally introduced into obstetrics by Sir James Simpson, was employed.[87] A stem of dried seaweed was inserted into the vagina where, owing to the warmth and moisture present, over a few hours, it swelled up, dilating the mouth and neck of the womb and inducing an abortion. A similar effect could be triggered by the use of slippery elm bark that increasingly figured in evidence after the mid-1920s. Reporting on this procedure in 1928, John Glaister observed that:

> Within the past few years, slippery elm bark has come to be used as a method of illegally producing abortion. It is used by forming a part of the bark into the shape of a thin pencil, pointed at one or both ends, and is inserted into the mouth of the womb. The effect of the combined warmth and moisture of the parts is to cause the bark to exude a mucilaginous or gummy material, and its presence in the mouth of the womb is to cause the organ to be so irritated that it begins to contract and thus void its contents if pregnant.[88]

Outcomes

As Angus McLaren has observed 'abortions usually only came to the attention of the authorities when something went tragically wrong'.[89] Perhaps unsurprisingly, of the complainants in Scottish High Court abortion cases during the period 1900–30, for whom information is available, some 33 per cent developed medical complications necessitating recourse to a doctor, some 25 per cent had to be hospitalised and 17 per cent died.[90] Typically, after a protracted course of drugs and repeated 'jags' with a metal instrument, often with little regard for sterilisation beyond a perfunctory dipping in Lysol, the client would be left in severe pain with excessive and persistent bleeding. As in many cases the abortion was incomplete, fragments of the foetus and afterbirth were left in the womb leading to life-threatening peritonitis and septicaemia.

At this juncture, friends or relatives would be likely to summon a local panel doctor.[91] However, if he suspected an illegal operation had been performed, in order to protect himself from prosecution as an accessory and from professional disbarment, he would often decline to conduct an intimate examination of the patient single-handed. Instead, he would either call in another medical practitioner (sometimes the police custody surgeon) to assist and to act as a witness of his efforts to clean out and disinfect the womb or, more normally, remove the patient to hospital for specialist treatment.[92]

INVOLVING THE LAW

The police and/or procurators fiscal were initially alerted in a variety of ways to the abortion offences tried before the Scottish High Court. As Table 5.3 indicates, there were three main sources of information. About one-third of all offences were reported to the police either by local medical practitioners/panel doctors summoned to attend patients suffering from the after-effects of an illegal and often incomplete abortion, or by hospital staff called upon to undertake emergency operations in cases where medical complications, including peritonitis and blood poisoning, had become life-threatening. Though many women were reluctant to disclose that they had submitted to an abortion or an attempted abortion for fear of prosecution, medical practitioners often pressurised them to admit that a procedure had taken place and to disclose the identity of the abortionists.[93] Hospital doctors could be even more demanding of their patients. For example, in 1916, it was alleged that Dr Alexander Russell, obstetric physician for the Glasgow Maternity Hospital had threatened to let a patient 'lie and die unless

Table 5.3 Sources of information relating to abortion offences contained in Scottish High Court indictments, 1900–30

Sources of Information	%
Local medical practitioner	15
Hospital doctor/superintendent	18
Anonymous tip-off	20
Relatives	8
Friends/neighbours	2
Police surveillance	2
Police investigations	24
Other	11

Source: NRS, AD15, Crown Office precognitions.

she told him who had performed an illegal operation on her'.[94] While in many instances doctors genuinely wanted to help locate dangerous abortionists, the desire to protect their professional reputations and to avoid being implicated in any crime may also have influenced such behaviour.

Anonymous tip-offs triggered police action in a further 20 per cent of offences. A typical example was the letter sent to the detective superintendent of Glasgow's Southern Division in 1911 that led to the arrest of Robert Carell and Mary Hall.

> Sir I wish to inform you of a crime which I overheard accidentally. I heard of it previously but I know for a fact it is true now. In a house in 49 Sandyfauld Street right hand door in close the woman is under the name of Carell . . . She has performed two illegal operations within a fortnight one is away and one is still to be found at above address in a very serious condition. Now this must be seen to at once as there is no time for delay as the midwife leaves Glasgow on Tuesday I expect for London. I know she is going abroad if you be smart you will find she is packed up and the young lady must be removed by Monday . . . If this is not attended to at once I will expose the detectives of the Southern Division. I will watch how this goes as it is gospel truth.[95]

A similar letter, received by Camperdown Police Office, Glasgow, in 1925, initiated the prosecution of Constance Ann McCurdie:

> Dear Sir,
> Please find out what has been done with a seven months child brought about by a illegal operation last Sunday at Mrs Cowie's 73 Cedar St the person who done this operation was sent by a Mrs Dick 92 Cedar St and payed the sum of 3 pounds. It would greatly oblidge [sic] decent mothers who lives beside such people their certainly was no Doctor or midwife called and no Burial the Husband was a party to the illegal operation and payed the money over. This should be looked into.[96]

Yet another example is captured in Figure 5.2.

The third main source of information was evidence obtained in the course of making an initial arrest. Frequently, police discovered correspondence, postcards, receipts, and diaries that revealed other offences. Thus, in the case against Dr George Bell Todd in 1912, in investigating the complaint by the father of a deceased client that she had undergone an illegal abortion, the police searched Todd's consulting rooms and found 120 named slips, along with letters from clients, identifying twenty-five women within the Glasgow jurisdiction alone who admitted to having been operated on by Todd, leading to nineteen separate charges being levelled against him.[97] On some occasions, in following up an initial lead, the police interrupted the commission of a further crime.

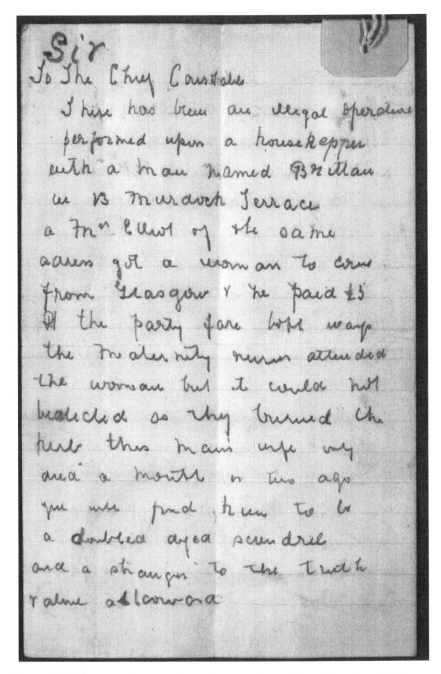

Figure 5.2 Anonymous letter to the police reporting an illegal abortion, 1925
[National Records of Scotland]
(Source: NRS, AD15/ 25/14/4/2, Crown Office precognitions)

For example, in 1923, when the police went to arrest Mary Drugan for performing an abortion on Elizabeth Smith, they discovered Margaret McGill in bed recovering from a recent termination.[98] Similarly, in 1924, in investigating two complaints against Robert Dobson, the police raided his house and caught 'him performing on a third client' and in the act of inserting a sea-tangle uterine tent into her.[99]

Finally, there were a few instances where information on illegal abortions was obtained accidentally as a result of police involvement in unrelated offences. In 1909, the Aberdeen police arrested James Brander for being drunk and incapable. On searching him, however, they discovered 'pieces of bent and twisted wire' along with correspondence clearly implicating him in illegal practices involving abortion.[100] Likewise, in 1929, when the police raided the premises of James Crichton to seize indecent prints, they found him 'in the back office inserting slippery elm bark into the private parts of a woman'.[101]

THE LEGAL FRAMEWORK

In the period 1900–30, under Scottish criminal law, any one who 'feloniously cause[d] or procure[d] a woman to abort [was] guilty of a very serious crime, whether it be effected by drugs or by the use of instruments'. Even where a termination was not achieved, such actions remained criminal and, if any attempt to procure an abortion led to the death of the client, this could in law constitute murder. The woman herself might also be prosecuted if she was aware of the purpose for which the procedures were being conducted. However, whether the woman alone could be relevantly charged with taking drugs to secure abortion had not, according to the legal authorities, been 'absolutely decided'.[102] The Offences Against the Person Act 1861, which explicitly criminalised attempts by a pregnant woman to effect her own abortion, did not apply in Scotland.[103] North of the Border, abortion constituted a common law, rather than statutory, offence so that it was possible to interpret it more elastically. In particular, there had to be criminal intent, and legal authorities recognised that 'the causing of an abortion by a medical practitioner acting in good faith in order to save the woman's life, would not be punishable'.[104]

In constructing a prosecution case, the Scottish Crown Office and Procurator Fiscal Service were subject to a range of legal constraints. First, in Scotland, a higher standard of proof than in England was required. No person could be convicted of an offence unless there was evidence of at least two witnesses implicating the person with the

commission of the offence, or corroboration of one witness by irrefutable evidence. Given that the abortionist, the client and her family
had a joint interest in concealment, this posed a major problem for the
prosecution. Secondly, in 1908, in the case against Alexander Baxter,
the Lord Justice Clerk ruled that 'although a reprehensible act' perhaps
deserving to be criminalised by statute, the mere sending of medication
to another person which, if used, would be likely to cause abortion, did
not constitute an attempt to procure abortion under Scottish common
law. There needed to be a clear line of causation from the drugs to an
actual attempt to secure a termination and active participation of the
accused in their administration.[105] Thirdly, in the case against Margaret
Stewart and Kate Johnstone in 1926, Lord Moncrieff ruled that the role
of the latter in simply communicating to the client the name of a stranger
who might perform an operation, without receiving any remuneration,
did not provide sufficient grounds for conviction on a charge of 'acting
in concert' to procure an abortion. Evidence of some form of procurement and remuneration was needed.[106]

Finally, in 1927, in his ruling in the case against Peggy Anderson, Lord
Anderson of Glasgow determined that, in contrast to English law where
an offence might be committed irrespective of whether the woman was
pregnant,[107] in Scottish law, conviction could be obtained only if it was
proved that the woman was actually pregnant at the time of an abortion
or attempted abortion. The victim of the crime was the potential child so
that, if there was no potential child, there was no crime.[108] While it had,
in fact, been customary in abortion cases to include in the indictment a
statement that the woman had been pregnant at the time of the alleged
offence, this judgment conflicted with the previous assumption of most
law officers and medical experts in Scotland that, in the words of John
Glaister, 'the crime of abortion would lie whether the woman was or
was not with child, provided by operation or otherwise the instrument
or drug was used with the criminal intent to procure miscarriage or
abortion'.[109]

CONSTRUCTING A PROSECUTION CASE

In conducting their investigations, framing their indictments and presenting the case for the prosecution, the Crown Office and Procurator
Fiscal Service remained mindful of these constraints. Abortions and
attempted abortions cited in High Court proceedings typically involved
the collusion of a number of people. The client herself often agitated
to be operated on in the face of contrary advice from friends, relatives

and/or partners, sometimes pestering, and even blackmailing an abortionist to treat her condition. For example, in 1908, in the case against Alexander Baxter, the witness, Elizabeth Radcliffe, openly admitted that: 'Abortion was [her] own idea'.[110] In summing up in the trial of Charles Alder in 1915, the judge concluded that the woman involved 'not only committed the fault which led to the trouble, but if there was a crime, she was also a party to the crime'.[111] Similarly, in 1918, in the case against Elizabeth Watson, there was clear evidence that the client, Elizabeth Somerville, had played a highly proactive role in the abortion. According to the Procurator Fiscal for Dumbarton, she had made all the arrangements for the procedure herself, having had a previous abortion from the same woman and having informed neighbours that 'she had every intention of getting rid of what she was carrying'.[112] Yet, in none of these cases was the client prosecuted as her evidence was crucial to securing a successful conviction.[113] Indeed, on the one occasion in 1925 when a woman was admonished at a Sheriff Court for illegally undergoing an abortion, the Lord Advocate viewed it as a significant departure from normal practice. The Crown Agent confirmed that the case *was* 'competent' but highly unusual for the 'reason that the evidence of the woman is generally required by the prosecution'.[114]

At other times, neighbours or acquaintances might also play a very active role in the process, giving advice on self-treatment or even prescribing some preliminary medications, arranging for the client to make contact with the abortionist and, not infrequently, witnessing the operation itself. For example, in 1918, Sarah Wright had prescribed large doses of quinine mixed in whisky to two widows before referring them on to the abortionist, Constance McCurdie, and was clearly at the centre of a network of contacts procuring customers for the accused in return for a fee.[115] In 1925, Annie Dick, who had a reputation around Argyle Street in Glasgow for knowing 'someone who could procure an abortion', had written a line to an abortionist asking if 'she would oblige a poor woman who was greatly worried over being pregnant'. Subsequently, she attended the operation and wrapped the foetus in newspaper and disposed of it on the kitchen fire.[116] In 1928, according to the complainant, Euthemia Henderson, her sister-in-law, Lucy Henderson, had first obtained drugs for her from a chemist that she administered in a cup, 'with some stout and a red hot poker'. Thereafter, Henderson was alleged to have introduced her to the accused, Margaret Shaw, by whom she herself had previously had an abortion. She had negotiated the fee and been present at several procedures designed to procure an abortion and witnessed the discharge of the foetus.[117] Again, in 1929, Mary McGowan introduced her friend, Agnes Logan, to an abortionist and arranged for an operation to take place in Kilmarnock. In addition, she attended some of the procedures involving the use of a crochet pin, receiving payment in kind in the form of her entrance fee to the Ayr Races.[118] In all such cases, however, it was the abortionist alone who was prosecuted, with the other participants deployed as witnesses.

On several occasions, the 1908 ruling in *H.M. Advocate* v. *Baxter* had an impact on the prosecution case. For example, in 1919, the draft indictment against Frederick Keller and Jane Hudson charged them with 'instructing a pregnant woman to take certain drugs and adopt certain treatments to procure her abortion'. The Advocate Depute minuted that while, in his view, 'the giving of such advice [was] just as reprehensible as the actual administration of the drug', he feared that, in view of the ruling in *H.M. Advocate* v. *Baxter*, the charge might 'be held irrelevant and a decision to that effect might lead to an increase in this method of procuring abortion'.[119] Accordingly, the Crown Agent urged the Procurator Fiscal to focus the indictment and medical evidence more on the possible use of an invasive instrument in the procedure, and the likely effects of an aggressive regime of douching.[120]

In a period when there existed no pregnancy test and no 'certainty of the signs in the earlier months',[121] the Anderson ruling could also prove problematic for the law officers building a prosecution case. Thus, in 1929, in preparation for the trial of James Crichton, charged with inserting a piece of slippery elm bark into the private parts of Agnes Thomson, the medical evidence as to her pregnancy was uncertain. The most that John Glaister was prepared to testify to was that her womb was 'compatible with the early stage of pregnancy', that she was 'a well-developed woman and her private parts indicate[d] that there had been trafficking therein'.[122] Nonetheless, the Crown concurred with the Procurator Fiscal for Glasgow that 'if evidence of this type were rejected then abortions could be procured or procurations attempted in the early stages of pregnancy with impunity'.[123] In the event, Crichton was duly convicted and sentenced to twelve months imprisonment.

Assembling evidence

Underpinning the prosecution case were the productions: articles lodged as evidence in court. Typically, these would include a variety of drugs and/or instruments found at the residence or premises of the accused and allegedly employed in procuring an abortion. The instruments might range from a simple piece of twisted wire or crochet pin to more sophisticated medical equipment such as a Higginson's syringe, uterine sound or vaginal speculum. Documentary material was also produced, including anonymous letters to the police and procurators fiscal [See Figure 5.2], incriminating correspondence (letters, postcards, and telegrams) between the participants in the abortion process, client lists, payment records, and appointment diaries kept by the accused. The prescription records of chemists who had dealt with abortionists were sometimes lodged as evidence as were the attendance registers of midwives who were prosecuted.[124] Where the accused had falsely claimed medical qualifications in order to secure clients, business cards [See Figure 5.1], newspaper advertisements, and even nameplates might be used as evidence. In addition, as advances in methods of identifying human blood were increasingly adopted from the early 1920s,[125] a range of stained bedding, towelling and clothing exhibits were submitted by the Crown Prosecution. The medical reports of practitioners who initially attended women suffering from complications caused by abortion or attempted abortion were also produced. These were often supplemented by the ward journals and observations of hospital staff who subsequently treated the more serious and life-threatening cases.

However, the most vital productions were the medical reports submitted by the leading Scottish forensic pathologists of the day.[126] Forensic reports in abortion cases heard at the High Court in Edinburgh were obtained from Henry and Harvey Littlejohn, successive Professors of Medical Jurisprudence at the University of Edinburgh, sometimes assisted by James Haig Ferguson, a prominent gynaecologist. For the few abortion cases heard at the High Court in Aberdeen and Dundee, the Crown usually employed Matthew Hay and Charles Marshall, respectively Professor of Forensic Medicine at the University of Aberdeen and Professor of Materia Medica and Therapeutics at the University of St Andrews. Meanwhile, for the overwhelming majority of cases – those heard at the High Court in Glasgow – the Crown Prosecution secured the services of John Glaister senior, Regius Professor of Forensic Medicine at the University of Glasgow [see Figure 5.3],[127] normally assisted by John Anderson, Director of the Pathological Department and Clinical Laboratory at the Victoria Infirmary.

From 1911 until Glaister's death in 1931, their forensic reports, also engrossed in the precognitions, dominated Scottish High Court proceedings relating to abortion, performing a number of functions crucial to the success of the prosecution case. Along with occasional observations from the Glasgow City Analyst, and employing increasingly sophisticated forensic techniques, they reported on the content of the pills and

Figure 5.3 John Glaister (senior) in his laboratory, *c.*1920s
[licensor: www.scran.ac.uk]
(Source: www.scran.ac.uk)

liquids used in evidence by the Crown and their likely impact on a pregnant woman if taken in the doses prescribed by the accused.[128] They also
commented on the potential for instruments recovered in the course of
police investigations to procure an abortion,[129] and where possible on

any body tissue adhering to them.[130] For the Crown Office, this aspect of the medical reports was crucial as the insertion of an instrument implied direct interference with the woman's body by the accused that did not necessarily apply to the administration of drugs. At other times, Glaister and Anderson were prompted to speculate on whether witness evidence of foetal discharge was consistent with an abortion having been performed.[131] In addition, they reported on their examination of the client's body. In particular, they were asked by Crown Counsel to confirm that she had been pregnant and, if possible, the duration of her pregnancy, whether an abortion had taken place, and to consider to what extent injuries to her private parts could be attributed to interference by any instruments seized by the police and listed in the Crown's productions.[132] Where a post-mortem was involved, they reported on the likely relationship between the immediate cause of death, usually blood poisoning, and a previous abortion.[133] Finally, from 1922 onwards, with the increasing use of the precipitin test, Glaister and Anderson, along with other forensic pathologists, commented on the presence of human blood on the instruments, clothes, towels and sheets found at the scene of an alleged abortion, and on the stained newspaper that was habitually used to wrap the aborted foetus and afterbirth before disposal.[134]

A range of factors served to complicate the task of the medical experts. Witnesses were often reluctant to disclose details of procedures for fear of incriminating themselves or of the adverse publicity that might be attracted by court proceedings.[135] Occasionally, medical practitioners also resisted giving evidence on the grounds of protecting patient confidentiality.[136] At other times, it was difficult to establish the impact of a particular procedure where there was a history of self-treatment by the complainant.[137] Delays between the abortion and police investigation posed additional problems. It usually meant that the aborted foetus was not available for forensic examination, and impaired the ability of the prosecution to establish the complainant's pregnancy at the time of the abortion and the degree to which her injuries had been caused by 'the insertion of instruments into her private parts'.[138] Similarly, where a post-mortem had to be held, a delay could render it impossible to establish how the abortion had been procured and the precise link between the termination and death. In many instances, the forensic experts could only speculate on the course of events.[139] Witnesses were often vague about the metal instruments that had been used, partly because they had normally been in a foetal position facing away from the abortionist during the procedure and partly because abortionists were careful to try to conceal the instruments in their hands or within the nozzle of a douche in order to reduce their client's distress and the risk of prosecution.[140] The presence of other medical conditions in the complainant that might have produced a miscarriage also presented a challenge to the prosecution case. For example, on a number of occasions, defence counsel contended that an abortion had been triggered by a venereal disease associated with a morally reprehensible lifestyle.[141] Finally, the application of new forensic techniques might at times be constrained by a shortage of time, funding and/or reagents as well as by personal factors. Thus, the human antiserum, which was required to test samples of blood for human origin, was not always readily available and evidence suggests that, in the early post-war years, John Glaister senior had some reservations about the precipitin test.[142]

VERDICT AND SENTENCING

Five per cent of the Scottish High Court abortion trials in the period 1900–30 were deserted either because the indictment was held to be 'irrelevant' or a key witness had absconded. A further 21 per cent produced a verdict of not guilty or not proven. In the absence of court transcripts one cannot be certain why a conviction was not obtained. Typically, these were cases where the indictment lacked specificity with respect to the timing and/or method of abortion, where there was a lack of witnesses to the actual procedure, where medical evidence was either inconclusive or conflicting, where the key witness had a history of self-medication, or where her testimony was inconsistent with that of other witnesses or with the productions presented in court by the Crown prosecution.

Of the 74 per cent of abortionists convicted, around a half received a sentence of penal servitude ranging from three to ten years but most commonly between three and five years. These punitive sentences involving hard labour were reserved for cases where an abortion had proved fatal,[143] where there had been a previous arrest or conviction for procuring or attempting to procure a termination, where the abortion had been associated with another sexual offence such as rape, and where a number of charges had been laid and it was clear the accused was viewing the practice as a business.[144] Judges could also impose heavier sentences where, as in the case of midwives and medical practitioners, the actions of the accused contravened a professional code of conduct.[145]

Meanwhile, the remaining defendants found guilty by plea or jury verdict received ordinary prison sentences ranging from four months to five years. The overwhelming majority received either twelve or eighteen months. The level of punishment was again determined by a range of factors, such as the degree of injury sustained in the course of the process and the extent to which invasive (especially metal) instruments had been used to interfere with the client's genitalia. There is also some evidence that the sentence could be influenced by how far advanced the client's pregnancy had been at the time of the abortion.[146] In addition, her sexual history, especially where there was a record of previous attempts to abort and a promiscuous lifestyle, might also be a consideration, as might pressure from purity groups such as the National Vigilance Association for Scotland. Across the period, there was a clear trend towards lighter sentences, especially after 1918, with less recourse to penal servitude and the increasing imposition of lighter prison sentences. This did not relate to any legislative changes, and evidence is lacking as to how far this may have in part reflected changing social and judicial attitudes to the crime and to more general shifts in the debate surrounding women's reproductive rights.

CONCLUSION

Kate Fisher has warned that the historical treatment of abortion is at risk of being distorted by 'the awareness of the dangers and horrors of "back street" abortions and the moral rhetoric about the right to life of the unborn foetus'.[147] In her view, it is not useful or valid to assume that in early twentieth-century Britain 'abortion was an illegal, dangerous and morally questionable method of fertility control employed by women only reluctantly'.[148] This study serves to endorse her findings. Though, on occasions, a witness in the Scottish High Court might condemn abortion as morally repugnant, more usually it was perceived as an acknowledged and familiar coping strategy within working-class communities. Consequently, two competing discourses inform the precognitions and trial papers of the period: that of female social networks who viewed abortion as a routine, if clandestine, aspect of the ongoing struggle with deprivation and unwanted pregnancy; and that of the legal and medical establishment who approached the issue of abortion as a criminal and moral offence and who perceived it as a threat to social stability, public health and racial progress.

This study also challenges the stereotype of the abortion 'victim' as a vulnerable and isolated, sexually inexperienced and exploited young woman at the mercy of a back-street abortionist, and pressurised by her lover into securing a termination. In fact, evidence from the High Court would suggest that a significant proportion of women involved in illegal abortion procedures were older women who were married, separated, or divorced and who were able to draw on the support of a network of friends, neighbours and local 'wise women' in securing and undergoing an abortion. In pursuing self-treatment, in procuring abortionists and on occasions even attempting to delimit the instruments used, women clients often played an extremely proactive role in the abortion process. It is arguable that, if women seeking abortions *were* 'victims', it was less the abortionists who victimised them than the social, medical and financial constraints that denied them access to efficient and affordable methods of contraception.

Perhaps the most notable feature of the cases heard in the Scottish High Court in the period 1900–30 was the absence of prosecution of those women who sought and submitted themselves to abortion procedures. This was in marked contrast to the legal regimes prevailing in Denmark, France, Germany, and Sweden, as well as in Canada and the United States.[149] Though Scottish common law allowed for aborting women to be charged, as in the Netherlands,[150] this was not obligatory, and the centrality of corroboration to the legal process effectively meant that they served instead as leading witnesses for the Crown Prosecution. However, this did not signify any sympathy on the part of the judiciary with the plight of women who, faced with the prospect of an unwanted pregnancy, had opted for a termination, and there is no evidence of any call for a more liberal treatment of abortion offences from the Scottish judiciary prior to 1930. While they normally evaded prosecution and imprisonment, aborting women did not go unpunished. As Jones observes, the process of securing a dying declaration from a woman who had undergone an illegal abortion 'involved intrusive, relentless questioning, and threats to withdraw medical help that epitomised the disciplining, shaming function' of the prosecution process.[151] Where they survived their abortions, they were frequently 'hounded in hospital' and forced to give evidence in court about the most intimate details of their private lives, and often to implicate friends and relations, with a consequent loss of reputation, employment, and social contacts. In most trials, reporters were requested only informally by the Clerk of Court not to publish details of witnesses. Where this request was ignored, the witness's 'character' and career could be ruined and her family stigmatised. Furthermore, at no point did the legal process engage with the emotional and psychological impact of abortion on the women involved. It was their evidence of the crime and not their welfare or indeed, still less the rights of the aborted child, which dominated the legal proceedings.

NOTES

1. See, for example, Knight, 'Women and abortion', 57–68; McLaren, 'Abortion in England', 379–400; Jones, 'Abortion in England, 1861–1967', PhD thesis; Fisher, ' "Didn't stop to think" ', 213–32; Usborne, *Cultures of Abortion*; McLaren, 'Illegal operations', 797–816.

2. See, for example, Davis and Davidson, ' "A fifth freedom" ', 31–3; Norrie, 'Abortion in Britain', 475–95; Stockley, 'The increasingly strange case of abortion', 330–7; Brown, 'Scotland and the Abortion Act', 135–51.

3. See, for example, *The Scotsman*, 28 May 1923, 29 December 1928. Reporting in 1939 on the situation in England and Wales, the Birkett Committee speculated that some 40 per cent 'of the abortions in this country may be due to illegal interference' and that 'it has recently become more frequent' [*Report of the Inter-Departmental Committee on Abortion*, 1939, 11,13].

4. Usborne, *Cultures of Abortion*, 136.

5. Hall, 'Articulating abortion in interwar Britain', 13.

6. McLaren, 'Illegal operations', 797.

7. Usborne, *Cultures of Abortion*, 15.

8. This pattern is consistent with that of Edwardian England [Knight, 'Women and abortion', 58].

9. As in Weimar Germany, the reasons for women seeking an abortion were frequently disregarded by interrogators 'who were primarily concerned with effective policing and prosecution and the apportionment of guilt' [Osborne, *Cultures of Abortion*, 136].

10. A few of the youngest women also feared being disowned by their parents and rendered homeless if they proceeded with their pregnancy.

11. Some 22 per cent of the women cited as prosecution witnesses in Scottish High Court abortion cases either testified to, or were reported as having indulged in some form of self-treatment prior to seeking the services of an abortionist. For the widespread practice of self-treatment elsewhere in the United Kingdom and Europe, see Fisher, ' "Didn't stop to think" ', 217–20; Knight, 'Women and abortion', 59–60; *Report of Inter-Departmental Committee on Abortion*, 41–3; Usborne, *Cultures of Abortion*, 99–101; Herzog, *Sexuality in Europe*, 20–1.

12. For similar perceptions outwith Scotland, see Usborne, *Cultures of Abortion*, 145–6; Fisher, ' "Didn't stop to think" ', 221–2; McLaren, *Twentieth-Century Sexuality*, 76; Hall, 'Articulating abortion in interwar Britain', 15.

13. See, for example, NRS, AD15/12/31, precognition of Marie Condie, 22 March 1912; NRS, AD15/22/46, precognition of Isabella Jackson, 18 August 1922; AD15/30/100, precognition of Sarah Smith, 22 October 1930.

14. '[T]o put her right' was one of many euphemisms for abortion used by witnesses in their precognitions. Other expressions included 'to get it put

away', 'to bring it down' and 'to make it come away'. The term 'abortion' was rarely used outside official circles and medical publications before 1939 [Jones, 'Abortion in England, 1861–1967', PhD thesis, 151].

15. NRS, AD15/09/164, precognition of Elizabeth Ettles, 24 February 1909. For the role of press advertisements for curing 'irregularities' in facilitating self-treatment in England, see Knight, 'Women and abortion', 61.

16. Pennyroyal is a species of flowering plant the leaves of which were used to make pills that were widely advertised as a cure for 'menstrual disturbances'. According to the superintendent of Stobhill Hospital, they were commonly taken 'by women in the early stages of pregnancy in the belief that they bring on the monthly illness and clear them of the pregnancy' [NRS, AD15/21/65, precognition of Dr John Johnston, 14 April 1921].

17. Bitter aloes is a bitter purgative, derived from a species of tropical plant, with a distinctive tendency to cause abortion when used in large doses and was commonly used along with ergot.

18. Diachylon is composed of lead oxide. According to Professor John Glaister, its use as an abortifacient by working-class women had become increasingly common since the late nineteenth century [NRS, AD15/20/60, report by John Glaister, 19 January, 1920; Glaister, *Textbook of Medical Jurisprudence and Toxicology*, 1921 edition, 445–6]. Diachylon was readily at hand in working-class homes as a plaster for use on cuts and sores.

19. Bitter apple is a Mediterranean and South Asian plant of the gourd family, producing a fruit with a bitter pulp that was used as a purgative.

20. NRS, AD15/11/22, precognition of Willamina Snowden, 9 January 1911.

21. NRS, AD15/12/31, precognition of Annie Abernethy, 21 March 1912.

22. NRS, AD15/18/45, precognition of Elizabeth Gordon, 12 April 1918. Pearl ashes were a caustic solution made up from a compound of potassium hydroxide administered mainly by douching. Isinglass is a gelatine derived from the air bladders of sturgeon which, when used with pearl ashes, prolonged and magnified the irritant effect of the latter on the womb.

23. NRS, AD15/23/33, note by Procurator Fiscal, Glasgow, 7 December 1922. 'Hickory-Pickory', a colloquial name for hiera picra, was a purgative drug derived from bitter aloes and canella bark.

24. NRS, AD15/23/65, precognition of Margaret McGill, 6 April 1923; report by John Glaister and John Anderson, 4 May 1923. Ergot, a rye fungus, was used in obstetric practice to induce labour. It acted on the muscles of the womb, causing them to contract and expel its contents. According to Professor Henry Littlejohn in 1908, ergot had 'a popular reputation as an abortive' [NRS, AD15/08/47, precognition of Henry Littlejohn, 27 July 1908].

25. NRS, AD15/27/59, precognition of Nellie Belbin, 31 January 1927.

26. Syrup of squills was made from the bulbs of *Urginia maritima* and was

used as an expectorant. Steel drops were tincture of steel and also taken to activate the menses. For a fuller discussion of the preparations commonly used in self-treatment in Scotland, see especially NRS, AD15/21/65, report by Dr J. M. Johnston, Medical Superintendent, Stobhill Hospital, 14 April 1921.

27. Knight, 'Women and abortion', 60. In contrast, in Canada, the 'use of instruments was by all accounts the leading method' of self-induced abortion [McLaren, 'Illegal operations', 800].

28. Royal College of Physicians of Edinburgh [hereafter RCPE] Archives, RCP/FEL/3/1 – Trial transcript in the case of Charles Alder, evidence of Henry Littlejohn, 18 October 1915.

29. NRS, AD15/28/45, precognition of Mary Ann Moss, 23 May 1928.

30. One witness who ran a dairy shop in Smith Street, Glasgow, later reported that: 'Questions of pregnancy are commonly talked about by the women customers who frequent my shop and I have heard discussion about what can be done for those in a pregnant condition' [NRS, AD15/31/32, precognition of Isabella Steel, 14 January 1931].

31. NRS, AD15/09/59, precognition of Sarah Milne, 7 October 1909.

32. NRS, AD15/12/31, precognition of Mary Orman, 22 March 1912.

33. NRS, AD15/28/53, precognitions of Mary McKan, Lily Reposo, Elizabeth Christie, Esther De Marco, 8 and 9 March 1928.

34. NRS, AD15/11/107, depositions of Christina and Annie McDougall, 20 June and 3 July 1911; JC26/1911/27, HCJ processes, copy of advert. As in The Hague, 'midwife' 'became a label used by abortionists to convey the impression of expertise and asepsis' [de Blécourt, 'Cultures of abortion in The Hague', 204].

35. NRS, AD15/12/31, precognitions of Elizabeth Maclean and Louisa Johnston, 16 and 18 March 1912.

36. NRS, AD15/26/51, precognition of Margaret McGill, 6 November 1925.

37. NRS, JC34/1/61, Appeal transcript in case against Annie Lawrie and Agnes Wilson, 2 November 1929, p. 52.

38. RCPE Archive, RCP/FEL/3/17, Trial transcript in case of *Lord Advocate* v. *Alder*, 18 October 1915, pp. 7, 18.

39. NRS, AD15/29/72, 'Statement of facts' by Procurator Fiscal, Glasgow, 4 December 1929.

40. NRS, AD15/11/22, precognitions of Mary Taylor and Mary Livingstone, 7 January 1911. Fortune tellers were often consulted by women who had missed their menses. The fear of being pregnant might be elicited during palm reading or the laying out of cards and, in some instances, an abortionist recommended. See, for example, the experience of Mary Livingstone in 1910. Margaret Leitch read her cards and said: 'I see a cradle' and promised Livingstone a line to an abortionist who 'would give me a mixture to bring back my courses' [NRS, AD15/11/22, precognition of Mary Livingstone, 6 January 1911]. For the role of fortune tellers in the

procurement of abortions elsewhere in early twentieth-century Europe, see Usborne, *Cultures of Abortion*, 110–11; de Blécourt, 'Cultures of abortion in The Hague', 206–9.

41. NRS, AD15/11/164, precognition of Ann Borland, 26 August 1911.

42. NRS, AD15/18/62, precognitions of Mary McMillan and Sarah Wright, 8 October 1918.

43. NRS, AD15/26/63, 'Statement of facts' by Procurator Fiscal, Dunbartonshire, 5 June 1926; undated note of introduction, Jeannie Milligan to Catherine Clark.

44. NRS, AD15/11/164, precognitions of Mary Smith and Jessie Watson, 25 August 1911, 16 September 1911.

45. NRS, AD15/12/137, precognition of Mary Johnston, 10 February 1912.

46. NRS, AD15/19/99, precognition of Joan Miller, 9 October 1919.

47. McClaren, 'Illegal operations', 804.

48. See, for example, de Blécourt, 'Cultures of abortion in The Hague', 209; Knight, 'Women and abortion', 67. For an alternative viewpoint, based on English evidence, that stresses the need to acknowledge a much more proactive role played by men in the process, see Jones, 'Abortion in England', Ch. 4.

49. NRS, AD15/11/164, precognition of William Murray, 23 August 1911.

50. NRS, AD15/12/31, precognitions of John Gemmell and Mungo Borthwick, 27 and 29 July 1912. Borthwick's evidence to the effect that he had told his wife 'she could please herself' reflected a devolvement of decision-making that was a feature of many narratives surrounding abortion presented to the High Court.

51. Glaister, *Textbook of Medical Jurisprudence and Toxicology*, 1921 edition, 451.

52. NRS, AD15/26/63, precognition of Christina Gerry, 26 May 1926.

53. NRS, AD15/12/31, precognition of Maggie Cameron, 30 March 1912.

54. RCPE Archives, RCP/FEL/3/17, Transcript of trial, *Lord Advocate* v. *Alder*, p. 24.

55. NRS, AD15/30/100, precognition of Helen Lyons, 27 October 1930.

56. This was comparable to the level of fees south of the Border [Jones, 'Abortion in England', 46].

57. See, for example, NRS, AD15/29/23, 'Statement of facts' by Procurator Fiscal, Glasgow, in the case against Gladys Peadon, 25 May 1929.

58. NRS, AD15/12/31, precognition of Bessie Duncan, 27 July 1912.

59. NRS, AD15/28/76, precognition of Euthemia Henderson, 13 June 1928.

60. NRS, AD15/30/96, precognition of Mary Shannon, 5 September 1930.

61. NRS, AD15/16/26, precognition of Ellen Adey, 24 February 1916.

62. See, for example, JC34/1/61, Appeal papers in the case against Annie Lawrie, 2 November 1929.

63. For example, in 1911, Mary Russell charged a client as much as £8 (more than twice the average pre-war rate) on being informed that she

was five months' pregnant, plus 'an extra 10/- to bury the wain' [NRS, AD15/11/107, deposition of Annie McDougall, 3 July 1911].

64. See, for example, *The Scotsman*, 5 May 1916, report of High Court trial of Dr John Dickie and Ann Taylor.

65. See, for example, NRS, AD15/22/46, precognition of G. Tolmie, 26 August 1922.

66. The ages of the male defendants ranged from twenty-seven to seventy-two while those of the female defendants ranged from thirty-three to sixty-seven. Both the average age and age range for male and female abortionists in England were very similar [Jones, 'Abortion in England', PhD thesis, 44].

67. In England, few of the female abortionists were associated with medical or health-related occupations. Housewives and widows made up the majority [Jones, 'Abortion in England', 42].

68. NRS, AD15/11/107, precognition of James Vance, Detective Officer, 23 June 1911.

69. NRS, AD15/19/21, precognition of Gladys Wolhuter, 23 June 1919.

70. NRS, AD15/16/16, National Vigilance Association for Scotland to Lord Advocate, 3 February 1916; AD15/27/84, precognition of Assistant Inspector of Midwives, 2 November 1927.

71. NRS, AD15/16/16, 'Note of Information' by Procurator Fiscal, Glasgow, 21 January 1916; AD15/19/99, Procurator Fiscal, Glasgow, to Crown Agent, 24 July 1919.

72. NRS, JC26/1911/146, Rector of St Mary Magdalene's, Dundee to Procurator Fiscal for Dundee, 27 November 1911. Another witness, however, accused Anderson of promoting crime 'by helping all those Fallen Women that frequent[ed] that notorious Tea Rooms at the corner of South Tay Street' [ibid., Alice McInroy to Procurator Fiscal, Dundee, 9 September 1911].

73. NRS, AD15/28/76, precognition of Phoebe Duncan, policewoman, Glasgow Central Division, 13 June 1928.

74. NRS, AD15/29/23, James Adair, Procurator Fiscal for Glasgow, 'Statement of facts', 25 May 1929.

75. *The Scotsman*, 15 June 1929.

76. For example, on being arrested in 1928 for the crime of procuring an abortion, Constance McCurdie protested that 'It was quite easy done. Just the work of a minute. I was hard up' [NRS, AD15/25/34, precognition of Margaret Watson, policewoman, 10 July 1925].

77. NRS, AD15/09/164; JC26/1909/1, precognitions and processes in case against James Brander.

78. NRS, AD15/11/67, AD15/12/31; JC26/1911/67, JC26/1912/117, precognitions and processes in case against George Bell Todd; *The Scotsman*, 4 June 1912. For other cases involving medical practitioners, see NRS, AD15/13/39, JC26/1913/134; AD15/16/26, JC26/1916/59, precognitions,

processes, and trial transcript in cases against Thomas Campbell and John Dickie.

79. See, for example, AD15/08/47, JC26/1908/126; AD15/19/99, JC26/1919/36; AD15/28/8, JC26/1928/35, precognitions and processes in cases against Alexander Baxter, Frederick Keller and John Wilson.

80. NRS, AD15/12/137, JC26/1912/14; AD15/22/83, JC26/1922/4, precognitions and processes in cases against James Leslie Brongo; *Aberdeen Post Office Directory for 1910–11*, 177.

81. Retailers of 'hygienic' and 'rubber' articles also featured amongst abortionists in the Netherlands [Blécourt, 'Cultures of abortion in The Hague', 202].

82. NRS, AD15/15/35, JC26/1915/98, precognitions and processes in case against Charles Alder; RCPE Archives, RCP/FEL/3/17, Transcript of trial *Lord Advocate* v. *Alder*, 18 October 1915.

83. Other lesser-used preparations included black draught (a mixture of senna and magnesia), cascara (a purgative derived from the dried bark of the American blackthorn), diachylon (lead oxide), jalap (a purgative derived from the roots of the jalap bindweed), mercury, and syrup of squills. For an overview of the range of drugs used by 'illegal practitioners' to procure an abortion, see Glaister, *Textbook of Medical Jurisprudence and Toxicology*, 1921 edition, 445–6]. See also above, notes 22 to 26.

84. NRS, AD15/21/65, precognitions of Mary Rennie and Dr A. W. Russell, 9 and 14 April 1921.

85. For example, according to one witness in 1911, the 'mode' of the abortionist, Jane Anderson, 'was to give pills to cause abortion, and if the pills did not have that effect then she syringed the patient with quinine and took away the foetus or unborn child by force' [NRS, AD15/11/164, precognition of Mary Lawson, 26 August 1911]. In a few cases, an injection of glycerine was also administered.

86. Glaister, *Textbook of Medical Jurisprudence and Toxicology*, 1921 edition, 449. On many occasions, defence witnesses were not able precisely to identify the instruments that had been inserted into them. Vague descriptions such as 'like a piece of twisted wire', 'like wire and twisted with small hook on end', 'sort of straight wire thing', were common.

87. This technique tended to be favoured by abortionists who had previously experienced some form of medical training. See, for example, NRS, AD15/26/13, report by James Adair, Procurator Fiscal, 7 June 1926.

88. NRS, AD15/28/76, medical report by John Glaister, 27 June 1928. For the use of this procedure elsewhere in the United Kingdom, see *Report of Inter-Departmental Committee on Abortion*, 1939, 61–2.

89. McClaren, 'Illegal operations', 798.

90. Apart from septicaemia, death was most commonly caused by severe haemorrhaging, shock, and embolism.

91. In some instances, if pain and bleeding persisted, abortionists were in

the habit of advising their client to report herself to a 'medical man' or present herself at a hospital where she might be taken in as an ordinary case of spontaneous abortion, thus avoiding responsibility for illegal and injurious procedures.

92. See, for example, NRS, AD15/09/59, AD15/18/45, AD15/28/8, AD15/28/54, Crown Office precognitions. In his textbook on medical jurisprudence and toxicology, John Glaister stressed the need for the medical practitioner to protect his professional reputation when attending cases of miscarriage by bringing in a fellow practitioner if there was any suspicion of an illegal procedure having taken place or, at the very least, by 'quietly arranging that a female neighbour or nurse should be called in so that she [might] be able to speak to the facts of the onset of the abortion . . .' [Glaister, *Textbook of Medical Jurisprudence and Toxicology*, 1921 edition, 459].

93. See, for example, NRS, AD15/28/53, precognition of Dr J. McConnochie, 9 February 1928. See also, NRS, AD15/28/45, precognition of Mary Moss, 23 May 1928, where it was claimed Dr James McDonald had 'threatened to tell her mother if she refused to sign a statement'.

94. NRS, AD15/16/16, precognition of Sarah Fraser, 8 March 1916.

95. NRS, JC26/1911/27/2/1, HCJ processes in the case against Robert Carell and Mary Hall.

96. NRS, JC26/1925/23/3, HCJ processes in the case against Constance McCurdie.

97. NRS, AD15/12/31, precognition of Detective Chief Inspector, 30 March 1912.

98. NRS, AD15/23/65, precognition of Detective Lieutenant, St Rollox Division, 24 May 1923.

99. NRS, AD15/26/13, report by James Adair, 7 June 1926.

100. NRS, AD15/09/164, precognition of William San, Sergeant, Aberdeen Police, 16 February 1909; JC26/1909/1, HCJ processes, correspondence from Mrs Barclay.

101. NRS, AD15/29/72, 'Statement of facts' by Procurator Fiscal, Glasgow, 4 December 1929.

102. Macdonald, *A Practical Treatise on the Criminal Law of* Scotland, 175–6.

103. For a fuller discussion of the contrast between Scotland and England in respect of abortion law, see Davidson and Davis, *The Sexual State*, 98–102.

104. Angus, *A Dictionary of Crimes*, 1. In 1897, in the case against Minnie Christina Graham, who claimed to be medically qualified, the Lord Justice Clerk held that any prosecution had to prove not only that the use of drugs and instruments was the cause of abortion but that such use was 'wicked and felonious' [*High Court of Justiciary (1897) 5 Scottish Law Times* (hereafter SLT) 219, 13 December 1897]. For an overview of the legal position of medical practitioners in Scotland with respect to carrying

out therapeutic abortion in the first half of the twentieth century, see especially, Davis and Davidson, ' "A fifth freedom" ', 31–5.

105. *H.M. Advocate* v. *Baxter,* High Court of Justiciary, 9 November 1908, 16 SLT 475. In this case, the Advocate Depute had warned about the lack of precedent for proceeding but the Lord Advocate, having reviewed correspondence from Baxter that clearly indicated his intention to post a 'bairn shifter' in the form of ergot for use in an illegal abortion, pressed for a prosecution on the grounds that it was a 'case of extreme gravity' and 'not to prosecute would lead to a failure of justice' [NRS, AD15/08/47, notes by Lord Advocate and Advocate Depute, 2 June and 14 September 1908; A. Baxter to F. Foy, n.d.]. After the ruling, the diet was deserted.

106. *H.M. Advocate* v. *Johnstone*, Court of Justiciary, 2 March 1926, 1926 Justiciary Cases (hereafter JC) 89.

107. Under English statute law, the crime was not the abortion itself but the doing of an act with intent to procure abortion, the latter not requiring a victim before it could be held unlawful.

108. High Court of Justiciary, 7 September 1927, *H.M. Advocate* v. *Anderson*, No. 1, 1928. This ruling was subsequently homologated by three High Court judges in 1936 [*H.M. Advocate* v. *Semple and Others*, 24 November 1936, 1937 SLT 48] but eventually rejected by the High Court of Justiciary in 1995.

109. NRS, JC26/1918/41, report by John Glaister, 25 November 1918. In the case against Peggy Anderson, the indictment had merely referred to the defendant's 'belief that her client was pregnant'. The existence of the pregnancy per se had not been specified in the charge [JC36/57, Trial transcript, 6 September 1927].

110. NRS, AD15/08/47, precognition of Elizabeth Radcliffe, 30 July 1908.

111. RCPE Archive, RCP/FEL/3/17, Transcript of trial *L.A.* v. *Alder*, p. 159.

112. NRS, AD15/16/26, 'Statement of facts' by Procurator Fiscal for Dumbarton, 27 April 1918.

113. In support of this policy, the Crown was able to cite the ruling of Lord Shand in 1888 that 'in a trial on a charge of procuring abortion, the evidence of the woman on whom the act was said to have been committed was competent, though she was not charged with the crime'[(1888) 15RJ 80].

114. NRS, AD15/25/29, Crown Office minutes, 22 and 23 March 1925. In England and Wales also, it was very unusual for a woman to be tried or convicted of procuring her own abortion [Jones, 'Abortion in England', 126], despite the fact that, under sections 58 and 59 of the Offences against the Persons Act 1861, women who self-administered any 'poison or other noxious thing' or colluded in the use of any substance or instrument with intent to procure a miscarriage', were guilty of a felony. According to the *Report of the Inter-Departmental Committee on Abortion* in 1939 in its summary of prosecution practices in England and Wales (p. 49): 'proceed-

ings are rarely instituted against a woman who has had an illegal abortion. If the abortion was self-induced, the difficulty of securing sufficient evidence to justify prosecution appears usually to be insurmountable. If it is procured by an abortionist, the view taken by the police is . . . that the prosecution of the abortionist, who may have a widespread practice, should be their primary aim, and since the woman's evidence is required against him, proceedings against her are not taken.'

115. NRS, AD15/18/62, note by Procurator Fiscal, Glasgow, 19 October 1918.
116. NRS, AD15/25/34, precognitions of Catherine Cowie and Annie Dick, 17 July 1925.
117. NRS, AD15/28/76, precognition of Euthemia Henderson, 13 June 1928.
118. NRS, AD15/29/55, precognitions of Mary McGowan and Constable Janet Dunlop, 15 May and 8 June 1929. Significantly, in this case. the policewoman had not cautioned McGowan and charged her as an accomplice to the crime, but merely precognised her on the assumption that she would only be a witness. As a result, although the Chief Constable of Ayr pressed for her to be indicted, the Crown Office was forced to suspend any proceedings against her.
119. NRS, AD15/19/99, Crown Agent to Solicitor General, 18 November 1919.
120. Ibid.
121. Glaister and Glaister Jr, *Text-Book of Medical Jurisprudence and Toxicology*, 1931 edition, 450.
122. NRS, AD15/29/72, report by John Glaister, 22 November 1929.
123. Ibid., 'Statement of facts' by J. Drummond Strathern, Procurator Fiscal for Glasgow, 4 December 1929.
124. Under the Midwives (Scotland) Act 1915 midwives were compelled to keep a register of all miscarriages that they attended. Failure to record such episodes was viewed as a disciplinary offence by the Central Midwives Board for Scotland and as incriminating evidence by the Crown Prosecution. It was also an offence not to call for medical assistance when 'an abortion threatened'.
125. For an overview of such advances, see especially, Crowther and White, *On Soul and Conscience,* 55–62; Duvall, 'Forensic medicine in Scotland', PhD thesis, 19–20, 88–92.
126. On the institutional framework for forensic medicine in interwar Scotland, see especially, Duvall, 'Forensic medicine in Scotland', Ch. 2.
127. On the career of John Glaister senior, see especially, Crowther and White, *On Soul and Conscience*, Chs 2–4.
128. See, for example, NRS, AD15/20/60, report by John Glaister, 19 January 1920; JC34/1/61, Trial transcript, evidence of John Glaister, pp. 86–91, 22 October 1929.
129. In cases involving a midwife they commented on how appropriate such

instruments were 'in the normal practice of her profession' [See, for example, NRS, AD15/23/65, report by John Glaister and John Anderson, 25 May 1923].

130. Typically, their reports would detect 'epithelial cells such as are found in the private parts of a woman' [See, for example, NRS, AD15/19/84, report by John Glaister and John Anderson, 30 July 1919; AD15/23/33, report by John Glaister and John Anderson, 29 November 1922].

131. See, for example, NRS, AD 15/24/49, report by John Glaister, 17 March 1924.

132. In submitting their reports they often portrayed lay abortionists as dirty and unhygienic.

133. See, for example, NRS, AD15/16/16, joint medical report by John Glaister and John Anderson, 15 November 1915; AD15/22/46, post-mortem report by John Glaister and John Anderson, 31 July 1922.

134. See, for example, NRS, AD15/27/59, reports by John Glaister and John Anderson, 7 and 12 February 1927; NRS, JC26/1931/37, joint report by John Glaister and John Anderson, 13 October 1930.

135. See, for example, NRS, AD15/22/46, correspondence between Procurator Fiscal, Glasgow, and Crown Agent, 16 and 17 November, 1922.

136. See, for example, NRS, AD15/16/26, note by Dr Nathaniel Brewis, 28 February 1916; AD15/26/51, note by Procurator Fiscal, Glasgow, 25 November 1925. As with venereal disease, abortion proved a key issue in the medico-legal debates over the boundaries of medical confidentiality in early twentieth-century Britain. See Ferguson, 'Speaking out about staying silent', 105–09.

137. See, for example, RCPE Archive, RCP/FEL/3/17, Trial transcript, evidence of Dr Harvey Littlejohn, 86–7; NRS, AD15/18/62, Procurator Fiscal, Glasgow, to Crown Agent, 17 December 1918; AD15/25/34, Procurator Fiscal, Glasgow, to Crown Agent, 22 July 1925.

138. See, for example, NRS, AD15/30/53, further Statement by Dr F. Martin, 11 May 1930.

139. Glaister appears to have been more resigned to this role than Littlejohn who disapproved of 'entering into questions of possibilities with respect to pathological evidence' [NRS, AD15/15/35, Procurator Fiscal, Edinburgh, to Crown Agent, 27 August 1915].

140. See, for example, NRS, AD15/18/62, note by Crown Office, 24 October 1918; AD15/25/29, precognition of John Glaister, 18 March 1925; AD15/28/76, precognition of Euthemia Henderson, 13 June 1928. In their defence, abortionists frequently claimed that they had merely been using their hands in order to examine their client for signs of pregnancy. Where the complainant denied feeling any 'prick' or pain, this was especially difficult to rebut.

141. See, for example, NRS, AD15/30/100, reports by John Anderson and Andrew Allison, 2 October 1930.

142. Duvall, 'Forensic medicine in Scotland', 92; Crowther and White, *On Soul and Conscience*, 56; Glaister and Glaister Jr, *Text-Book of Medical Jurisprudence and Toxicology*, 1931 edition, 398.

143. Increasingly, a charge of murder was replaced by one of culpable homicide to take account of lack of intent.

144. For example, in the trial of Elizabeth Walker in 1925, while reaching a unanimous verdict of guilty, the jury 'strongly recommended mercy' in view of the fact that she was a married woman with six children. The judge declined to show leniency on the grounds that 'she had been making a trade of procuring abortion' and that it 'was a crime as to which any laxity might lead to results dangerous to individuals and demoralising to the community'. He accordingly imposed a sentence of three years' penal servitude [*The Scotsman*, 30 March 1925].

145. For example, in the trial of Dr George Bell Todd in 1912, in passing sentence of seven years' penal servitude, Lord Guthrie claimed that he was 'doing only his duty . . . in the interests of the State . . . and also in the interests of the noble profession which the prisoner had dishonoured' [*The Scotsman*, 4 June 1912]. The heaviest sentence was the 10 years' penal servitude imposed in 1922 on James Ormiston, alias Scott, a former police inspector in Leith.

146. Defence counsel was known to argue in mitigation that the abortion was 'at the very beginning of pregnancy, which was in fact sufficient to take it in some parts of the world out of the category of crime altogether' [*The Scotsman*, 4 June 1912].

147. Fisher, ' "Didn't stop to think" ', 213.

148. Ibid., 213.

149. *Report of the Inter-Departmental Committee on Abortion*, 1939, 158–65; Mclaren, 'Illegal operations', 798; Usborne, *Cultures of Abortion*, 228.

150. de Blécourt, 'Cultures of abortion', 199.

151. Jones, 'Abortion in England', 31.

6

'An Open and Notorious House of Lewdness': Dora Noyce and the Danube Street Brothel

INTRODUCTION

On 22 September 1973, Dora Noyce (seventy-three), described in the press as 'the oldest girl in the oldest profession', was fined the considerable sum of £250 in Edinburgh Sheriff Court[1] under section 13 of the Criminal Law Amendment Act 1885, for keeping a brothel at 17 Danube Street.[2] She admitted twenty-eight previous convictions, dating back to 1934. Over the years, after 'bouts of police surveillance', Dora Noyce had been regularly fined for her activities and, at intervals, sentenced to periods of imprisonment. On this occasion, given that she had only recently completed a four-month prison sentence, the sheriff accepted the view of defence counsel that she was 'incorrigible' and 'unrepentant' and that a fine to render her activities 'less profitable' would be the most appropriate punishment and least burdensome to the taxpayer.

As was customary after her court appearances, Noyce, by then a great grandmother, conducted an impromptu press conference in Deacon Brodie's immediately after she had been discharged, ensuring that her business received widespread publicity. She remained undaunted by the prospect of further police raids on her establishment followed by further criminal convictions and ever-increasing fines. She told reporters, 'in an impeccable Edinburgh voice', that she had 'been intermittently in the business for thirty years' and had 'no intention of closing down'.[3] She was proud of building up an establishment of 'national and international repute'. According to Noyce, she provided 'a service in a clean and honest house' that was 'really rather a refined affair'. She likened her 'house of leisure and pleasure' – she hated the term 'brothel' – to the YMCA, 'except for one little item', arguing that it provided a 'discreet' and 'homely', rather than predatory, environment in a city that was starved of entertainment after 10 p.m.[4]

Dora Noyce and her Danube Street brothel played a central role in the sexual folklore of late twentieth-century Scotland. This chapter seeks to explore the true story behind her career as a madam, the operation of the brothel, and the nature of the social and legal response to her enterprise in the post-war years.

DORA NOYCE: THE MADAM

Dora Noyce was born Georgie Hunter Rae in 1900, the youngest of five children, to Alexander Rae, a cutler, and his wife, Mary Hunter.[5] She grew up in poverty in Rose Street, Edinburgh, a 'notorious promenade for prostitutes',[6] in an area of the central New Town that had increasingly become the focus for soliciting after World War I.[7] Some time after World War I she established a relationship with Ernest Noyce, a joiner's handyman, with whom she had a daughter (Violet Ellen) in 1923, and whose name she adopted (though there is no evidence that they ever married).[8] By then, Noyce had already adopted the name of Dora and was officially recorded as a 'housekeeper' living in Cowan's Close, a slum area in the St Leonard's District of South Edinburgh.[9] Noyce later admitted that she had first become involved in prostitution in the 1930s but little is known of her interwar activities. Then, in 1943, she purchased a terraced house in Stockbridge at the northern edge of the Georgian New Town for a little over £4,000 and subsequently ran it as a brothel for over thirty years despite the best efforts of the law and local residents to close it down. In locating in Stockbridge, Noyce was following the example of previous brothel-keepers who had located their operations at some distance from the city centre. They had been less reliant for custom on soliciting in the streets and, instead, relied on 'word of mouth' and repeat business from clients who arrived by car or, more often, by taxi.[10]

At the same time, Noyce reinvented herself, adopting the 'modulated tones' of the 'upper class groomed by one of the better finishing schools' and looking 'like a Morningside matron, dressed in twinset and pearls'.[11] Bob McCulloch, one of many taxi drivers who delivered her clients to Danube Street, records that she was (or affected to be) both morally and politically conservative. According to McCulloch, she took 'a very strong moral stance on many issues. She deplored anything vulgar, such as blue films and strip shows', and regarded herself as 'a bit of a square', viewing sex as a facet of romance rather than just a

Figure 6.1 Dora Noyce leaving Edinburgh Sheriff Court in December 1976 *[licensor: www.scran.ac.uk]*
(Source: www.scran.ac.uk)

crude commercial transaction.[12] Politically, she was a staunch Tory and a firm believer in private enterprise. Indeed, she was prone to turn up at the garden fetes of her local Tory MP, much to his embarrassment, and was wont to display party posters at election time in the windows of her brothel with the somewhat ambiguous slogan: 'Life is better under the Conservatives'.[13]

THE BROTHEL: 17 AND 17A DANUBE STREET

Noyce's establishment in Danube Street was on four floors.[14] It was described as 'shabby, Victorian, and fairly dark' giving the impression of 'middle-class genteel decrepitude'.[15] Dora occupied an apartment on the third floor with her dogs. The ground floor was a communal area where customers were received and entertained with a drink while Dora negotiated appropriate fees for a range of sexual services and generally co-ordinated and policed the activities of her 'girls' and their clients.

Most regular customers were then escorted to bedrooms on the second floor. In addition, there was a basement at 17a that was sublet to the prostitutes and divided into small cubicles. Evidence suggests that they could have their own clients there who would enter by a separate basement door. According to a former police officer who patrolled the area, the basement was much less regulated than the main brothel and posed greater risks for clients.

At its peak the brothel was reputed to have supported fifteen resident 'girls', with a further twenty-five coming in on a regular shift basis, available from 6 or 7 p.m. at night.[16] It was especially busy when ships on NATO exercises berthed in the Firth of Forth, when international rugby matches were being played, and during the Edinburgh Festival. It was rumoured that, when the aircraft carrier, USS *John F. Kennedy*, was in port, 'there were sailors queuing almost the length of Danube Street', with 'girls' arriving in taxis from as far away as Glasgow, Livingston and Falkirk. It was claimed that, on one occasion, £4,000 had been earned in the brothel before the captain declared the establishment off-limits in response to complaints from local residents to the American consulate in Edinburgh. Somewhat mischievously, Noyce also briefed the press that business was brisk during the General Assembly of the Church of Scotland. At other times, the overwhelming majority of customers were regulars including, allegedly, members of the magistrate's bench along with many other clients from the city's professional elite.[17]

The atmosphere in the brothel was relaxed but closely regulated by Noyce who insisted on polite and 'discreet' behaviour.[18] One customer later reminisced about his first 'punt' to Danube Street:

> She [Dora Noyce] opened the door and welcomed me in, it was hard to believe it but there were about 20 ladies to choose from all sitting about and chatting, there was even a plate of sandwiches and biscuits that was for the use of customers ... Too overcome to say much, I sat down in the chair near the door, and took it all in ... There were ladies in two piece, and some in hot pants and bikini tops, and some with designer clothes on, quite a mixture ... Dora was like a mother to them, and her authority stood out even then, and after five minutes she asked me, 'do any of the pretty ladies appeal to you son', I was gobsmacked and pointed to the lady nearest me and said yes, and was taken downstairs to a small dingy room which had a double bed and a wardrobe.[19]

Details of the sexual transactions are hard to document.[20] One of the prostitutes testified in the late 1970s that 'the average time given to clients was about 20 minutes – but it could be up to an hour', with a minimum charge of £10.[21] A neighbour claimed that she had witnessed twenty-six men visiting the brothel in the course of five hours.[22]

There is little information about the prostitutes that Noyce employed and the process by which they were recruited. As Dora Noyce always pleaded guilty to the charges against her, the social historian is deprived of the kind of detailed evidence on the brothel and its inmates that would almost certainly have been reported in the course of a trial. Noyce herself always portrayed her business as 'a high class establishment' and 'really rather a refined affair'. She claimed that her 'girls' were well groomed and well spoken and that they had entered the 'profession' by choice and sexual proclivity rather than through deprivation or economic necessity: 'I have never started a girl on the game. The girls come to me mostly because they are dissatisfied with marriage and their husbands, because they want companionship and because they are a bit over sexed anyway.'[23]

However, in her attempts to convey an acceptable image of her enterprise to the prosecution and public, and to distance herself from the enduring stereotype in the media of the 'vicious madam' entrapping young women and subjecting them to a life of sexual exploitation, Noyce may well have exaggerated the degree of agency enjoyed by her 'girls'. Other evidence suggests that the women employed in her brothel were primarily driven by financial need, and not infrequently associated with criminal elements in society. Indeed, some cynics later surmised that Noyce's periodic stays in Greenock or Saughton prison must have given her an ideal opportunity to recruit new 'girls' for her establishment.[24] Certainly, local residents did not share her rather glamorised picture of her employees. From their perspective, regularly witnessing a stream of men being serviced every fifteen minutes, often in tiny, insanitary cubicles, the operation was 'basically squalid and the girls for the most part usually poor and unhappy creatures'. According to one former CID officer, 'most of them came from broken homes and had a history of abuse'.[25]

BROTHEL-KEEPING AND THE LAW

Local by-laws as well as statute law were employed in the prosecution of brothel-keepers in Edinburgh. Under section 278 of the Edinburgh Municipal and Police Act 1879, it was illegal to maintain a brothel. Additional powers of search and arrest with respect to brothel-keeping were also granted to magistrates under the Burgh Police (Scotland) Act 1892. More importantly, under the provisions of the Criminal Law Amendment Act 1885 it was an offence in Scotland for any person to keep or assist in keeping a brothel, for a landlord knowingly to let premises for use as a brothel, or for the tenant or occupier of any premises knowingly to permit them to be used 'for the purposes of habitual prostitution'.[26] The penalty for a first offence was a fine of £100 or imprisonment for three months or both. A second or subsequent conviction was liable to a fine of £250 or imprisonment for six months or both. In Scotland, the higher penalties could be imposed only in the Sheriff Courts and not in other courts of summary jurisdiction.

During the interwar period the number of convictions each year in Edinburgh for brothel-keeping rarely exceeded ten and was often very much lower. Burgh Court records reveal that brothels involved with the law were distributed throughout the city and not restricted to one particular 'red light' district in the city centre. Instead, they existed in areas such as Stockbridge, Murrayfield, Newington and the outskirts of Leith, where rents were lower and clients could gain ready access by car or taxi. The brothels often operated in conjunction with dance halls and clubs in the city centre, such as the Havana Dance Club in Princes Street, the Savoy in Cockburn Street, or the Kosmo Club in Swinton Row, where female employees were 'booked out' to perform sexual services in a variety of locations.[27]

According to William Merrilees, latterly Chief Constable for the Lothians and Borders, in the early decades of the twentieth century there were many brothels in Edinburgh 'some which had been in business for as long as thirty years without suffering interference'.[28] In the 1930s, however, as a detective inspector, he collaborated with the newly appointed Procurator Fiscal, James Adair, in a sustained campaign to prosecute brothel-keepers and to close down their establishments as part of a more general drive to clear up 'vice-ridden Edinburgh'.[29] As a result, Merrilees claimed that, by 1939, 'all brothels in the city of any consequence had been disposed of'.[30]

After the war, the vice duties performed by the police in Edinburgh were reorganised so as to enable the force to adopt a more efficient and co-ordinated approach to offences such as prostitution and brothel-keeping.[31] Nonetheless, the annual reports of Edinburgh city police indicate that convictions for brothel-keeping in the city were typically no more than one or two per year.[32] Dora Noyce was to figure in the majority of such cases. Ginty Kerr, a former superintendent in the Lothian and Borders Police, recalled how:

The police would go and routinely take observations once every six months and they would fix Dora for running a brothel; and once every six months she would go to court and the Sheriff would fine her the maximum £250, which was a lot of money in those days [I only earned £700 when I joined the police, so £250 was a third of a year's wages for me] and at the twelve month interval she would get a month in the jail, so she would tootle along to the women's wing of Saughton and she would serve her time there and her main girl would manage the premises in Danube Street. And then she would come back and pick up where she left off; and at the eighteen-month interval she would get a £250 fine, and so it would go on. It would alternate.[33]

There was therefore, in effect, a policy of relative tolerance in Edinburgh towards the Danube Street brothel. Indeed, in 1966 the earl of Dalkeith questioned the Secretary of State for Scotland in Parliament as to whether this leniency towards a persistent offender was 'tantamount to running a licensed brothel system without any of the advantages of supervisory safeguards'.[34]

A range of reasons can be advanced to explain how Dora Noyce managed to preserve her establishment for so long. First, she did her utmost to prevent the brothel becoming an issue of public order. According to former police officers who patrolled the area she ran 'a very tight ship' and did her utmost to 'minimise hassle from her girls'.[35] As far as possible she ensured that clients arriving in taxis were dropped off further down the street, and the brothel itself was indistinguishable from the surrounding properties in the New Town. The political correspondent, Iain MacWhirter who, as an adolescent, had taken a prurient interest in observing the establishment, recollected that:

> There was nothing there at all, apart from those cheerless black New Town facades. No red lights, no guilty-looking men in macs; no floozies with come-hither stares. Only a man mending a Vauxhall Victor. The only screwing that was going on was on its carburettor.[36]

Even a Conservative councillor admitted that, with the exception of brief periods when Dora Noyce was in jail, there were very few complaints from neighbouring residents.[37]

Secondly, Noyce ensured that the brothel did not become a public health issue in a period of growing public and political concern at the rising incidence of sexually transmitted diseases. Though debate increasingly focused on concepts of 'promiscuity' and 'permissiveness' and the spectre of widespread casual sex with an endless chain of infection, the role of prostitution, with the spread of disease attributed to a small cluster of feckless and immoral vectors, remained a leitmotif of public health reports.[38] In Scotland, during the 1950s and early 1960s, many venereologists and health officials favoured closer regulation of prostitutes as a means of reducing the reservoir of infection within the community. It was already common practice for 'habitual prostitutes' appearing before the courts to be remanded in custody for medical examination under section 26 of the Criminal Justice (Scotland) Act 1949. Scottish law officers subsequently ruled that such powers had been intended as an aid to sentencing and not infectious-disease prevention. Nonetheless, until the late 1960s in Edinburgh, all women convicted of prostitution continued to be referred to the VD clinics, irrespective of whether they had any symptoms.[39] Dora Noyce preferred to pre-empt this process. She sent her 'girls' for regular health checks at the Family Planning Clinic in nearby Dean Terrace or, when appropriate, for treatment at Ward 46 of the Royal Infirmary of Edinburgh.[40] As a result she avoided 17 Danube Street being associated with the moral panics surrounding the emergence of new forms of sexually transmitted infection within the Edinburgh community after 1960.

The third and overriding reason for the survival and success of 17 Danube Street was the close working relationship that Dora Noyce established with the police, often to their mutual benefit.[41] There appears to have been an informal agreement that, in return for information about the criminal underworld garnered in the course of servicing clients, raids on the brothel would be restricted and Noyce possibly given some discreet forewarning. In addition, she was able to use her contacts with senior detectives to fend off overtures from organised crime intent on taking over the brothel for the purposes of blackmail and extortion.[42] For their part, the police saw advantages in having a focus of prostitution that was well regulated but could be occasionally prosecuted without the need for protracted and costly surveillance and that reduced the number of prostitutes soliciting in the city centre. As elsewhere in Scotland, the Edinburgh police authorities were reluctant to be seen as moral arbiters, and police chiefs were adamant that the force should focus only on activities relating to prostitution that had caused 'annoyance' and public complaint, which Noyce sought to minimise. The apparent absence of trafficking and intimidation associated with the Danube Street brothel, and the fact that it was run by a woman who appeared to care for her employees, may well have also tempered the view of the police who traditionally reserved their animosity for male pimps and ponces living off immoral earnings.[43] An additional factor may have been the sympathetic treatment accorded her activities and court appearances by the Scottish press, often emphasising the pastoral rather than exploitative nature of her role as madam and the therapeutic rather than criminal aspects of the brothel's sexual services.

Certainly, the relatively tolerant treatment experienced by Dora Noyce was in sharp contrast to the vigorous application of the Criminal Law Amendment Act 1885 and Immoral Traffic (Scotland) Act 1902 by Glasgow police authorities. After extensive surveillance employing anti-vice patrols and using prostitutes as key witnesses, they launched a sustained campaign against male brothel-keepers. The press made much of the colour and ethnicity of defendants, many of whom were West Indian or Maltese, and there were distinctly xenophobic, if not racist, overtones in the rhetoric of some of the court reporting.[44] Moreover, after the 1950s, an increasing proportion of such cases were conducted in the Sheriff Courts, thus attracting higher penalties including periods of imprisonment.[45] As the Tory councillor and journalist, Brian Meek, later reflected, this contrast seemed to 'undermine the accepted stereotypes': 'Prim, proper Edinburgh [was] prepared to turn a blind eye while friendly warm-hearted Glasgow [took] a line which could have come straight from the pulpit of a Victorian Welsh chapel'.[46] The fact that brothel-keeping in Glasgow was predominantly a male preserve and was widely suspected of funding the criminal underworld no doubt goes some way to explaining this contrast.[47]

AFTERMATH

On Dora Noyce's death in July 1977 the brothel soon became embroiled in a mass of publicity and legal activity. Despite her best efforts to avoid conflict with local residents, over the years there had been growing resentment at the disturbance created by drunken clients, often going to the wrong address and not infrequently 'urinating and vomiting in doorways'.[48] Some neighbours had pretended to photograph them and threatened to send pictures to their wives and girlfriends. Concerns had also been raised about the possible impact of the brothel on the morals of children living in the neighbourhood and on local property values.[49] In the early 1970s, a Danube Street Association had been formed to campaign for the brothel's closure on the grounds that, as a commercial enterprise, it contravened its feu charter. The campaign proved abortive but, in 1975, a number of residents did successfully appeal for a reduction in rates on the grounds of 'loss of amenity and disturbance'.[50]

By August 1977, the community was complaining to the police and council officials that, despite Dora Noyce's death, her former employees had remained in the house and were continuing to operate it as a brothel, with little regard for the quality of life of the neighbourhood. It was claimed that there was a ceaseless queue of taxis depositing loud and unruly 'punters' in Danube Street, with incessant screaming and dogs barking. Some residents were so incensed that they verbally abused and assaulted the prostitutes and broke some of the brothel's windows, and were subsequently charged for breach of the peace.[51] *The Guardian* reported that a silent vigil was being planned, fuelled by fears that 17 Danube Street might be taken over by 'a vice syndicate from the Midlands'.[52] Violet Eager (née Noyce), Dora's beneficiary, had also added her voice to the campaign to close down the brothel, claiming that the stigma associated with her mother's establishment was affecting her family and grandchildren.[53]

In September, further demonstrations and increasingly heated confrontations between residents and prostitutes took place amid rumours that the brothel might be acquired by 'criminal elements' from Glasgow.[54] Meanwhile, the inmates had sought to secure their legal position by dividing the house into separate rented accommodation with separate bell pushes on the front door. This, their solicitor argued, not only protected their tenancy rights but also rendered the establishment immune to prosecution as a 'brothel'. In the view of the council, this threatened to contravene regulations governing listed buildings, and the planning department duly served an inspection notice to investigate complaints of 'unauthorised erections' – a double entendre widely celebrated in the media.[55]

More importantly, Violet Eager had initiated legal action against the nine remaining inmates in order to close the brothel and protect herself from prosecution. As the owner of the building, as long as it was still being operated for the purposes of prostitution, she was liable to prosecution under section 13 of the Sexual Offences (Scotland) Act 1976. At the end of October, the sheriff duly issued an interdict against the inmates of 17 and 17a Danube Street forbidding them to use the establishment for the purposes of prostitution.[56] They were subsequently fined for breaking the interdict and lost their appeal against it in December. Local residents gave compelling evidence that male clients were continuing to visit the house in significant numbers for sexual services and that it was 'still being used communally as a brothel'. The sheriff principal agreed and was in no doubt that the establishment continued to conform to the definition of 'brothel' in Scots law as defined in *Hume's Commentaries* – namely, 'an open and notorious house of lewdness, for the reception of loose and dissolute visitors'.[57] The defendants were left in no doubt that any further breach of the interdict would attract severe penalties including jail sentences, and, shortly after receiving notice to quit in December 1977, they departed.[58] The house was subsequently sold for £15,000 and divided up into private flats.[59]

Nonetheless, much to the dismay of the Edinburgh Tourist Board, for decades after, 17 Danube Street remained a popular destination for visitors both from the United Kingdom and overseas, and 'an enduring landmark in the sex geography of Edinburgh'.[60] Dora Noyce had become somewhat of a local hero in the press, and the story of her life was subsequently celebrated in a play written by Hector MacMillan in 1981–2 for the Lyceum Theatre, entitled *Capital Offence*, that mocked the moral hypocrisy of Edinburgh's elite and, perhaps predictably, occasioned 'an ostentatious walk-out from the Grand Circle' on its opening night.[61] Some social commentators have similarly viewed Dora Noyce and her Danube Street brothel as 'a metaphor for the capital's love–hate attitude to sex and the sex industry'. It is claimed that in Edinburgh, where the social influence of the Catholic Church has been far more limited than in Glasgow, a certain Presbyterian hypocrisy has continued to hold sway, and that the city remains 'in the grip of a dual identity: respectable and God-fearing on the one hand, rebellious and scornful in its debauchery on the other'.[62]

CONCLUSION

The story of Dora Noyce and 17 Danube Street highlights three important aspects of the relationship between the law, sex and society in later twentieth-century Scotland. First, it illustrates well the degree to which the legal environment surrounding sexual behaviour continued to be configured primarily within the local state. It is clear that the impact of legislation designed to penalise brothel-keeping, such as the Criminal Law Amendment Act 1885, was mediated to a significant extent by the attitude and agenda of local councillors, local police and health authorities, and the local media.

Secondly, the extent to which the police and procurators fiscal desisted after 1950 from a sustained legal attack on Dora Noyce and her establishment, on the lines of William Merrilees's interwar campaign, reflected the growing reluctance of the agencies of law enforcement to become involved in moral issues, notwithstanding the forebodings of many civic dignitaries and church leaders. In line with the proceedings of the Wolfenden Committee (1954–57) 'public nuisance' increasingly supplanted 'immorality' as the primary instigator of police action.

Thirdly, the relationship between Dora Noyce and the law suggests that underpinning the more institutional picture of prostitution and brothel-keeping in Scotland conveyed in court records and press reports there existed a more complex story of collusion and accommodation between the sexual underworld and the authorities. By its very nature, this is a story that can only be partially told. For a full picture the social historian must necessarily await further research drawing on the future release of police and court records and additional oral testimony from those participants who have survived to tell the tale of 17 Danube Street.

NOTES

1. The monetary equivalent of over £2,000 in 2017.
2. *Edinburgh Evening News*, 21 September 1973; *The Guardian*, 24 September 1973.
3. *Edinburgh Evening News*, 21 September 1973; *The Guardian*, 24 September 1973.
4. For a discussion of the broader implications of this presentation of prostitution in terms of 'domestication' rather than 'predation', see Bondi, 'Sexing the city', 177–200.
5. NRS, Statutory Register of Births, 685/02 0611, 1900 Rae, Georgie Hunter.
6. NRS, Valuation rolls for 1905–6, VR100/235/2861; Merrilees, *The Short Arm of the Law*, 64. The word 'prostitute' is used in this chapter as the contemporary term employed by the police, magistrates and media to describe women who were prosecuted for soliciting or otherwise engaging in the sex trade.
7. Settle, 'The social geography of prostitution', 240–1.
8. NRS, Statutory Register of Births, 685/05 1113, 1923 Noyce, Violet Ellen; *The Scotsman*, 23 December 1977.
9. Ibid.
10. Settle, 'The social geography of prostitution', 256–8.
11. McCulloch, *My Fare* City, 50; Emslie, 'Nights at city's Blue Danube Street'; *Edinburgh Evening News*, 14 December 2005. Bob McCulloch recalled that she 'dressed well and sounded a little like Margaret Thatcher' [BBC Radio Scotland, '17 Danube Street', 19 December 2005].
12. McCulloch, *My Fare City*, 50.
13. *The Guardian*, 19 July 1977; *Glasgow Herald*, 16 September 2003.
14. Unless otherwise stated, the following section is based upon *The Scotsman*, 26 August 1977, 29 November 1977, 23 December 1977; McCulloch, *My Fare City*, 49–50; *Sunday Times*, 30 October 1977, 29 November 1977; interviews with Bob McCulloch, 13 November 2012 and Mark Taylor, 23 November 2012; BBC Radio Scotland, '17 Danube Street', 19 December 2005, interview with Tom Wood (former Deputy Chief Constable of Lothian and Borders Police).
15. BBC Radio Scotland, '17 Danube Street', 19 December 2005, interview with Tom Wood.

16. In this respect the Danube Street brothel appears to have differed from most brothels in Edinburgh that had traditionally been small flats with one or two rooms occupied by two or three women, run not by a 'madam-type character' but a poor working-class women seeking to benefit from letting her premises [Settle, *Sex for Sale*, 142–4].

17. Hector MacMillan, *Capital Offence*, first draft, 1981, Scottish Theatre archives, Glasgow University Library, Special Collections, STA H.p. Box 1/11, p. 88.

18. According to *The Guardian*, 24 December 1977, one of Noyce's house rules was that 'discretion is the better part of amour'.

19. http://www.ukpunting.com/index.php?topic=1494.0 (accessed, 22 August 2012).

20. The author visited 17 Danube Street in the 1980s. Although by then it was no longer a brothel, there were still manacles fixed to the walls in the basement, presumably a legacy of previous bondage practices offered to clients.

21. *The Scotsman*, 29 November 1977.

22. Ibid., 23 December 1977.

23. *The Guardian*, 24 September 1973. Significantly, Noyce portrayed her own introduction to prostitution in similar terms, stressing that she 'had a respectable upbringing' but that she 'liked men', implying that prostitution served to fulfil a hyperactive sex drive [McCulloch, *My Fare City*, 50].

24. *The Scotsman*, 19 July 1977.

25. *The Guardian*, 10 August 1977; anon., 'Dora and her girls', *Scottish Review*, June 2015.

26. For a summary of the law operating in post-war Scotland, see *Report of the Committee on Homosexual Offences and Prostitution*, 101–8; Gane, *Sexual Offences*, Ch. 9. A man inhabiting a house that was used for prostitution and living off 'immoral earnings' could also be prosecuted under the Immoral Traffic (Scotland) Act 1902.

27. Settle, 'The social geography of prostitution', 258. For a detailed account of the links between the clubs and Edinburgh brothels, revealed in the widely publicised trial of the Kosmo club in 1933, see Merrilees, *The Short Arm of the Law*, 96–106; Settle, 'The Kosmo Club case'.

28. Merrilees, *The Short Arm of the Law*, 64, 80.

29. For a detailed account of this campaign, see ibid., 107–14.

30. Ibid., 114. As Settle points out, however, 'police memoirs as a source must be used cautiously'. Merrilees was intent on depicting 'a heroic image of himself' in the battle against vice in the City and may well have exaggerated the demise of brothel-keeping [Settle, 'The Kosmo Club case', 573].

31. Edinburgh City Archives (hereafter ECA), ED 6/1/14, *Edinburgh City Police Annual Reports for 1959*,15; *1960*, 15.

32. ECA, ED 6/1/11–16, *Edinburgh City Police Annual Reports for 1945–71*.

33. BBC Radio Scotland, '17 Danube Street', 19 December 2005, interview with Ginty Kerr.

34. *Hansard [HL]*, ser. 5, vol. 738, 21 December 1966, cols 1402–3.

35. BBC Radio Scotland, '17 Danube Street', 19 December 2005, interviews with Ginty Kerr and Tom Wood. The relative absence of drug dependency among Dora's employees, as compared with the sex industry in Edinburgh after 1980, also contributed to the orderliness of the brothel. None of the formal complaints lodged with the police relating to 17 Danube Street mentioned drugs or needles.

36. *The Scotsman*, 1 August 1996.

37. *The Guardian*, 24 September 1973.

38. Davidson, *Dangerous Liaisons*, 245–7.

39. Ibid., 274–5.

40. Interview with Bob McCulloch, 13 November 2012; Radio Scotland, '17 Danube Street', 19 December 2005, interview with Ginty Kerr. According to Kerr, Dora Noyce also arranged for treatment for any of her 'girls' who had alcohol problems through her contacts with the Crichton Royal Infirmary in Dumfries.

41. The following is based on an interview with Bob McCulloch, 13 November 2012; Settle, 'The social geography of prostitution', 253; Merrilees. *The Short Arm of the Law*, Chs 4–7; BBC Radio Scotland, '17 Danube Street', 19 December 2005, interview with Tom Wood. In the same programme, Ginty Kerr recalled that police stationed at Gayfield Square police station, at the top of Leith Walk, in the 1960s regularly steered foreign seamen to Danube Street as a means of ensuring their safety and protecting public order.

42. Interestingly, in his play *Capital Offence*, Hector MacMillan strongly implied police collusion in the survival of the brothel, hinting that one of Dora Noyce's talents was her ability 'at sussing out who was on the take' [Scottish Theatre Archives, Glasgow University Library, Special Collections, STA H.p Box 1/11, first draft, 1981, 7, 22, 63].

43. Settle, *Sex for Sale*, 39–40. One police officer, who had regularly served warrants for Dora Noyce's arrest, later claimed that the 'girls' were well fed and 'never abused' and that she had made provision for them to maintain savings accounts as 'their "seed" money for a new life back in the community' [anon., 'Dora and her girls', *Scottish Review*, June 2015].

44. See, for example, *Glasgow Herald*, 5 May 1966, 30 September 1966, 3 February 1968, 10 May 1968, 3 March 1970, 23 September 1971, 12 January 1977. The most celebrated case was that of Dr S. D. K. Soni, an Indian from Uganda, charged in Glasgow Sheriff Court in 1969 under the Immoral Traffic (Scotland) Act 1902 with living on immoral earnings. A former senior casualty officer at the Western Infirmary and Glasgow Royal Infirmary, he owned or controlled at least eight furnished houses in Glasgow from which women worked as prostitutes [*Glasgow Herald*, 13 March 1969, 28 May 1969, 29 May 1969, 30 May 1969, 31 May 1969, 4 June 1969, 6 June 1969, 14 June 1969, 19 July 1969]. For the importance

of race to contemporary fears relating to brothel-keeping, pimping and prostitution, see Mort, *Capital Affairs*, 311–12.

45. Scottish Home Department/Scottish Home and Health Department, *Criminal Statistics Scotland, Annual Reports for 1950–74*, Table 5.

46. *Glasgow Herald*, 16 September 2003.

47. Scattered evidence in the Burgh Court papers suggest that, as in interwar Edinburgh [Settle, *Sex for Sale*, 144], in the post-war years most brothels were run by women. See, for example, the brothels at 3a Fettes Row and 17 Union Place [ECA, Edinburgh Burgh Court Records, cases of Isabel Clemson and Eileen McCann, 2 May 1950, 11 February 1953]. Clemson had a number of previous convictions for brothel- keeping stretching back to 1931.

48. *Glasgow Herald*, 24 September 1973.

49. Ibid., 10 December 1973.

50. *The Guardian*, 19 July 1977.

51. *The Scotsman*, 26 August 1977; *Glasgow Herald*, 11 August 1977.

52. *The Guardian*, 10 August 1977.

53. *The Scotsman*, 25 August 1977.

54. *Edinburgh Evening News*, 9 September 1977. These demonstrations were subsequently to be satirised in Hector MacMillan's play, *Capital Offence*, in which one placard reads 'I am coming soon, hold fast what you have – Revelations', much to the amusement of the police [Scottish Theatre Archives, Glasgow University Library, Special Collections, STA H.p Box 1/11, first draft, 1981, 30].

55. *The Scotsman*, 30 October 1977.

56. NRS, SC39/17/1977/96, Action for Interdict papers.

57. NRS, SC39/17/1977/96, sheriff principal's judgment on appeal, 16 December 1977, citing David Hume's *Commentaries on the Law of Scotland, Respecting Trial for Crimes* (1797); *The Scotsman*, 28 and 29 November 1977; 17 December 1977; *Edinburgh Evening News*, 6 December 1977.

58. *The Scotsman*, 23 December 1977.

59. Ibid., 20 March 1978.

60. *The Scotsman*, 1 August 1996. The brothel itself, and a somewhat sanitised version of its activities, have become part of the 'constructed heritage of the area'. As Liz Bondi observes: 'The story appears to add a touch of spice to the reputation of this now well-established middle-class area. It helps to make the area exciting rather than staid' and suggests 'that not so long ago this area was an urban frontier' [Bondi, 'Sexing the city', 195].

61. Glasgow University Library, Special Collections, Scottish Theatre Archives, STA H.p Box 1/11; http://hector-macmillan.com/capital_offence.html (accessed 18 December 2017).

62. Anon., 'Sex and the City', *Linlithgow Gazette*, 24 June 2002; Massie, *Edinburgh*, 177.

7

'Cure or Confinement'? Law, Medicine and the Treatment of Homosexual Offenders in Scotland, 1950–80[1]

INTRODUCTION

In recent years, the social politics and the legal and medical discourses surrounding homosexuality in twentieth-century Britain have attracted increasing attention from historians and social scientists. Within the growing literature, the medical perception and treatment of homosexuality and homosexual offences have been viewed from a variety of standpoints. Many studies address the subject as a central aspect of the politics surrounding either the regulation of dangerous sexualities or the process of homosexual law reform.[2] Others, often from a social constructionist viewpoint, have focused on the competing sexological and psychoanalytical discourses surrounding homosexuality and their impact upon public policy.[3] Anecdotal evidence of medical attitudes and therapies is also scattered in the written and recorded testimonies of homosexuals.[4] However, with the notable exception of the oral history undertaken by King, Smith and Bartlett,[5] and, more recently, by Meek,[6] there has been little systematic primary research into the medical perception and treatment of male homosexuality that prevailed in the surgeries, clinics, courts and prisons of the land since World War II. This is especially true in relation to the Scottish experience, despite the distinctive traditions of law and medical practice north of the Border, as well as, arguably, Scotland's distinctive civic and sexual culture.

This chapter seeks to begin to make good this omission by documenting the medical perception and treatment of homosexual offenders in Scotland in the period 1950–80, and, in particular, the role that medical evidence played in the prosecution and sentencing of such offenders. Two main sources of evidence are explored. First, the verbal and written evidence of Scottish witnesses before the Wolfenden Committee on Prostitution and Homosexual Offences (1954–57) is examined in order to identify how homosexual offenders were treated, or allegedly treated, in the 1950s. The Wolfenden Committee was appointed in 1954 in response to a moral panic surrounding an apparent escalation in urban vice and with a remit to consider the law and practice relating to homosexual offences and prostitution. Secondly, a systematic analysis is undertaken of the medical reports on homosexual offenders submitted by psychiatrists and other doctors to Scottish High Court trials and appeals during the period 1950–80, and of their role in court proceedings.[7] This will serve to throw important light on the degree to which medical views and practices pertaining to homosexual offenders in Scotland changed over the quarter of a century following Wolfenden and how far and in what ways they influenced the legal process.

THE VIEW FROM WOLFENDEN

Scottish evidence to the Wolfenden Committee varied as to the extent to which medical considerations played a part in the sentencing of homosexual offenders in the 1950s. James Adair, former Procurator Fiscal for Edinburgh and Glasgow, was of the opinion that: 'Some judges were very responsive to suggestions by medical men about treatment, while others agreed that these were not the concern of the judge.'[8] Certainly, under the Criminal Justice (Scotland) Act 1949, courts had explicit powers both to call for medical reports on offenders and to prescribe medical treatment (though not its specific nature) as part of a probationary sentence. Thus, an offender could, with his consent, be required under a probation order to undertake remedial treatment either as a resident or non-resident of an institution or as a patient of a named doctor.[9] Some legal witnesses before the Wolfenden Committee considered that, compared with legal practice in interwar Scotland,[10] there was an increasing trend in Scottish courts for medical reports to be used in cases involving homosexual offences, and that the practice was 'much more the custom in Scotland than in England'.[11] Dr W. Boyd, Consultant Psychiatrist to the Scottish Prison and Borstal Service, testified that he was:

> in charge of a Mental Health Service where both the Procurators Fiscal and the Sheriffs were willing to recognise that we could have cooperation, and many offenders were placed on probation on the condition that they attended hospital.[12]

Indeed, in Glasgow, whereas formerly the magistrates had tended to process homosexual offenders without any consideration of medical issues simply 'as men who were doing a dirty thing', and routinely to 'fine them a fiver each', in the 1950s, such cases were increasingly remitted to the Sheriff Court to ensure some level of medical examination.[13]

In line with the recommendation of the Scottish Advisory Council on the Treatment and Rehabilitation of Offenders that psychotherapeutic and other medical treatment should be more widely available for convicted sexual offenders,[14] the Scottish Home Department had, it claimed, by the mid-1950s, begun to expand psychiatric provisions within the Scottish prison system. The Department recommended that all first offenders should have a full medico-psychological assessment prior to sentencing.[15] Further, it advocated that all male prisoners convicted of homosexual offences should be interviewed at some point by a psychiatrist and that, if the offender was suitable for treatment and was willing to undergo it during his sentence, he should be admitted to a psychiatric hospital as an inpatient or given treatment at a psychiatric clinic as an outpatient. Similar psychiatric examination and treatment were viewed as desirable for all male borstal inmates.[16]

Despite such aspirations, however, Dr T. D. Inch, Medical Adviser to the Scottish Prison and Borstal Services, maintained that the resources for treatment within Scottish prisons remained 'pitifully inadequate' and 'barely scratching the surface of the problem'.[17] With first offenders, who often served short sentences, at best only a 'few psychotherapeutic talks' were possible. Apart from Barlinnie Prison, Glasgow, where a new medical psychiatric unit was being built, there were no special psychotherapeutic units in Scotland such as existed at Wormwood Scrubs and Wakefield, and many of the prisons were too small to justify in-house psychiatric provisions.[18] For any 'deep treatment', such as it existed, the Scottish Prison Service relied entirely on external psychiatric provisions within the NHS. Within the borstal system, treatment was, in practice, largely confined to casual, ad hoc advice conveyed by the governor, chaplain and psychiatrist to inmates, and to the enforcement of 'hard work and varied recreation, especially of an athletic nature' to counteract 'homosexual tendencies'.[19]

Scotland did vary from England and Wales in the type of medical treatment administered in prison to convicted homosexual offenders. According to the evidence of Scottish Prison Medical Officers, no use was made of electroconvulsive therapy (ECT) in Scottish prisons. Narcoanalysis (psychoanalysis undertaken during a light phase of anaesthesia) had been used to a limited extent during the war but had been deemed unsuited to 'civil life'.[20] However, in contrast to England and Wales, where the practice had been discontinued as too dangerous, oestrogen treatment had been used in Scottish prisons on sexual offenders for some time (especially at Perth), largely inspired by the work of F. L. Golla at the Burden Neurological Institute in Bristol.[21] It was only given to prisoners who signed an agreement to the procedure and then only under strict medical supervision. According to Inch, oestrogen treatment had never been pushed 'to its limits' – 'to the extent of producing atrophy of the testicles or even gynaecomastia (excessive enlargement of the male breasts) – but only to the point of eliminating or at least greatly reducing libido'.[22] The prime objective was to make the prisoners less anxious, more 'adaptable' and 'easier to handle', and to provide the 'small maintenance dosage that reliev[ed] tension' without producing any physical change in the patient. Significantly, such treatment regimes were not public knowledge. According to Inch, the Scottish Prison Service had 'never said anything'. 'We have', he noted, 'just kept very quiet about it.'[23]

The fullest and most compelling Scottish evidence to the Wolfenden Committee in favour of homosexual law reform did come from medical witnesses. Perhaps the most influential evidence was that submitted by Drs Inch and Boyd from the Scottish Prisons and Borstal Services.[24] Echoing the previous recommendations of the Scottish Advisory Council on the Treatment and Rehabilitation of Offenders, they aired serious doubts as to the value of imprisonment in reforming sexual offenders and favoured the decriminalisation of homosexual behaviour for consenting adults over the age of twenty-one.[25] In their view, a range of alternative provisions was necessary. In accordance with Freudian interpretations, there needed to be more child guidance and child psychiatric clinics to 'treat deviation as early as possible before fixation occurred'. Courts should have routine psychiatric reports on all homosexual offenders prior to sentencing, supplied by a properly staffed University or Regional Hospital Board clinic, and more extensive use needed to be made of probationary orders for treatment of first offenders under the Criminal Justice (Scotland) Act 1949. For the homosexual recidivist or 'homosexual psychopath', there should be a separate psychopathic institute, as in Denmark. Finally, treatment regimes had to be more effectively monitored and sustained by means of improved staff resources for aftercare and social work. Underlying their evidence was a belief that a less punitive policy would, in fact, produce a more liberal and sympathetic attitude to homosexuality in British society.

Evidence submitted by Drs Winifred Rushforth and W. P. Kraemer, respectively founder and Medical Director of the pioneering Davidson Clinic in Edinburgh, established in 1940 to provide family therapy and psychoanalytical treatment to the general public, also favoured the decriminalisation of homosexual behaviour between consenting adults as integral to changing social attitudes and to a refocusing of public debate on to issues of aetiology rather than punishment.[26] In their view, in many cases, homosexuality was 'neither a disease nor a matter of choice' but compulsive behaviour contingent on emotional immaturity.[27] They stressed the value of psychotherapy in bringing some homosexuals 'into a more mature state' in which they could relate to women. They considered that imprisonment merely reinforced the mental and social problems of homosexuals and should be used only for 'hardened offenders' who were 'a potential danger to young people'. They did not feel that prison predisposed homosexual offenders to effective treatment, and viewed the existing prison medical staff as unsuited to addressing sexual problems. At the very least, they advocated the general introduction of group psychotherapy for offenders. Significantly, however, their evidence still identified homosexuals as fundamentally dysfunctional and antisocial and, in part, their opposition to legal coercion was that it served merely to magnify not only the homosexual's sense of social isolation but also his sexual ego. As Dr Kraemer testified:

> I feel that if we make them into heroes and put them into prisons, . . . it is not really doing very much good, and it gives them a wrong idea of self-importance . . . [I]f you do that I feel it is bad for society and for the character of these men, too.[28]

In his view, many of such 'young heroes want[ed] to suck forbidden fruit' and prosecution often served to fuel a neurotic compulsion for punishment.

In his contribution to the British Medical Association's evidence to the Wolfenden Committee, John Glaister junior, Regius Professor of Forensic Medicine at the University of Glasgow, also combined a somewhat pathological view of homosexuality with support for its limited decriminalisation. He was a vigorous supporter of coercive measures, including segregation in colonies for 'the inveterate and degenerate sodomist, the debauchers of youth, and those who resort[ed] to violence to meet their desires'. Likewise, he endorsed a 'major attack by the law' on 'the confirmed invert and the male prostitute'. However, he did not feel that the incidence of homosexuality threatened the nation with 'racial decadence' and considered that consenting acts of adults in private (not including sodomy) were a matter 'of private ethics' and should be outwith the law. In his opinion, while society's disapproval was 'inevitable and desirable' and while homosexuality was certainly not something that should be encouraged, incarceration was not the answer in the majority of cases that involved minor offences. Glaister viewed prison as 'the last place for homosexual treatment'. On the contrary, he emphasised its propensity 'to incubate and foster homosexual tendencies'. Moreover, he also considered that the risk of prosecution often acted as an aphrodisiac for offenders. 'Many homosexuals', he averred, 'feel that to flout the law is fraught with adventure due to possible detection, and to their peculiar make-up this may tend to add a fillip to their sex life.'[29]

At the same time, much of the evidence presented on the effectiveness of existing medical treatments for homosexual conditions was far from compelling. The experience of the Scottish Home Department was that, within the prison population, only a minority of homosexual offenders, some 30 per cent, were suitable for medical treatment and only 11 per cent prepared fully to co-operate with a course of psychotherapy.[30] In particular, it was claimed that short-term prisoners proved reluctant to agree to a course of treatment that might be prolonged beyond the date of their release. Nor were the medical staff of the Scottish Prison and Borstal Services at all certain of the outcome of their therapies. They insisted that it was never their aim to try to change the sexual identity of a homosexual, which they regarded as 'expensive, dangerous' and, almost certainly, impossible. Dr Boyd admitted that, though they might 're-direct' the energies of homosexuals and 'allow them to make a more adequate adjustment to their responsibilities', he did not 'for a moment suggest they could "cure" homosexuality'.[31] In his experience, it was not possible to treat homosexuals as sex offenders in prison and he recommended that hardened offenders should be treated in separate psychopathic institutes.[32] Even with the more limited aim of trying to reduce the levels of sexual urge and mental anxiety in homosexual offenders, the medical science was hazy. As Drs Inch and Boyd freely admitted, 'we do not know what may be happening so far as the endocrine treatment is concerned and what the ultimate result may be', and, though evidence suggested that, in many cases, it alleviated 'a most uncomfortable feeling of tension and guilt', and rendered patients more amenable to psychotherapy, they had never undertaken a controlled experiment 'to see whether aspirin would [have been] equally successful'.[33]

The evidence of the Davidson Clinic suggested that the scope for addressing homosexual behaviour by means of psychoanalysis was also limited. Though its staff claimed relatively high levels of success, this was clearly based on a relatively modest definition of 'success' and on extremely selective and long-term, labour-intensive therapy, exploring the patient's history right back into infancy and his/her earliest family relationships.[34] While it was argued that men in their late teens and twenties, who were still developing emotionally, might benefit from treatment, sexually active men who 'had extensively practised their perversion' were viewed as unsuited to analysis. For later age groups, the view of Rushforth and Kraemer was that 'if there had been little or no perverted behaviour', treatment might, at the most, free the patient from undue anxiety and enable him to find a less compulsive, and more 'discreet' and 'creative way of living' that was of value to himself and the community. In their opinion, a person who had been homosexual for any length of time, even if he adjusted by means of marriage, remained fundamentally homosexual. Moreover, the Davidson Clinic had found that homosexual patients referred by the police or social workers were especially unresponsive to psychotherapy.[35] Significantly, its analysts either would not or could not furnish the Wolfenden Committee with any recorded case where sexual reorientation had been effected.[36]

Such uncertainties merely fuelled the scepticism surrounding the medical treatment of homosexuality within the Scottish judicial and penal systems.[37] Thus, in evidence to the Wolfenden Committee, several sheriffs argued that, in many instances, homosexuality was an issue of criminal wilfulness rather than medical dysfunction and should be addressed accordingly.[38] Insofar as they viewed it as a 'disease', they stressed its dysgenic impact upon the nation's health and demography and its essentially predatory and 'infectious' nature, with an initial sexual act engendering a cycle of addictive debauchery, often with ever-younger and more vulnerable partners.[39] Even where Scottish sheriffs and magistrates advocated greater recourse to medical treatment, they were insistent that it be part of normal criminal proceedings so that the element of deterrence remained and offenders could be compelled to comply with appropriate therapies.[40]

Significantly, the most influential attack on the 'medicalisation' of homosexuality came from James Adair, a member of the Wolfenden Committee, and former Procurator Fiscal. His virulent critique, which effectively amounted to a minority report, and which echoed the prejudices and concerns of many within the Scottish legal and political establishment,[41] was scathing of the tendency of psychiatrists to sentimentalise the problem of homosexuality and to play down its paedophilic aspects and damage to physical health. In his opinion, much of the evidence presented by 'mental specialists' was 'quite inexplicable and in not a few cases manifestly indefensible'. He considered that homosexuality had become the latest disease 'fashion' or 'craze' of 'medical men', and highlighted the uncertainties of medical and mental science 'and the limited knowledge and powers of the medical profession under existing circumstances to deal with homosexual patients'. According to Adair, a significant proportion of homosexuals seeking treatment were only doing so in order to evade the due process of law and were merely using medical therapy as a smokescreen for their perversion. Many, he argued, were already too old at eighteen for treatment, with their sexuality and behaviour 'for all practical purposes immutable'.[42] Adair was especially concerned to elicit from witnesses the physical damage done by sodomy and was adamant that it should be retained as a separate offence with heavy penalties.[43] Indeed, in some ways, he displayed an obsession with anal intercourse reminiscent of the medical discourses surrounding the prosecution of sodomy in late nineteenth-century Britain.[44]

THE VIEW FROM THE HIGH COURT

The extent to which the testimony submitted to the Wolfenden Committee accurately reflected the role of medical evidence in cases involving homosexual offences in Scotland in the 1950s, and the degree to which that role subsequently evolved, can in part be obtained from a study of court proceedings. A survey of cases brought in the lower courts under section 11 of the Criminal Law Amendment Act 1885 and under by-laws relating to indecency in public conveniences does reveal an increasing use by offenders of medical arguments in written pleas. Some emphasised that they were already seeking referral for psychiatric treatment;[45] others, especially those accused of contravening by-laws, increasingly proffered medical excuses for their behaviour, including hypertension, epilepsy, alcohol addiction, and, most commonly, prostate and bladder problems.[46] However, in the lower courts medical reports were rarely called for prior to formal summons or sentencing.[47] Limited and fragmentary evidence suggests that medical reports were deployed more regularly within the sheriff courts, but the absence of surviving case papers, coupled with issues of data protection, inhibits any systematic research in this area. This is the more disappointing in that it was before the sheriff courts that the bulk of prosecutions for 'homosexual offences' between consenting adults were tried.

What have been available to the author, under restricted access, are the psychiatric reports on defendants and convicted offenders submitted to the Scottish High Court and Court of Appeal over the period 1950–80 in cases involving sodomy or contravention of section 11 of the Criminal Law Amendment Act 1885. These reports form part of the judicial 'processes'; case papers in the proceedings before the court, including summonses, indictments and productions.[48] Inevitably, evidence drawn from such processes will be highly selective as the cases involved only the more serious crimes involving homosexual practices. Nonetheless, they do convey some impression of the weight attributed within the legal process to psychiatric opinion.

An examination of High Court cases relating to homosexual offences suggests that, over the period, there was, quite apart from routine medical inspection under the Mental Health Act in respect of fitness to plead, and forensic investigations of 'anal interference' where minors were involved, an increasing recourse to psychiatric evidence, commissioned both by the Crown and defence lawyers. By the 1970s, some 30 per cent of cases involved such medical evidence. This appears to have been especially so where the accused was a professional man such as a teacher or where he was socially well connected.[49]

Broadly speaking, there are four treatment strategies for homosexual offences that can be detected in the medical evidence to the Scottish High Court in the period 1950–80. First, there were isolated cases where homosexual offences were diagnosed as primarily a function of mental deficiency and where the offender was deemed a danger both to himself and society. In such cases, admission to an 'institution or colony for mental defectives' – typically Carstairs State Hospital, South Lanarkshire – was recommended.[50]

Secondly, there was a group of offenders for whom medical treatment (predominantly psychotherapy but sometimes supplementary hormone therapy) was recommended with the aim of changing the direction of their sexual preference. These were cases in which, typically, the offender was either under twenty-five or deemed to be psychosexually immature for reasons of upbringing, social conditioning, or the impact of random sexual advances or homoerotic experiences. These were offenders whose homosexuality was regarded, primarily within a Freudian perspective, as 'transitional' rather than innate, with restrictive home environments and sexual ignorance impeding normal heterosexual development and outlets. Even for this group, however, claims for the ability of medical treatment to secure a 'cure' or genuine sexual reorientation became more qualified as the period progressed. Thus, in the case of C. W. H., charged in Hawick in 1955 on two counts of contravening the Criminal Law Amendment Act 1885, the Physician Superintendent of Dingleton Hospital, Melrose, was adamant that there was a 'recognised cure' for homosexuality, that there were cases of successful treatment 'within [his] own purview', and that the panel's homosexual tendencies could be 'cured and eradicated'.[51] Such unconditional claims were seldom, if ever, heard in medical testimony in the 1960s and 1970s. It should be added that, during the period 1950–80, in medical evidence to the High Courts, aversion therapy using drugs or electric shocks was never explicitly recommended for this group of offenders.

Thirdly, there were offenders for whom medical treatment was recommended not to change their sexual orientation but to enable them better to adapt to their sexual problems and to life in general. Typically, these were cases where the accused was viewed as a latent homosexual who had successfully sublimated his urges over a long period but for whom an additional dysfunction, such as alcoholism or marital stress, had triggered overt homosexual behaviour, very often associated with acute anxiety and guilt. In such cases, 'latent homosexuality' was presented as 'an illness of the mind' and extensive psychotherapy, attached either to a probationary sentence or to admission to a psychiatric unit under section 55 of the Mental Health (Scotland) Act 1960, was often suggested as a means of enabling the offender to come to terms with his condition and to develop a self-awareness of social and other factors precipitating inappropriate urges and behaviours. A primary aim was to ensure that he did not remain socially isolated but was 'helped back into his place in society and to maintain his employment in the community'.[52]

Finally, there were medical offenders for whom medical treatment was advocated, often in association with a custodial sentence, as a means primarily of achieving greater continence and self-control. Typically, these were cases where homosexual behaviour was viewed as either obsessive and/or predatory. By the 1970s, group psychotherapy, such as that available at the Douglas Inch Centre in Glasgow, a forensic outpatient clinic in Glasgow specialising in psychodynamic therapy, was increasingly recommended for such offenders, but the predominant treatments advanced were aversion and sex-suppressant therapy. Thus, in the case of T. P., tried before the High Court in Glasgow in 1968 for contravention of section 11 of the Criminal Law Amendment Act 1885, the Physician Superintendent of Dingleton Hospital, Melrose, recommended that, in addition to his prostate gland being investigated, the panel (a person charged with a crime or offence in Scots law) should be referred to the Royal Edinburgh Hospital for aversion therapy. In his view: 'It might be that some kind of negative conditioning, like electric shocks, in relation to homosexual stimulation might turn him against this form of sexual activity.'[53] In other cases, such as that of A. H. L., tried for a series of offences against teenage boys in 1977, supervised drug therapy, such as the use of Anquil, designed 'to curb his sex drive', was recommended.[54]

In assessing the impact of psychiatric evidence on sentencing for homosexual offences in this period, the picture is complicated by the fact that many such offences were part of wider charges involving the sexual assault or corruption of young children. Indeed, one of the more notable features of such trials was the conflation of homosexual offences with what would now be regarded as paedophilia. Moreover, the severity of charges brought in the High Court inevitably lessened the likelihood of non-custodial sentences being passed.

In general, where an offence was deemed sufficiently serious as to warrant a prison sentence, the duration of such a sentence was not determined on therapeutic grounds. However, there was a small but increasing number of cases where medical evidence does appear to have elicited the use of section 3 of the Criminal Justice (Scotland) Act 1949 to impose probationary orders with associated psychiatric treatment. In many such instances, the younger, the more self-reflective and co-operative the defendant, the less fixated his sexual behaviour, and the less protracted the recommended treatment,[55] the more likely it was that such evidence would affect sentencing. Thus, in the case of H. C. M.,[56] accused in 1953 of sodomy and lewd and libidinous practices with soldiers from Redford Barracks, medical testimony for the defence stressed the panel's self-awareness that there was 'something far wrong with him psychically' and his willingness to leave the country after treatment to go for further 'special' therapy in Denmark.[57] No treatment, it was alleged, would be forthcoming within the Scottish prison system.[58] It was also argued that, as a 'passive homosexual', in medical circles, the defendant would be viewed as having 'a definite constitutional disease' rather than the criminality often diagnostic of the 'active homosexual'.[59] In the event, H. C. M. was sentenced to three years' probation on condition that he entered Moray Royal Institution at Perth for treatment for twelve months as a voluntary boarder.

In the case of T. A., convicted in 1954 of eight charges of gross indecency in a public convenience and three of attempted sodomy in Hawick, under section 11 of the Criminal Law Amendment Act 1885, the defence also requested a psychiatric report with a view to mitigating sentence.[60] Despite the involvement of males below the age of twenty-one, again the willingness of the panel to 'have himself put right' and to co-operate in treatment was decisive, as was his awareness, in the view of the psychiatric witness, that homosexual relations would always be intrinsically unfulfilling and 'accompanied by feelings of shame and disgust'. T. A. was put on three years' probation, subject to spending twelve months in a mental hospital. Subsequently, a revised court order requiring attendance only as an outpatient was issued on the grounds of his responsiveness to oestrogen treatment and psychotherapy.

Similarly, in the case of R. H., tried in 1956 at the High Court in Edinburgh on charges of sodomy and lewd and libidinous practices, mitigating evidence in favour of treatment as a voluntary boarder in a mental hospital was submitted both by Professor Sir David Henderson, Physician Superintendent of the Royal Edinburgh Hospital, and Dr William Boyd, Consultant Psychiatrist to the Scottish Prison Service. The panel was portrayed as the victim of predatory and precocious male teenagers, and not, given his previous heterosexual relationships, as a 'true homosexual'. His sexual proclivities were seen as a function of his deprived upbringing – sharing a bed throughout adolescence with his brother – and his dysfunctional relations with girls, rather than a deep-seated fixation, indicating a likely positive outcome for treatment. Accordingly, R. H. was remitted to Hawkhead Hospital, Renfrewshire, for residential treatment for one year under a three-year probationary order. As with T. A., treatment proved so effective that this was duly revised in favour of outpatient therapy.[61]

A fourth case illustrates that, by the end of the period, medical options were being deployed even in cases involving younger male adolescents. In the case of I. S. N., charged with sodomy and lewd and libidinous practices in 1979,[62] a number of considerations were advanced by a Consultant Psychiatrist of the Douglas Inch Centre; that the behaviour was immature rather than predatory; that a custodial sentence would not be in the long-term interests of society; that progress in therapeutic techniques had considerably increased the chances of effecting behaviour modification, and that such techniques were available at the centre. Accordingly, sentence was deferred while the panel attended the centre for group therapy and individual counselling. Though, after six months, psychiatric reports could not report any 'dramatic change in his personality [or] sexuality', the accused was eventually admonished and dismissed so as to enable him to 'continue to work on his problems and consolidate his gains'.[63]

However, such attitudes were often contested by psychiatric witnesses for the prosecution. In the case of H. C. M., after he had breached his probation order and reoffended, the Lord Justice Clerk endorsed the view of Sir David Henderson that 'lenient treatment' having failed, a 'stringent penalty of imprisonment' was called for. In his opinion, 'a little severity just for once might put him in a proper frame of mind' for benefiting thereafter from therapy. The defence counsel's plea that the panel should 'be allowed to leave the country in order to his undergoing treatment in a foreign clinic for his mental condition' was summarily dismissed.[64]

The medical case for the prosecution also prevailed in the case of J. G., tried before the High Court in Edinburgh in 1973 for sodomy and attempted rape. The defence psychiatrist from Woodilee Hospital, near Glasgow, pressed for a sentence of compulsory admission to a psychiatric unit for two to three years under the Mental Health (Scotland) Act 1960, on the grounds that his 'personality disorder, . . . associated with sexual deviation of a homosexual nature', could be expected to respond to treatment. However, Dr H. G., Consultant in Charge of Stobhill General Hospital and Clinical Lecturer in Psychological Medicine at the University of Glasgow, while conceding that homosexuality amounted to 'mental illness', did not regard the panel as a suitable case for treatment, given 'the long duration of his homosexual orientation'.[65] A sentence of four years' imprisonment was imposed. Similarly, in the case in of I. N., the consultant psychiatrist giving evidence on behalf of the Procurator Fiscal was dismissive of any recourse to medical treatment in sentencing. While he conceded that the defendant's behaviour might be modified, he considered it unlikely that his sexual orientation would be changed since 'he [was] not genuinely disposed to change it':

> He is talking of treatment at present because he wishes to avoid prison . . . I do not think it would help his prospects of learning to conform to society's wishes if, having thoroughly broken the law because he believes it is a bad law, he were to be encouraged to view medical treatment as a means of escaping punishment. If convicted, he would do best to thole his assize and seek help at a later date out of a genuine wish to change.[66]

Adverse medical evidence could also be decisive in appeal cases. The appeal of J. R. in 1964 against a sentence of six years' imprisonment on sodomy charges involving minors was dismissed largely on the basis of a report from the Physician Superintendent of Bangour Village Hospital, near Edinburgh. In his view, the panel 'did not regard his condition as an illness and [did] not consider he require[d] any treatment'. Though an 'established homosexual', he was so much in denial and lacking in insight that treatment was unlikely to be effective, although a prison sentence might at least encourage him to revert to a 'non-practising role'.[67] Similarly, the appeal of R. M. K. W. in 1974 against a sentence of two years' imprisonment foundered on the report of the consultant psychiatrist at Rosslynlee Hospital in Midlothian to the initial trial that, in view of the fact that the panel had defaulted on treatment arising out of a previous charge and failed to co-operate with the psychiatric services, the court should proceed with sentencing without regard to his previous psychiatric history.[68]

In a variety of other cases, too, favourable psychiatric evidence signally failed to affect sentencing, especially where minors were involved. In the case of J. B., tried before the High Court in Dundee in 1961 on charges of sodomy and lewd and libidinous practices, extensive psychiatric evidence was produced relating to the impact of his previous imprisonment in Japanese prisoner-of-war camps, his vulnerability to blackmail from adolescent boys, and his willingness to enter a mental hospital for treatment but three years' imprisonment was imposed.[69]

In the case of J. J. T., indicted before the High Court in 1962 on charges of sodomy with a fourteen- year-old teenager, again the defence mobilised considerable medical evidence in favour of a non-custodial sentence. One hospital medical officer recounted the 'frequent bouts of depression and hopelessness' suffered by the defendant arising out of his latent homosexuality, and his previous receptiveness to psychiatric treatment. He stressed the need for a lengthy period of inpatient psychiatric treatment including regular psychotherapy rather than long-term imprisonment. This view was endorsed by a consultant psychiatrist. In the event, however, J. J. T. was sentenced to thirty months' imprisonment albeit, in this instance as in similar cases, the court ordered that medical reports should be forwarded to the prison authorities for information as the basis of possible further psychiatric investigation and treatment within prison.[70]

Similarly, in the case of P. C., charged at the High Court in Perth in 1965 with sodomy and lewd and libidinous practices, the presiding judge was not disposed to delay sentencing for a psychiatric report.[71] He rejected the argument of defence counsel that such a report might be useful in determining the effects of different terms of imprisonment on the grounds that, in his opinion, the offender would receive treatment in prison anyway. A sentence of six years' imprisonment was duly delivered.[72]

The following year, C. E. J. T., initially tried in a sheriff court for sodomy with an eighteen-year-old boy, also encountered unwillingness on the part of the judiciary to endorse a probationary sentence on the grounds of medical evidence. The sexual act had been consensual, and the psychiatric report argued that there was a good chance that 'this man [could] learn to suppress his homosexual interests entirely' as a psychiatric outpatient. Moreover, the sheriff had been disposed to place the panel on probation, but as 'society' took such 'a serious view of the crime of sodomy', the case was remitted to the High Court in Glasgow for sentencing 'as a matter of public policy'. In the event, a one-year prison sentence was imposed.[73]

A similar fate befell W. T. M., convicted in 1971 for a range of homosexual offences with males between the ages of fourteen and twenty-two. When the case had been initially heard before the Sheriff Court, strong evidence in favour of a non-custodial sentence, conditional on a two-year period of treatment, had been submitted by Dr H. G. In his opinion, W. T. M.'s homosexuality was 'a mental illness' and 'require[d] and [was] susceptible to treatment' but did not justify detention under a hospital order. A further report from Dr J. M. of Riccatsbar Hospital, Paisley, was even more supportive of a probationary sentence. In his view, the fact that the panel was bisexual and had previously enjoyed satisfactory heterosexual relationships, that 'his basic personality' and 'motivation towards normal behaviour' were 'good', and that he was 'very willing to co-operate', made the prognosis for treatment very hopeful. However, when, because of the nature of the charges, the case was remitted to the High Court in Edinburgh, a sentence of three years' imprisonment was imposed.[74]

The views of the judiciary with respect to psychiatric evidence were sometimes most clearly articulated during appeal proceedings. In the appeal by C. W. H. in 1955 against conviction for contravention of section 11 of the Criminal Law Amendment Act 1885, the transcript of the original trial clearly reveals that, despite the evidence of the Physician Superintendent of Dingleton Hospital that the panel's homosexuality was a mental disease with 'a pathological origin' and susceptible to treatment (including drug therapy), the sheriff was disposed to view the offences as a function of a 'moral' rather than 'psychological' defect. He reported to the appeal court that he was not satisfied that the offender's mental condition was abnormal or that 'it required, or would be susceptible to, medical treatment'. The appeal against a one-year prison sentence was accordingly dismissed.[75]

Similar sentiments were expressed by the presiding judge in his report to the Court of Appeal in the case of A. H. L. in 1977 against a seven-year prison sentence.[76] Psychiatric reports had emphasised that A. H. L.'s offences against young boys were due to his homosexual proclivities and could possibly be treated as a mental illness, preferably by attendance at a psychiatric clinic. In the view of Lord Wheatley, the priority was to take the offender 'out of circulation', whether or not effective treatment might be available in prison. He added a pointed postscript that the suggestion by psychiatrists that probationary treatment might be an option was wholly 'unrealistic' and merely served to raise 'unjustifiable hopes and corresponding disappointment', something he recommended that psychiatrists submitting evidence in court should firmly take on board.[77] Though, in this case, the psychiatric reports were forwarded on to the prison authorities, application to appeal was refused.[78]

CONCLUSION

It is problematic to draw firm conclusions from this overview of merely two perspectives on the medical perception and treatment of homosexual offenders in Scotland in the period 1950–80. Evidence to the Wolfenden Committee was arguably driven as much by concern to justify departmental procedures as to capture an accurate picture of contemporary medical and legal practices. In addition, not only may the evidence from the High Court be far from typical but also the use of trial processes and appeal papers, as with all legal records, poses a range of methodological challenges.[79] It could be argued, for example, that owing to the closure of High Court precognitions, the narratives derived from medical reports have been given undue priority and that the study lacks due regard to 'the multiple texts that make up a legal record'. Finally, the evidence presented here was very much shaped and informed by legal discourses and desiderata.[80]

Nonetheless, some tentative conclusions can perhaps be drawn. First, it is clear that, in testimony to the Wolfenden Committee, the evidence of medical and legal witnesses from Scotland reflected the more general ambivalence towards medical strategies for homosexual offences articulated in its proceedings and final report. While many witnesses did embrace the need for the medical treatment and rehabilitation of offenders, and appear to have been increasingly sympathetic to more psychodynamic forms of psychotherapy, their mindset remained heavily rooted in taxonomies of deviance shaped by established notions of sexual pathology rather than in more progressive ideas of sexual expression and inclusion. Cure or sublimation, with their implications of self-rejection or self-denial, remained at the basis of therapy.

Secondly, an analysis of court records suggests that the impact of medical evidence on trial proceedings for homosexual offences was complex. From the 1950s, such evidence did play an increasing role in cases, and psychiatric reports figured ever more prominently in trial processes. However, medical testimony was by no means monopolised by the defence and could also be mobilised very effectively by the Crown

Office. The evident lack of consensus over the aetiology of homosexuality and the efficacy of medical treatment further ensured that medical evidence was often marginalised within legal proceedings. Indeed, many cases reflected enduring tensions between medical conceptions of homosexual behaviour 'as a pathology or intrinsic condition' and judicial conceptions of it as embodying 'criminal sexual "acts" rather than identities'.[81] As a result, psychiatric issues continued to be framed within legal discourses that often reflected broader moral assumptions and concerns surrounding homosexuality within Scottish civil society, the very same assumptions and concerns that were to delay homosexual law reform north of the Border until 1980.[82]

NOTES

1. This chapter is a revised version of a chapter originally published in I. Goold and C. Kelly (eds), *Lawyers' Medicine: The Legislature, the Courts and Medical Practice, 1760–2000* (Oxford: Hart Publishing, 2009) 125–42.

2. See, for example, Weeks, *Sex Politics and Society*, Chs 6, 8; Higgins, *Heterosexual Dictatorship*, 51–8; Davenport-Hines, *Sex, Death and Punishment*, Ch. 8. For an overview of the social politics of homosexual law reform in Scotland, see Davidson and Davis, *The Sexual State*, Chs 3–4.

3. See, for example, Waters, 'Havelock Ellis, Sigmund Freud and the State', 165–79; Waters, 'Disorders of the mind', 135–51; Crozier, 'Taking prisoners', 447–66; Houlbrook, *Queer London*, 195–8, 257–62.

4. See, for example, Jivani, *Its Not Unusual*, 122–8; Cant (ed.), *Footsteps and Witnesses*, 49; Davidson, T., (ed.), *And Thus Will I Freely Sing*, 154–9.

5. King, Smith and Bartlett, 'Treatments of homosexuality in Britain', 427, 429.

6. Meek, *Queer Voices in Post-War Scotland*.

7. I wish to thank the Lord Justice General for permission to consult and cite selected Scottish High Court trial processes and appeal papers held at the National Records of Scotland.

8. The National Archives, Public Record Office, Kew [hereafter PRO], HO345/9, Proceedings of the Wolfenden Committee on Homosexual Offences and Prostitution [hereafter PWC], Summary Record of 21st Meeting, March 1956. On the issue of variance in judicial practice, see also *Report of the Wolfenden Committee* [hereafter *RWC*], 63, para. 182; Henderson, *Society and Criminal Conduct*, 25.

9. PRO, HO345/9, CHP/108, PWC, evidence of Faculty of Advocates, March 1956; NRS, HH60/268, evidence of Scottish Home Department, October 1954.

10. Evidence suggests that, prior to World War II, the police and judiciary

in Scotland were often extremely hostile to the efforts of psychiatrists to secure medical treatment rather than imprisonment for their clients. See, for example, Merrilees, *The Short Arm of the* Law, 121–2. This attitude was strongly reinforced by the judgment of the Lord Justice Clerk in the case of *H.M. Advocate* v. *M.* in March 1944. M. had been charged on indictment in the Sheriff Court of the Lothians and Peebles at Edinburgh with a number of homosexual offences under the Criminal Law Amendment Act 1885. The sheriff had been sympathetic to sentence being deferred until the likely response of the panel to psychotherapeutic treatment under a probationary order had been assessed. The Lord Justice Clerk determined, however, that it was not the court's prerogative merely to approach such cases 'from the purely medical standpoint' and with a 'single eye to the possible rehabilitation of the offender'. Instead, he ruled that 'the duty of the Court was to give effect to the law which punished such offences as crimes' without delay and he imposed a sentence of eighteen months' imprisonment [NRS, ED15/109, note by Scottish Home Department, 18 March 1946].

11. PRO, HO345/15, CHP/TRANS/42, PWC, evidence of K. M. Hancock, Director of the Scottish Prison and Borstal Services, 1 November 1955; HO345/16, CHP/TRANS/60, evidence of Association of Sheriffs Substitute, 9 April 1956. See also, Moran, *The Homosexual(ity) of Law*, 116. It was obligatory to have a medical report on any person under the age of twenty-one involved in such cases.

12. PRO, HO345/15, CHP/TRANS/41, PWC, evidence of Dr W. Boyd, 1 November 1955.

13. PRO, HO345/16, PWC, evidence of Magistrates of Corporation of Glasgow, 9 April 1956.

14. Scottish Advisory Council on the Treatment and Rehabilitation of Offenders, *Psycho-Therapeutic Treatment of Certain Offenders*, 6–9.

15. NRS, HH60/268, PWC, memorandum by Scottish Home Department, October 1954. In the opinion of Dr T. D. Inch, Medical Adviser to the Scottish Prison and Borstal Services, offenders who were mentally defective, neurotic or psychotic should be hospitalised and the 'homosexual psychopath' subjected to an indeterminate sentence within a 'special institution or colony'. The routine provision of medical reports was also advocated by some magistrates but not by the Crown Agent [PRO, HO345/16, evidence of Magistrates of the Corporation of Glasgow, 9 April 1956; evidence of L. I. Gordon, Crown Agent, 9 April 1956].

16. HH60/268, PWC, memorandum by Scottish Home Department, October 1954.

17. NRS, HH57/1287, PWC, note by Dr T. D. Inch, 13 October 1955. On the scarcity of psychiatric resources in Britain, see also *RWC*, 62, para. 180; Westwood, *Society and the Homosexual*, 89.

18. PRO, HO345/15, CHP/TRANS/41, PWC, evidence of Dr W. Boyd, 1 November 1955. In view of this, the policy of the Scottish Home

Department, in direct contrast to that of the Home Office, was to integrate the prison medical service with mainstream and psychiatric medicine within the NHS. The lack of adequate resources for the implementation of probationary treatment for sexual offenders in Scotland was an enduring problem. In 1959, a Glasgow psychiatrist reported that, owing mainly to a shortage of qualified staff, provisions were still 'ludicrously inadequate ... The usual treatment is to administer some drugs and to perform a little elementary psycho-analysis' [*The Scotsman*, 6 June 1959]. See also, Henderson and Batchelor, *A Textbook of Psychiatry*, 206; Wardrop, *Psychiatry and Probation*, 8.

19. NRS, HH57/1287, PWC, Note by Scottish Home Department on Scottish Prisons and Borstal Institutions, October 1955.
20. Ibid.
21. For Golla's use of hormone treatment, see Golla and Hodge, 'Hormone treatment of the sexual offender', 1006–7.
22. NRS, HH57/1288, memorandum by Dr T. D. Inch, 'Sexual Offenders: Treatment in Prisons'; PRO, HO345/15, CHP/TRANS/42, PWC, evidence of Dr T. D. Inch, 1 November 1955. More routinely, homosexual offenders suffering from anxiety states were treated with largactil and sodium amytal [NRS, HH57/1288, Dr H. S. Walter, Psychiatric Clinic, Aberdeen Royal Infirmary to Dr G. I. Manson, Medical Officer, HM Prison, Peterhead, 3 December 1957].
23. PRO, HO345/15, CHP/TRANS/42, PWC, evidence of Dr T. D. Inch, 1 November 1955. The subsequent disclosure by the Wolfenden Committee of the use of hormone therapy produced some colourful headlines. See *Sunday Pictorial*, 16 February 1958: 'Sex Pills for Scots in Jail'.
24. NRS, HH57/1287, note by Dr T. D. Inch for PWC, October 1955; PRO, HO345/15, CHP/TRANS/42, PWC, evidence of Drs T. D. Inch and W. Boyd, 1 November 1955.
25. Significantly, this was not a view shared by many Scottish Prison Medical Officers [PRO, HO345/15, CHP/TRANS/42, PWC, evidence of Drs T. D. Inch and W. Boyd, 1 November 1955].
26. PRO, HO345/7, CHP/36 and 345/16, CHP/ TRANS/62, PWC, evidence of Drs W. Rushforth and W. P. Kraemer, 10 April 1956. In 1956, the clinic was staffed by five medically qualified therapists and six lay therapists. Both medical and lay therapists underwent a period of training during which they themselves had to undergo 'a complete and successful personal analysis'. The clinic employed a mixture of Freudian and Jungian techniques, with drugs used 'only exceptionally as an adjunct to treatment'. Its practice was heavily influenced by the work of Melanie Klein, the pioneering Viennese psychoanalyst. In evidence, it was claimed that the clinic was the only 'analytical group' then operating in Scotland. The Davidson Clinic accepted in the region of a hundred new patients a year, of which about 10 per cent were 'overt homosexuals', largely referred by the police, a minister,

or a GP. The lay therapists, who were unpaid during their training, were not formally recognised within the Edinburgh medical establishment or by the University.

27. PRO, HO345/16, PWC, evidence of Dr W. P. Kraemer, 10 April 1956.

28. PRO, HO345/16, CHP/TRANS/62, PWC, evidence of Dr W. P. Kraemer, 10 April 1956.

29. British Medical Association Archives, B/107/1/2, memorandum by Professor John Glaister (Jr), 30 June 1955.

30. The reasons listed for unsuitability for treatment were: not recommended by specialist (44.7%); too dull or inadequate character (23.4%); absence of any anxiety over sexual practices or of any real wish to change (8.5%); denial of tendency or tendency not apparent (17%); too old and unadaptable or practice too well established (4.3%); belief that conviction has cured offender (2.1%)[PRO, HO345/9, CHP/88, PWC, evidence of Scottish Home Department, 30 October 1955; PRO, CAB129/66, Cabinet Memorandum, Sexual Offences, Secretary of State for Scotland, 17 February 1954]. For comparative data for England and Wales, see *RWC*, 66, para. 197.

31. Professor Glaister also considered the likelihood of cure for 'innate inverts' as utopian. He felt it likely that 'there will always be a nucleus in our midst, just as we have other groups of handicapped persons' [BMA Archives, B/107/1/2, memorandum by J. Glaister (Jr), 30 June 1955].

32. PRO, HO345/15, CHP/TRANS/42, PWC, evidence of Dr W. Boyd, 1 November 1955.

33. PRO, HO345/15, CHP/TRANS/42, PWC, evidence of Drs K. M. Hancock and T. D. Inch, 1 November 1955; evidence of Dr W Boyd, 1 November 1955. Evidence on the outcome of treatment was also compromised by the lack of follow-up surveillance of released prisoners. Inch testified that: 'As regards the after effects, certainly none of them have yet come back to us but we do not know, and we have no means of knowing, whether they continue treatment afterwards or not. . . . I am unfortunately quite unable to say what the permanent end result is.' [PRO, HO345/15, CHP/TRANS/42, PWC, evidence of Drs K. M. Hancock and T. D. Inch, 1 November 1955; NRS, HH57/1288, Departmental minute, 5 December 1957].

34. PRO, HO345/7; 345/16 PWC, evidence of Drs W. Rushforth and W. Kraemer, 10 April 1956.

35. Ibid. They anticipated that group psychotherapy might prove more effective but predicted that bringing together a group of homosexuals within the clinic would provoke a public outcry.

36. Indeed, Winifred Rushforth considered that the primary role of the clinic was not to try to alter sexual orientation but to facilitate the patient's understanding of his homosexual feelings and anxieties.

37. Sir David Henderson attributed the failure of psychiatrists to 'gain the complete confidence of the legal profession' in homosexual cases to this lack of any clear evidence of a 'cure'. See, Henderson, *Society and Criminal*

Conduct, 25. This disparity between medical and legal expectations also prevailed south of the Border [Westwood, *Society and the Homosexual*, 90].

38. Thus, according to Sheriff Hamilton,: 'It [was] fashionable to say that homosexual offenders [had] a "mental kink" and require[d] treatment but apart from the odd case of physical ailment such as prostate gland enlargement, the only "treatment" which [might] be beneficial [was] such as [would] strengthen the willpower to resist offending' [PRO, HO345/8, PWC, memorandum prepared by The Association of Sheriffs-Substitute, 1955].

39. Thus, Sheriff-Substitute Middleton of Dumfermline and Kinross challenged the committee as to whether there was ever a homosexual case 'where the relationship [was] confined to two individuals, and there [was] no danger to other members of society' [PRO, HO345/16, evidence on behalf of Association of Sheriffs-Substitute, 9 April 1956].

40. PRO, HO345/8 & 16, CHP/44 & CHP/TRANS/60, PWC, evidence of Association of Sheriffs-Substitute, March 1955, 9 April 1956; PRO, HO345/16, PWC, evidence of Stipendary Magistrate, Glasgow, 9 April 1956.

41. For a discussion of the broader debate over homosexuality in Scottish society, see Davidson and Davis, *The Sexual State*, Chs 3–4.

42. See especially, *RWC*, 117–21; PRO, HO345/12 and 16, PWC, 15 October 1954, 10 April 1956; HO345/2, J. Adair to W. C. Roberts, 4 October 1956; HO345/10, note on WC discussion meetings, 11 and 12 September 1956.

43. See PRO, HO345/9, PWC, minutes of 21st Meeting, March 1956.

44. See, Crozier, ' "All the appearances were perfectly natural" ', 65–84.

45. See, for example, Edinburgh City Archive [ECA], Burgh Court Papers, case against W. B. A., letter of defendant to Clerk of Court, 25 May 1960. Significantly, some 36 per cent of the patients attending the Jordanburn Nerve Hospital in the 1950s for problems relating to homosexuality, for whom medical correspondence survives, were referred either by solicitors or general practitioners in relation to criminal proceedings [Lothian Health Services Archive, Edinburgh University Library, LHB7/CC1, Royal Edinburgh Hospital medical clinic and outpatient letters, 1950–58].

46. ECA, Burgh Court Papers for 1960 and 1970.

47. This lack of medical investigation was one of many criticisms of the judicial system levelled by the Scottish Minorities Group in their campaign for homosexual law reform.

48. Though previously in the public domain, because of their sensitive nature, in accordance with data protection legislation, these records are now closed for 100 years unless special access is granted by the High Court of Justiciary.

49. See, for example, NRS, JC9/36, 38; JC26/1956/65, trial papers in the case

against H. C. M. On the correlation of class and medical evidence, see also, Higgins, *Heterosexual Dictatorship*, 160–1.

50. See, for example, NRS, JC9/37; JC26/1954/145, trial minutes and papers in the case against J. H.

51. NRS, JC34/4/189, appeal papers in the case against C. W. H., report of proceedings at Sheriff Court, Hawick.

52. See, for example, NRS, JC26/1962/90, trial papers in the case against J. J. T., report by Dr M. A. E. S., Eastern District Hospital Psychiatric Unit, 26 October 1962; NRS, JC26/1973/293, trial papers in the case against J. G.

53. JC9/57; JC26/1968/216, trial minutes and papers in the case against T. P. For reference to the use of aversion therapy, see also JC26/1970/204, trial papers in the case against R. C. In such cases, aversion therapy was clearly perceived as suppressing antisocial behaviour rather than effecting a genuine reorientation of sexual preference.

54. NRS, JC26/1977/386, trial papers in the case against A. H. L. For the use of drug therapy, including oestrogen therapy, see also NRS, JC26/1956/65; JC26/1979/402; JC26/1979/200.

55. Sir David Henderson, who had given evidence in Scottish trials over many decades, reported that, where psychoanalysis had been recommended, once its duration and uncertain outcome had been explained, the Court usually took the view that treatment should be undertaken only after a prison sentence had been served. [Henderson and Batchelor, *Textbook of Psychiatry*, ninth edition, 206].

56. NRS, JC9/36, JC9/38, JC26/1956/65, trial minutes and papers in the case against H. C. M.

57. Specifically, oestrogen treatment under Dr Christian Hamburger, the Danish endocrinologist. 'An institution in Ireland' was also recommended.

58. Significantly, the Lord Justice General declined to have this point elaborated, interjecting that: 'I think I know the position in prison'. Evidence in other cases suggests that this was, in fact, the situation in the 1950s. See, for example, evidence of C. W. F. W., a habitual homosexual offender, to the effect that he was promised treatment but 'as soon as I have got into prison nobody has in any way been concerned with the matter except that I should serve the sentence . . . I have been compelled to be my own doctor in this matter.'[NRS, JC34/4/209, appeal papers in the case against C. W. F. W.].

59. Medical evidence for the defence was submitted by Dr A. P. Cawadias, an endocrinologist, author of *Hermaphroditos: The Human Intersex*, and former Vice-president of the Royal Society of Medicine. In practice, there is some evidence that law officers viewed the 'active' partner more leniently and perceived the 'passive' partner as the 'real transgressor' in bringing another man to orgasm. [See, Bancroft, *Human Sexuality and Its Problems*, 714] This viewpoint was undoubtedly reinforced by the medical discourse surrounding the increase in sexually transmitted diseases, which identi-

fied passive homosexuals as major 'reservoirs of infection'. See Davidson, *Dangerous Liaisons*, 251].

60. NRS, JC9/37, trial minutes in the case against T. A.
61. NRS, JC9/39; JC26/1956/122, trial minutes and papers in the case against R. H.
62. NRS, JC26/1979/194, trial papers in the case against I. S. N.
63. This is in marked contrast to the case of T. F. in the same year, charged with similar offences before the High Court in Edinburgh. In this instance, psychiatric reports stressed that the panel had long-standing predatory paederastic tendencies, that he regarded his casual sexual acts with adolescent males as socially acceptable, and that, given his previous convictions, it was not considered that 'psychiatry ha[d] anything to offer as an alternative to imprisonment'[JC9/82; JC26/1979/402, trial minutes and papers in the case against T. F.].
64. NRS, JC26/1956/65, trial papers in the case against H. C. M.
65. NRS, JC26/1973/293, trial papers in the case against J. G.
66. NRS, JC26/1979/194, trial papers in the case against I. N.
67. NRS, JC/34/9/184, appeal papers in the case against J. R.
68. NRS, JC34/21/230, appeal papers in the case against R. M. K. W.
69. NRS, JC26/1961/3, trial papers in the case against J. B.
70. NRS, JC26/1962/90, trial papers in the case against J. J. T. See also, JC34/4/209, appeal papers in the case against C. W. F. W.
71. The possible conflict between the need for prompt sentencing and for adequate medical evidence was an issue that had been raised by the Wolfenden Committee. See *RWC*, 64.
72. NRS, JC34/11/42, appeal papers in the case against P. C., transcript of trial in Sheriff Court.
73. NRS, JC26/1966/67, trial papers in the case against C. E. J. T.
74. NRS, JC9/66; JC26/1971/344, minutes and trial papers in the case against W. T. M.
75. NRS, JC34/4/189 appeal papers in the case against C. W. H.
76. NRS, JC9/78; JC26/1977/386; JC34/26/300, minutes, trial papers and appeal papers in the case against A. H. L.
77. This very much echoed the views of the Wolfenden Report. See *RWC*, 61–2.
78. Such a case resonated with earlier warnings by the psychiatrists, David Henderson and Ivor Batchelor, that a co-ordinated approach to cases involving sexual anomalies would 'never be accomplished so long as angry judges thunder[ed] moralistic platitudes from the Bench, and indiscreet psychiatrists indulge[d] in optimistic theorising . . .' [Henderson and Batchelor, *Textbook of Psychiatry*, 207].
79. On these challenges, see especially, Robertson, ' What's law got to do with it?', 161–85.
80. However, alternative narratives of how law and medicine interacted over

homosexual issues in post-war Scotland, exploring clinical records and gay archives, would appear broadly to endorse the picture drawn from the proceedings of the Wolfenden Committee and the Scottish High Court of Justiciary. See, Davidson, 'Psychiatry and homosexuality', 403–24; Davidson, ' "The cautionary tale of Tom" ', 122–38; Meek, *Queer Voices in Post-War Scotland*.

81. On this tension, see Cook, 'Law', 79.
82. The Sexual Offences Act 1967, which decriminalised male homosexual acts in private in England and Wales between consenting adults over the age of twenty-one, did not apply to Scotland. Similar provisions for Scotland had to await the Criminal Justice (Scotland) Act 1980. For details of the constraints operating in Scotland after 1967, see Davidson and Davis, *The Sexual State*, Ch. 4.

8

'Liable or Likely to Deprave and Corrupt the Morals of the Lieges': Sex Shops and Moral Panic in Late Twentieth-century Scotland

THE ANN BOLEYN SEX SUPERMARKET

Having made test purchases earlier in the day, at around 5.30 p.m. on 10 May 1971, armed with an arrest warrant, police officers from the Maryhill Division of Glasgow entered a shop called Anne Boleyn at St George's Cross in the district of Woodside, the first sex shop to be opened in Scotland. Chief Inspector Connor led the raid accompanied by four other officers. They took the names of the ten customers already on the premises, who included four girls aged between sixteen and eighteen, and removed, in six large polythene sacks, all the goods considered to be obscene, amounting to some £800 to £900 worth of sex toys and aids. The owner, John Cameron, and the manager, John Irvine, were charged with selling obscene items in contravention of section 162 of the Glasgow Corporation (General Powers) Order Confirmation Act 1960, and a report sent to the Procurator Fiscal.[1] Though the shop was supposed to be open until 10 p.m., it was closed after the police had departed. However, the takings for the first day of business were in excess of £130 and, in the early afternoon, the shop had been so busy that, for a time, no more customers could be admitted.

The opening of Scotland's first sex shop produced a wave of moral outrage from local civic and church leaders, widely reported and supported in the media. A group of Glasgow councillors led by Mary Goldie, a former councillor for Woodside, organised a petition to the Secretary of State for Scotland of nearly 7,000 signatures, protesting at the likely impact of the sex shop on the locality: in particular, its potential to 'demoralise and corrupt' children and to act as a magnet for 'undesirable elements'. The petition called upon the government either to legislate for the closure of such shops or to ensure that they were closely regulated under licence. Meanwhile, along with similar representations to the Scottish Office, the Glasgow Presbytery of the Church of Scotland and the Glasgow Standing Conference of Youth Organisations organised a prayer meeting and protest march of over 200 young people [see Figure 8.1] to press for the closure of the 'sex supermarket' and a ban on any future enterprises that threatened the moral health and integrity of the community. In addition, the correspondence columns of Scottish newspapers voiced widespread concern that sex shops would cater to the most basic instincts of the sexual deviant, further encourage the proliferation of pornography and sexual abuse, and threaten the 'moral fibre of the Scottish nation'. A particular fear was that sex shops would serve as a conduit for a metropolitan permissiveness alien to the sexual norms of Scottish civil society.[2]

John Cameron, however, was undeterred by such opposition. He was by nature an entrepreneur and risk-taker. A member of the Institute of Patentees and Inventors, he ran a stone-cleaning business, claiming to have cleaned some 80 per cent of the buildings in Glasgow over the previous fifteen years. In addition, he had formed a firm called Cameron's Commandos, which dealt with bird control, and had virtually cleared the centre of Glasgow of starlings. As his defence counsel later observed, it was not therefore 'unnatural that a man of Cameron's enterprise should go into a new and very daring venture such as a sex supermarket. He had merely extended his business from dealing with the birds to include the bees.'

Between May and July 1971, Cameron sought to expand his operations and to open sex shops in all the major towns and cities in Scotland. All his efforts to secure premises for the sale of 'contraceptives and virility aids' proved abortive. In Edinburgh, Councillor Kidd, a leading purity activist, supported by local Church leaders and women's groups, threatened to organise public demonstrations and pressed for a by-law to prohibit the establishment of any sex shops in the city.[3] Cameron's assurances that the majority of customers would be middle aged, that he would not allow young people to enter his shop, and that he was not looking for a location in the city centre but in 'a nice quiet residential area' did nothing to placate his critics. A visit by Councillor Kidd to the Anne Boleyn premises in Glasgow merely reinforced his vehement opposition to such outlets. On leaving, he very publicly warned Cameron: 'Don't come to Edinburgh. This is filth ... If you open in Edinburgh you'll be bankrupt. The people of Edinburgh just wouldn't tolerate this ... People who use these things [sex aids and appliances] should be destroyed. They don't know what love is.' Kidd refused a parting gift of 'rejuvenating pills', protesting that 'it's nourishment I want!'[4] His views continued to be endorsed by a wide range of religious and educational organisations across Scotland. In July, the Roman Catholic Archdiocese of St Andrews and Edinburgh submitted a petition of 1,537 signatures to Edinburgh's Lord Provost's Committee opposing the establishment of a sex shop in the city. It argued that it would 'lead to the spread of immorality among the young and the various diseases pertaining to loose morals, that it would be against all Christian ethics' and that, in encouraging sexual pleasure and indulgence for its own sake, 'it would strike at the roots of family life on which our nation depends'.[5]

Meanwhile, the Ann Boleyn sex supermarket at St George's Cross had been enjoying brisk business. In the first few weeks of its operation, its takings had exceeded £1,600 with a 250 per cent profit. In addition, mail orders, especially from the Highlands, had grown significantly.[6] Cameron, however, was increasingly frustrated by his inability to open a chain of sex shops in the central belt of Scotland and by the lack of response from male adults in Glasgow who, he claimed, preferred to spend their disposable income on drink rather than products that might give their wives more sexual fulfilment. In response, reportedly viewing himself as 'the Saviour of the Sexually Discontented Tartan Hordes', he decided to head for the Highlands in a gaily coloured, converted single-decker bus loaded with 'kinky underwear, contraceptives and sexual appliances'.[7] As the *Scottish Daily Record* captured the event: 'It's Sex on Wheels as John Heads for the Hills.' He planned to park in fields outside towns to avoid the main streets 'where trouble might start', and to attract custom by placing adverts in local newspapers. There was a predictable outcry from church leaders, Father George McCurrach affirming that 'the people of the Highlands [were] much less prone to indulge in mucky fantasies stimulated by pornographic goods or literature than some people [might] be in the bigger cities'.[8]

It is unclear whether or not Cameron's Highland venture ever came to fruition but it is recorded that the Anne Boleyn sex shop eventually closed down in late November, with £400 worth of sex aids being given away in twelve minutes![9] The case against John Cameron and John Irvine for selling 'indecent or obscene articles' was subsequently heard at Glasgow Central Police Court in January 1972. Both men pleaded guilty to the offence. Counsel for the accused argued that, in many respects, they had done a service to the community by preventing 'hard core pornographers' moving in from London and the Continent. In contrast, the Anne Boleyn stock was depicted as relatively harmless, 'rather guilty novelties and junk', including a 'bust developing cream

Figure 8.1 The protest march in Glasgow against the opening of a sex
supermarket, 8 May 1971 *[courtesy of The Herald]*

(Source: *Glasgow Herald*, 10 May 1971)

which had the same ingredients as a packet of cornflakes'. It was also claimed that, although in reality the shop was merely selling various 'appliances, creams and gadgets', it had provided emotional support for people suffering from a variety of sexual problems who felt let down by medical practitioners and psychiatrists. Thomas McLaughlan, the Stipendary Magistrate, was unimpressed, advising Cameron that, in view of his previous career in the cleansing business, he would do well to 'clean up his own mind'. John Cameron was fined £20 and John Irvine, his manager, was admonished.

A NEW MORAL CRUSADE

The campaign against the opening of sex shops in Scotland and the prosecution of John Cameron coincided with a broader crusade against the spread of pornography and sexual display in British society. A new moral authoritarianism, advanced by a powerful coalition of puritanical groups, such as the National Viewers' and Listeners' Association (hereafter NVLA), the Festival of Light and the Responsible Society, sought, increasingly by recourse to the law, to reassert a Christian-based moral order/rearmament that would relocate sex within the framework of conjugal love and faithfulness and protect the innocence and moral fibre of the nation's youth.[10] At the centre of their campaign was a desire to strengthen the law against pornography and to ensure that law's rigorous enforcement.[11]

This backlash against the permissive values and cultural ethics of the 1960s was also experienced in Scotland where the puritan lobby south of the Border attracted significant support from both church and civic leaders. The Free Church of Scotland and the Free Presbyterian Church of Scotland actively supported the views of the NVLA and the Festival of Light. They viewed the intrusion of pornographic material into bookshops and magazine stands as a conspiracy of publishers to undermine 'the morality of the nation'. They commended the moral evangelicalism of Lord Longford's inquiry into pornography and pressed for more stringent laws to contain the problem.[12]

The Church of Scotland was conducting its own moral crusade against pornography, inspired by a Scottish Festival of Light, attended by more than 2,000 people in George Square, Glasgow, in January 1972.[13] In February, it launched the Scottish Petition for Public Decency, protesting at the 'increasing commercial exploitation of sex' and 'the public portrayal of intimate or unnatural sexual behaviour'. It called upon the government to review the law on obscenity and to criminalise the activities of retail outlets, such as sex shops, that sought to display sexually explicit items for public consumption. The petition, presented to the Secretary of State for Scotland in June 1972, was signed by over 200,000 adults and attracted support from nearly all the Scottish churches and from more than half of all Scottish MPs.[14]

The Scottish Home and Health Department (hereafter SHHD) adopted a cautious response to the moral panic induced by the prospect of sex shops/supermarkets opening across Scotland. In their view, local legislation, vigorously applied, appeared sufficient to meet the problem insofar as it existed in the towns and cities. Clauses relating to obscenity in local corporation acts, such as the Glasgow Corporation (General Powers) Act 1960, the Dundee Corporation (Consolidation Powers) Order Confirmation Act 1957, and the Edinburgh Corporation Order Confirmation Act 1967, could be applied to sexual aids and appliances as well as to publications and videos.[15] Officials warned that more coercive measures against sex shops would necessarily involve a broader national debate about censorship involving the appropriate balance between concerns for public morality and the protection of civil liberties.[16] They also anticipated difficulties in defining a 'sex shop' for the purposes of legislation, as distinct from other more general retail outlets that might incidentally stock some explicit magazines or contraceptives. In addition, the SHHD explored the possibility of using planning powers to regulate the location and operation of future sex shops in Scotland. However, in line with the views of local authority associations and of the Department of the Environment in Whitehall, the Scottish Development Department advised the SHHD that such powers were not an 'appropriate line of approach to the issue'.[17] Accordingly, petitioners were informed that the Secretary of State viewed fresh legislation on sex shops as premature although the Scottish Office would continue to monitor the situation.[18]

In the event, the issue of sex shops soon dropped down the agenda of the Scottish policy community. A Scottish appendix to the Longford Report on Pornography in 1972, written by members of the Church of Scotland's Moral Welfare Committee, concluded that although sex shops, 'stocking large quantities of pornography' had opened in 'some of the major cities', shortly afterwards they had closed their doors 'not merely due to public protest and prosecution (and both happened) but because of the low turnover which proved insufficient to meet the high running costs'.[19] During the remainder of the 1970s, Scottish governance was increasingly preoccupied with other policy issues relating to sexuality and sexual health, including homosexual law reform, sex education, the aftermath of 1960s legislation on abortion and family planning, and the challenge presented by the rising incidence of a new generation of sexually transmitted diseases.[20] While efforts to contain the spread of pornography continued, the focus of debate increasingly centred less on the specific threat of sex shops to public morality and more generally on the protection of Scottish society, and especially the younger generation, from indecent displays.[21]

LEGISLATING FOR SEX SHOPS: THE DEMAND FOR ACTION

By 1980, however, the situation had changed significantly with mounting pressure on the government to introduce legislation to prohibit the spread of sex shops. Margaret Thatcher and her new Conservative administration were targeted by a major campaign by 'moral crusaders', headed by Mary Whitehouse, seeking to legislate against pornography and its outlets.[22] Campaigners were especially incensed by the recommendation of the Williams Committee on Obscenity and Film Censorship that, in order to control public access to pornography and avoid the public display of indecent material, under certain conditions 'separate premises' [sex shops] would be permitted to sell all but a small class of hard-core pornography involving child exploitation and physical injury.[23] A broad spectrum of public and political opinion in Scotland shared their concerns. In representations to the Scottish Office, the Church of Scotland argued that any move to license designated sex shops would merely encourage their proliferation and be seen as extending the 'official seal of approval' to the obscene material they stocked. In its view, 'society legitimately [had] a morality . . . which [could] be harmed immeasurably by the quality and quantity of pornography in its bloodstream', and sex shops presented a major threat of contamination.[24] Similarly, moral vigilantes, such as the Glasgow Branch of the National Viewers' and Listeners' Association, warned that material from sex shops would 'leak out into schools, factories, youth clubs, public toilets and litter bins', constituting a new and vicious form of environmental and spiritual pollution.[25]

Concern over the issue was fuelled by the opening of a chain of sex shops in Scotland by Paul Spring and his company Centre Wall Ltd which had, by 1982, franchised some 120 outlets across the United Kingdom. Shops were opened in Aberdeen, Dundee, Edinburgh, Glasgow, Kilmarnock, and Paisley. In all these locations the opening of the shops was met by public protests, often accompanied by anti-porn marches and petitions, but, initially, the efforts of local councillors to prevent their operation by the use of by-laws proved largely abortive.[26] In Glasgow, a wide-ranging 'anti-porn' campaign was co-ordinated by the local secretary of the National Viewers' and Listeners' Association. Involving community and church leaders, tenants and parent-teachers' associations, and women's groups, it strove to prevent the opening of sex shops in Dumbarton Road and Clarkston Road by picketing, by petitioning (some 24,000 signatures) the Secretary of State for Scotland, and by use of the media.[27] In retaliation, Centre Wall Ltd endeavoured to frighten off their opponents by publishing the names and personal details of the leading campaigners in sexual contact magazines with messages designed to create distress and embarrassment. One such message read: 'Middle-aged lady bored with straight-laced way of life seeks young men to refresh her. Husband approves, may join in if needed.'[28]

In the case of Aberdeen, Councillor Richard Gallagher sought to invoke an 1884 city byelaw relating to obscenity to close down the city's first sex shop – Aids to Loving – located in Chattan Place. It had reputedly sold out within sixty hours of its opening and clearly received a mixed reception in the local community – with over 200 neighbouring residents petitioning for its closure, while some 1,000 signatures were allegedly obtained by the owner supporting his venture. Gallagher's campaign rested on three main arguments. First, he claimed that the so-called 'marital aids' sold in the shop were obscene and offensive and designed to promote 'unnatural sexual acts'. Secondly, he protested at the inconvenience caused by the shop's popularity, claiming that 'it causes so much interest . . . that one Sunday afternoon the stream of traffic along Chattan Place was rather like the old days when people flocked to see the arrival of a warship in the harbour'. Thirdly, underpinning Gallagher's case was a belief, shared by civic leaders across Scotland, that sex shops were quintessentially a product of London vice and sexual exploitation, and that their import into Scottish life had to be resisted at all costs.[29] His objections were duly submitted to the Lord Provost's Committee but the Director of Law and Administration subsequently reported that the district council had no powers to insist that Aids to Loving should cease trading. As the council did not own the shop, it could not dictate the nature of its business nor could the opening of a sex shop in existing retail premises be interpreted as a 'change of use' and subject to planning controls.[30]

LEGISLATING FOR SEX SHOPS: PLANNING PERMISSION VERSUS LICENSING

Scottish Office officials sympathised with the concern of local councils to contain the spread of pornography. They were highly sceptical about the more libertarian aspects of the Williams Report. They shared the view of Scottish peers, church leaders and moral pressure groups that, rather than a reduction in legal controls, there needed to be greater recognition of the link between pornography and sexual crime and greater vigilance and protection against the display of material that threatened to demoralise children, offend the sensibilities of many citizens and undermine Christian family values.[31] The Scottish Office, however, was reluctant to initiate any general review of the law relating to obscenity in Scotland. Even on the specific issue of sex shops, it was resistant to calls from Scottish MPs to arm local authorities with additional powers. Malcolm Rifkind MP, Minister for Home Affairs and the Environment at the Scottish Office, argued that, though needing to be modernised and consolidated, the clauses in the Burgh Police (Scotland) Act 1892 and related local acts concerned with obscenity had hitherto proved adequate in controlling pornography in Scotland, and that these powers could appropriately be deployed to prosecute sex-shop owners who displayed obscene material.[32]

Nonetheless, by March 1981, Rifkind was under increasing pressure from backbench Scottish MPs from all parties to include new provisions for sex shops as an amendment to the Local Government Miscellaneous (Scotland) Bill, then being considered by Parliament.[33] The amendment proposed that anyone seeking to operate a sex shop, or a shop dealing in sex magazines or sex aids, should be required to obtain planning permission, with particular reference to its proximity to schools, churches and shopping precincts. Planning permission, when granted, would be subject to a range of conditions relating to access, display, and external advertising. Initially, in line with briefing from the Department of the Environment and his own officials, Rifkind resisted the use of planning controls as an option, stressing that, in many cases, the opening of a sex shop would not legally constitute a 'change of use' and that, while 'moral considerations' were central to the concerns surrounding sex shops, a local authority could not 'exert moral approval or disapproval in exercising planning powers'.[34] Though the amendment was defeated, however, the debate appears to have convinced Rifkind that the strength of moral outrage in Scotland was such that more immediate action was necessary and that, rather than await a future review of licensing regulations, the use of planning processes should be further explored, whatever its imperfections.[35] This view was to be increasingly at odds with that held in Whitehall and the Scottish Development Department who favoured the alternative strategy of a system of licensing.

In April 1981, in response to Rifkind's call for action, E. L. Gillett, Secretary of the Scottish Development Department, reviewed the policy options available.[36] He argued that sex shops presented few grounds for planning objections, such as their noise or smell, or their impact on traffic congestion. Though, on rare occasions, it might be shown that the proliferation of sex shops might change the character of an area, this objection would not apply to a single sex shop opening in an ordinary shopping street. Moreover, '[T]he community's "dislike" of the arrival of a sex shop on grounds of morality would not be a material planning consideration.' There would also be a problem of definition in that it was 'difficult to draw the line in what [was] probably an infinite progression (or regression!) from chemist or corner newsagent to the suppliers of erotic apparatus and hard porn'. Furthermore, given that the Secretary of State for Scotland would be associated with legal appeals from sex shop proprietors against decisions made on moral grounds – appeals that would almost certainly be successful – he would be seen as endorsing their activities and be vulnerable to criticism from powerful elements in Scottish society.

Gillett also identified the likely problems arising from any system of licensing. First, as with a scheme to extend planning regulations, there was the issue of definition, and what ratio of erotic literature and aids to general stock would render a shop a 'sex shop'. Secondly, the fundamental aim of licensing would be to control sex shops and ensure 'their appropriate distribution within the community'. It would not secure their prohibition and would not therefore satisfy those in Scotland who wanted a total ban. Legislation to license sex shops would also run counter to the express wishes of the Lord Advocate and Crown Office. The current prosecution policy in Scotland was to indict anyone opening or operating a sex shop on the charge of indecency, either under Scottish common law or the Burgh Police (Scotland) Act 1892 and subsequent local confirmation acts.[37] Thus, in April 1981, proceedings were at various stages against proprietors in Aberdeen, Dundee, Glasgow and Kilmarnock. There was therefore a real problem of 'licensing an activity (and thereby conferring some form of official sanction) when those who engage[d] in it [might] be liable to criminal prosecution'. As Gillett concluded: 'It would certainly be awkward should local authorities license premises for sale of sexual or sex-related aids only to have the licence holders prosecuted for the sale of indecent and obscene material.'[38]

By the summer of 1981, the divergence between Whitehall and St Andrew's House in their choice of policy options had further widened. The Home Office and the Department of the Environment had decided to explore a system of licensing. In the first instance they proposed to monitor the effectiveness of a licensing scheme for sex shops and cinema clubs being introduced by the Greater London Council, prior to national legislation being contemplated.[39] While conceding that licensing might be the best option in the long term, Rifkind considered that waiting for the 'possibility of future legislation [would] lay the government open to the charge of complacency'. Instead, he continued to press for an amendment to the Town and Country Planning (Use Classes) (Scotland) Order 1973 to give local authorities some powers to contain what his Church of Scotland lobbyists were describing as 'an epidemic of "sex shops"' north of the Border. He argued that, at the very least, this should enable authorities to regulate the number (if any) and location of sex shops in their area.[40] When, later in the year, the Home Office and Department of the Environment decided that public concern and the pressure from Conservative backbenchers were such as to justify the immediate inclusion of a national licensing scheme in the forthcoming Local Government (Miscellaneous Provisions) Bill on the grounds that 'it was preferable for the government to take the initiative and claim credit', Rifkind's office stuck to its position.[41] He and his officials remained convinced that a licensing scheme for premises that were viewed by the bulk of Scottish public opinion as 'socially unacceptable', and whose activities were the subject of criminal proceedings, would convey the distorted and costly impression that Scottish governance was complacent about the issue of pornography. It was also aware that a total ban on sex shops was desired by many Scottish local authorities, and considered that this was more likely to be obtained by means of local planning decisions rather than any centralised system of licensing. In addition, the SHHD anticipated that in the forthcoming Civic Government (Scotland) Bill existing local powers for prosecuting the activities of sex shops on grounds of obscenity would be consolidated and significantly increased penalties introduced, thus lessening the need for new provisions.

In the autumn of 1981, the Secretary of State for Scotland, George Younger MP, continued to press Whitehall departments for a planning solution to the problem.[42] He recognised that he might be left with 'difficult and unpopular decisions in appeal cases' but considered the risk slight 'compared with the credit of taking [prompt] action' to control sex shops. However, he soon encountered vigorous opposition from two quarters. Lord McCluskie, Judge of the Court of Session and High Court Judge, advised that he could find no evidence that 'moral outrage at, or disapproval of, the nature of goods or activities' in a premises on the part of 'even a substantial sector of the local population would be a relevant consideration for planning purposes'. He argued that there were already safeguards to protect children under the Indecent Displays (Control) Act 1981 and that there was no hard evidence that sex shops were frequented by anyone other than the 'cross-section of the population' attracted by other retailers. McCluskie considered it legally unsafe to rely on the planning option even as an interim measure. If decisions were successfully appealed there would be serious political repercussions and the outcome would be perceived as 'a victory for pornographers over the ineffective forces of government'.[43]

Meanwhile, the Secretary of State for the Environment, Michael Heseltine MP, was weighing into the debate in favour of a licensing scheme.[44] He endorsed the view that existing planning criteria applied to change of use with respect to premises such as food outlets and pet shops and were not relevant to sex shops. He argued that, although the public might not see the distinction, the courts would and the pornographers would be quick to appeal. Heseltine made pointed reference to the fact that, already in Scotland, sex-shop owners had successfully appealed against conviction in a number of cases under statute and common law relating to the sale or display of indecent or obscene material.[45] The likelihood was that proprietors would prove even more evasive faced with a legally insecure planning process.

By late November 1981, the licensing option had been firmly adopted for England and Wales. Control of the issue had accordingly shifted from the Department of the Environment to the Home Office, headed by William Whitelaw MP. It was proposed that, in order to respond to the growing pressure for action from Conservative backbenchers, a national licensing scheme for sex shops, modelled on clauses in the Greater London Council (General Powers) (No. 2) Bill, would be introduced immediately as an amendment to the Local Government (Miscellaneous Provisions) Bill. Under the new legislation, any existing or future proprietor of a sex shop would have to apply for a licence. The district council would then consider the application with reference to certain specified criteria including the suitability of the applicant, the number of similar premises in the area, and the character of the locality and nearby premises. Scotland was to be excluded from the scheme and left to decide on its own course of action.[46]

Initially, the Scottish Office was not disposed to follow the Home Office's lead. Younger continued to argue that such a scheme 'would alienate the majority of protesters in Scotland' who sought 'not control but prohibition' and that, according to the Crown Office, it would conflict with ongoing Scottish criminal proceedings.[47] Instead, it was proposed that, while a planning option might no longer be politically feasible, Scottish ministers would continue to resist the introduction of a licensing scheme. Should the Scottish Office be subject to further pressure during the introduction of the Civic Government (Scotland) Bill, it would seek to reassure the public that, under Clause 51 of the Bill, penalties for selling or distributing indecent or obscene material were to be substantially increased in line with the Obscene Publications Acts 1959 and 1964 in England and Wales, and that, should it prove imperative at some future date, under Clause 46, the Secretary of State would have the power by statutory order to add sex shops to the list of premises required to be licensed.[48]

However, at a strategy meeting on 25 February 1982, attended by Scottish Office ministers and senior officials as well as representatives from the Crown Office and Lord Advocate's Department, in view of the impending legislation south of the Border and the likelihood that Scottish peers would press for a similar measure to be included in the Civic Government (Scotland) Bill, it was decided that a licensing scheme for sex shops in Scotland, was, after all, the best option.[49] Accordingly, on 2 March, after fresh appeals in the House of Lords for immediate action, the Earl of Mansfield, Minister of State in the Scottish Office, committed the government to introducing an appropriate amendment at the committee stage of the bill in the Commons.[50]

Within the Scottish policy community there still remained a number of concerns relating to the licensing option. First, there were concerns that licensing should not be seen as condoning the activities of sex shops,[51] and that they should be clearly differentiated in legislation from other licensed activities that might be 'said to be socially desirable'.[52] Secondly, there was felt to be an urgent need to reconcile licensing with existing common and local statute law relating to shameless indecency and obscenity, as well as with offences under the recent Indecent Displays (Control) Act 1981.[53] Clarification was sought to ensure that the licensing process would not in any way obstruct criminal proceedings already in progress. Thirdly, while it had been reluctantly agreed within the Scottish Office that a total ban on sex shops on moral grounds would require a general revision of the laws on obscenity, politicians such as Malcolm Rifkind were eager to ensure that any licensing scheme would empower local authorities to rule on a particular application that 'no such establishment was appropriate' with respect to the nature of the area. Finally, there was widespread agreement that penalties for offences associated with sex shops had hitherto been trivial and needed to be significantly increased.[54]

SEX SHOPS AND THE CIVIC GOVERNMENT (SCOTLAND) ACT 1982

As finally enacted, section 45 of the Civic Government (Scotland) Act 1982 went a long way to address these concerns. In line with Rifkind's desire to emphasise the particular importance of the issue and the moral distinction between sex shops and other forms of licensed activity, the provisions relating to the licensing of sex shops in Scotland were accorded a separate clause and substantive schedule within the Act.[55] It permitted (but did not compel) district or island councils to adopt a licensing scheme. A 'sex shop' was defined as any 'premises, vehicle, vessel or stall used for a business which consist[ed] to a significant degree of selling, hiring, exchanging, lending, displaying or demonstrating sex articles'. Such articles included 'anything intended for use in connection with, or with the purpose of stimulating or encouraging sexual activity' or 'acts of force or constraint associated with sexual activity'. Also included were sound and video recordings concerned primarily with the portrayal of sexual activity or of genital organs, and urinary and excretory functions. However, the legislation did not apply to any article that was manufactured primarily for the purposes of birth control.[56]

An applicant for the grant of a licence was required to give notice in a local newspaper so that objections could be lodged with the council. He/she had to be over eighteen years old, to have resided in the United Kingdom for at least six months, and to be deemed a 'suitable' character to hold a licence. An application could be refused on a number of grounds: the nature of the locality; the use to which any premises in the vicinity was put (for example, a school or church); or the layout, character or condition of the proposed sex shop. In addition, and of critical importance, a council could decline to award a licence if the number of shops in the locality was equal to or exceeded the number considered appropriate for the locality, and the schedule stated explicitly that this might be 'nil'. There was no right of appeal against such an outcome.[57] Local authorities were accorded wide-ranging powers of entry, search, and inspection with respect to premises operating as sex shops in their area, along with powers to regulate the hours of opening, the nature and location of displays and advertisements, and the visibility of the interior of sex shops to passers-by. In accordance with the concerns previously voiced by the Lord Advocate and Crown Office, schedule 2 of the Act highlighted that the licensing process could not afford a defence to a charge in respect of any offence relating to indecency and obscenity at common or local statute law. Penalties for those operating a sex shop without a licence or contravening the conditions of a licence were severe, with fines of up to £10,000 on summary conviction of an offence.

AFTERMATH

In the event, over the following decades, very few sex shops were licensed in Scotland. The evidence suggests that by 2004 only eighteen out of thirty-two local authorities had embraced the licensing provisions of the Civic Government (Scotland) Act 1982, of which only two actively licensed a sex shop. According to an official survey, by the early years of the new millennium only five licensed sex shops existed in Scotland, of which four were located in Edinburgh.[58]

As with its handling of other aspects of the sex industry, such as saunas, lap-dancing bars, and prostitution,[59] Edinburgh appears to have adopted a fundamentally pragmatic attitude to sex shops. Applications for licences were generally considered individually on their merits and, much to the displeasure of the Church of Scotland, not on strictly moral grounds.[60] Some applications were rejected because the location of a proposed sex shop was considered to be inappropriate. Thus, in 2000, Edinburgh City Council initially resisted the opening of a second branch of *Leather and Lace* in Easter Road. The owner of the premises, Vincent Delicato, had been operating a licensed sex shop in Drummond Street since 1995.[61] He argued that there was increasing demand for sex aids and toys, especially from middle-aged couples, that there was nothing predatory or depraved about his clientele, and that there was no evidence that his business was causing harm to the community. However, his Easter Road application met with vigorous opposition from local residents who complained that the sex shop would be adjacent to a dense residential area with schools, churches and family retail outlets. In addition, women's groups, including Scottish Women Against Pornography [hereafter SWAP], objected that sex videos and toys merely reinforced a negative image of women and endorsed sexual exploitation and violence. As with many other similar campaigns, there was also a belief that sex shops facilitated paedophilia by providing a venue for predators and by marketing videos that fed their proclivity for eroticising young girls as sexually voracious.[62] In the event, Delicato appealed the council's decision in the Sheriff Court and was eventually accorded a licence. However, his applications to open licensed sex shops in Gorgie Road, in Fountainbridge and Leith Walk all proved abortive. In these instances, evidence of the proximity of schools and family restaurants, such as McDonald's, proved compelling. His reported connections with London sex-industry entrepreneurs merely strengthened public disquiet over his activities.[63]

At the same time, there is also evidence that the Licensing Committee and Lothian and Borders Police saw advantages in licensing sex shops as a means of regulating the trade. As with their handling of Dora Noyce and her Danube Street brothel, the police authorities preferred a policy of 'tolerance' towards the shops if it enabled them more easily to monitor the sale and distribution of pornography and sex toys and prevented 'the trade from being driven underground'.[64] There also appeared to be a conviction that it was preferable to cluster sex-related outlets in specific areas. Thus, despite strong opposition from local community groups and SWAP, the sex shop *Erogenous Zone* was licensed to operate in Bread Street adjacent to the so-called 'Pubic Triangle' of saunas and lap-dancing bars.[65] As a result, despite Edinburgh's reputation for sexual primness, as one social commentator noted, its sex shops were 'not hidden away from view down darkened alleys where customers glance[d] around furtively before sneaking down. The outlets plied their trade from busy main roads.'[66]

In contrast, from the start, the majority of Glasgow City councillors were totally opposed, primarily on moral grounds, to the licensing of sex shops.[67] In an effort to ensure that the licensing process effectively secured a blanket ban on such premises, decisions on applications were based on the principle that all of Glasgow should be treated as a single locality, with 'zero' being the appropriate number of sex shops.[68] Thus, in 1984, two applications for licences for existing outlets in Clarkston Road, Cathcart, and Dumbarton Road, Partick, were rejected. The applicant, Robert Mitchell of Creedward Limited, claimed that his shops dealt only in contraceptives, films, vitamin pills, magazines and marital aids and not in hard-core pornography or 'whips and chains' and that, far from catering for a small group of sexual deviants, his shops had an annual turnover of some £200,000 with up to 1,200 customers a week. He questioned the legality of the Licensing Committee assessing his application on moral and religious grounds but, in the event, it was the lobbying of church and moral activist groups that prevailed. Similarly, in 2003, Glasgow City Council rejected an application from

Darker Enterprises (owned by the Sullivan brothers, reportedly leading players in the British pornography industry with eighty-six sex shops in England and Wales) to open a licensed sex shop in Gordon Street, near Central Station. There was widespread opposition to the proposal from the local community, predominantly on moral and religious grounds. Local businessmen also considered it would deter tourism while Network Rail considered that the 'congregation of undesirables' near the station would intimidate women and children and pose a traffic hazard. Initially, licensing officials supported the application but they were quickly overruled by the council who continued to declare 'all of Glasgow to be a single locality, with zero the right number'. The Sullivans protested that Glasgow City Council was contravening the spirit of the Civic Government (Scotland) Act. They argued that, while zero might be set for the number of sex shops in a particular locality, it could not be imposed for the entire council area. Darker Enterprises had successfully challenged a blanket ban in Cheltenham on the grounds that the legislation was designed to regulate sex shops and not to ban them outright, and the company threatened to take Glasgow City Council to court – 'even to Europe'– if it continued to refuse licences. Nonetheless, as late as 2009, Glasgow was still maintaining its ban on sex shops, albeit the justification for such a policy had to some degree shifted from predominantly moral objections to concern for the more abusive aspects of the sex industry. As the deputy leader of the city council reflected:

> In Glasgow the local authority has set the provision for sex shops as nil due to the underlying belief that there would be an overwhelming contradiction in licensing such exploitative activities, while at the same time trying to promote a Scotland grounded on human rights and equality for all.[69]

Applicants for sex shop licences fared no better in Aberdeen. The council did consider each application on its local merits but rejected a series of proposals at the turn of the century for outlets in Mearns Street and Market Street in view of the likely impact upon 'local residents and their amenities' and the danger of the sex shops exacerbating existing problems associated with the 'sex trade around the harbour'. In addition, the Aberdeen Procurator Fiscal went on the offensive against businessmen who sold hard-core pornography in unlicensed premises and subsequently secured a number of convictions involving large seizures of stock and fines under the Proceeds of Crime Act 2002.[70]

In Dundee, there were no licensed sex shops and no record of applications. As with Glasgow, the city council effectively viewed the process as a means of imposing a total ban and treated the whole city as one locality for the purposes of the Civic Government (Scotland) Act.[71] Elsewhere in Scotland licences were rarely applied for and only one issued (in Fife). It was evident that only in the larger urban centres was there likely to be sufficient, concentrated demand to make a licensed sex shop economically viable. Even there, a range of constraints were said to operate to deter applications. These included growing competition from mail order, the internet and the Ann Summers chain,[72] the inevitability in many areas of a 'nil' formula being routinely imposed, ambiguities around the definition of 'sex shop' and hence the requirement for a licence, and the deliberately inflated level of licence fees set by many authorities.[73]

In 2001, the Scottish Executive appointed a task force to review the licensing provisions contained in the Civic Government (Scotland) Act. Its subgroup on sex shops considered that the licensing system should be retained to protect the public interest and to ensure that local communities were not exposed to 'offensive displays'. It noted, however, the 'regrettable lack of consistency' across Scotland in the approach of local authorities to the licensing of sex shops and the 'questionable application' of the process in many areas. In its recommendations the subgroup reaffirmed the original intentions of the act that 'as far as the licensing authority [was] concerned, approval or disapproval of sex shops [was] not an issue', and that it was not lawful for a local authority to interpret its powers in such a way as to create an effective ban on sex shops throughout their area.[74] The subsequent report of the task force in 2004 endorsed the subgroup's views. It recommended that the process of licensing should be retained in the interests of public order and decency. In view of the limited number of licences for sex shops issued over the previous twenty years, it considered that the provision should remain optional. While some form of uniform national licensing system and/ or strict guidelines had been discussed by the subgroup, the task force concluded that it was more important that local views and conditions should be taken into consideration and that the power of local authorities to determine the appropriate number of sex shops for a locality as being 'nil' should be retained. The report also stressed, however, that this power was to ensure 'flexibility to ban sex shops from particular areas' after an application had been considered objectively on its merits, and not to establish a blanket ban.[75] It represented a small, if somewhat grudging, acknowledgment by Scottish governance of changing social attitudes to sex and sexual behaviour in Scottish society since the public outcry surrounding the opening of the Anne Boleyn 'sex supermarket' in Glasgow in 1971.

CONCLUSION

Two main reasons can be advanced for the moral panic that surrounded the issue of sex shops in Scotland after 1970. To some extent, it formed part of a more general backlash of moral conservatism against the perceived sexual excesses of the 1960s and the insidious sexualisation of mass culture. To many, sex shops, with their increasingly explicit pornographic materials and salacious sex aids, signified the commodification of what had traditionally been seen as the most intimate and spiritual act within a loving, Christian, marital relationship. Though the Scottish churches had gradually accepted the importance of sexual pleasure as an integral part of companionate marriage, they remained firmly opposed to the pursuit of sexual gratification for its own sake. Moreover, in the view of many within the policy community in Scotland, sex shops represented a magnet for sexual deviants and predators whose presence threatened to contaminate the neighbourhood and endanger the moral integrity of the community. It was widely believed that the explicit material stocked in the shops served merely to heighten the addictive sexual desires and frustrations of their clientele, leading in turn to sexual violence and paedophilia.

The moral panic surrounding sex shops was also very much a function of an enduring fear that the sexual mores of London (and specifically Soho) would spread north of the Border and threaten a distinctive sexual culture in Scotland, heavily influenced by Calvinistic values. As the Scottish subcommittee of the Longford Inquiry observed in 1972: 'It is our firm view that the cultural heritage of the Scot is strongly moralistic and that there is benefit to the nation from a standard of morality.'[76] Thereafter, the threat from metropolitan vice was repeatedly alluded to throughout the debates on the regulation of sex shops, especially by those seeking to ban their existence in Scotland altogether. Lord Ross of Marnock, former Secretary of State for Scotland, echoed the views of many Scottish peers and MPs, and indeed many civic and church leaders, when he urged that the Scots be allowed to deal with the issue 'in their own Presbyterian way' rather than meekly following the 'libertarian' approach of English legislators:

> As regards the whole traditions of Scotland it [the introduction of sex shops] is not something that is desirable. I know that there may well be quick money to be made by some London financier or by the same person who finances the Soho establishments. But we do not want them in Scotland . . . This is one of the cancers that we cannot allow to grow from the point of view of the morals and morale of Scotland.[77]

Similarly, Lord Wilson of Langside, former Solicitor General for Scotland and Lord Advocate, bemoaned the extent to which the depth of moral disquiet surrounding sex shops in Scotland had been ignored in favour of a licensing system that conformed to the sexual ethos and environment of the City of London. 'This way of governing Scotland' was, he declared, 'the kind of thing that create[d] Scottish nationalism.'[78]

NOTES

1. The following narrative is based upon, *Glasgow Herald*, 24 April 1971, 5, 10, 11, 12, 14 and 15 May 1971, 17 June 1971, 6 January 1972; NRS, HH43/287, M. Goldie to Secretary of State for Scotland (hereafter SSS), 14 April 1971, R. J. Inglis to I. L. Sharp, 18 May 1971; *Scottish Daily Record*, 16 and 18 October 1971.

2. According to Paul Ferris, in London ' "[S]ex supermarkets" were in business by 1970, promising carpeted decor and soft lighting through which well-adjusted couples would stroll, selecting an eight-inch giant vibrator here, some impractical underwear there, or perhaps the latest in fun-condoms crowned with Micky Mouse's head or Dumbo the Flying Elephant' [Ferris, *Sex and the British*, 236].

3. *Glasgow Herald*, 9 June 1971. Kidd was also at the forefront of a campaign to withdraw public funding from the *Traverse Theatre*, renowned for its avant-garde productions, and to prosecute theatre companies performing sexually explicit plays [Davidson and Davis, *The Sexual State*, 245].

4. *Glasgow Herald*, 10 June 1971.

5. Ibid., 15 July 1971.

6. *Scottish Daily Record*, 18 October 1971.

7. Ibid., 16 October 1971.

8. Ibid., 16 October 1971.

9. *Glasgow Herald*, 6 January 1972.

10. Weeks, *Sex, Politics and Society*, second edition, Ch. 14; Haste, *Rules of Desire*, Ch. 10; Holden, *Makers and Manners*, Ch. 5.

11. According to Marcus Collins, by the early 1970s 'pornography [had] succeeded prostitution as the principal symbol of sexual malaise' [Collins, 'The pornography of permissiveness', 100].

12. Free Church of Scotland (hereafter FCS), *Report of the Committee on Public Questions, Religion and Morals for 1971*, 138; Free Presbyterian Church of Scotland (hereafter FPCS), *Proceedings of Synod for 1971*, 16.

13. *Glasgow Herald*, 15 November 1971, 6 January 1972.

14. Ibid., 3 and 17 February 1972; *Pornography: The Longford Report*, 390–1.

15. NRS, HH43/287, minute by N. E. Sharp, 18 May 1971.

16. Ibid., R. J. Inglis to Mary Goldie, draft letter, 17 May 1971.

17. Ibid., R. J. Inglis to B. J. Biddis, 21 May 1971; B. J. Biddis to R. J. Inglis, 24 May 1971.

18. See, for example, ibid., R. J. Inglis to Mary Goldie, 25 May 1971.

19. *Pornography: The Longford Report*, 387.

20. Davidson and Davis, *The Sexual State*, Chs 4–8.

21. Ibid., Ch. 11.

22. See especially, Durham, *Sex and Politics*, Ch. 5.

23. *Report of Committee on Obscenity and Film Censorship*, paras 9:10–9:15, 13:4.

24. Church of Scotland Archives, (hereafter CSA), Charis House, box 35 misc., Reverend F. S. Gibson (Secretary to the Church of Scotland Committee on Social Responsibility) to Malcolm Rifkind, 9 March 1980; *Scotsman*, 15 November 1980.

25. *Glasgow Herald*, 27 October 1980.

26. See *Hansard* [HC], vol. 1, 23 March 1981, cols 692, 696–7, debate on Local Government Miscellaneous Provisions (Scotland) Bill; CSA, Charis House, box 35 misc., Scottish Home and Health Department (hereafter SHHD) to Director of Social Work, Church of Scotland, 22 July 1981; NRS, AD63/1514/8, F. R. Crowe, Crown Office to Lord Mansfield, 2 December 1981. The Crown Office estimated that by 1982, in addition to the seven shops operated by Centre Wall, there were in Scotland 'a similar number of independently owned shops specialising in pornography' [AD63/1514/9, F. R. Crowe to Lord Advocate, 10 February 1982].

27. *Glasgow Herald*, 3 March 1981, 24 June 1981.

28. NRS,   CS258/1982/17180,   CS258/1983/12880,   CS258/1983/13031, CS258/1984/1474, CS258/1984/6234, CS258/1984/6306, Papers relating to petitions for suspension and interdict against Centre Wall Ltd.

29. *Glasgow Herald*, 17 July 1980.

30. *Aberdeen Press and Journal*, 27 September 1980. Subsequently, Aberdeen City Police launched a series of raids on sex shops in the city, seizing some £20,000 worth of magazines, videos and sex toys and prosecuting Centre Wall personnel under the obscenity clauses in the Local Corporation Act [*Glasgow Herald*, 27 March 1981, 23 June 1981].

31. *Glasgow Herald*, 20 November 1979; *Hansard* [HL], vol. 404, 16 January 1980, cols 183–94.

32. *The Scotsman*, 15 November 1980; *Hansard* [HC], vol. 999, 17 February 1981, col. 108.

33. *Hansard* [HC], vol. 1, 23 March 1981, cols 688–700.

34. Ibid., col. 698; NAS, DD12/4188, minute by G. N. Bendon, Department of the Environment (hereafter DOE), 18 March 1981.

35. NRS, DD12/4188, M. Rifkind to SSS, 24 March 1981.

36. NRS, AD63/1514/5, memorandum by E. L. Gillett, Scottish Development Department (hereafter SDD), 14 April 1981.

37. Under common law in Scotland, it was an offence to 'publish, circulate,

or expose for sale any obscene work – book, picture, photograph, print or writing – devised and intended to corrupt the morals of the community and to create inordinate and lustful desires' [NRS, AD63/291, Summary of the law on obscenity, February 1955].

38. The Lord Advocate was adamant that if the ongoing proceedings were successful 'there [could] be no question of licensing anyone to commit crime'. In his view, no legislation should be proceeded with until 'the criminality of sex shops was decided judicially' [NRS, AD63/1514/5, minute by Mrs C. Duncan, 30 April 1981].

39. NRS, AD63/1514/6, minute by D. J. Essery, Scottish Economic Planning Department, 1 June 1981.

40. Ibid., M. Rifkind to Giles Shaw, Parliamentary Undersecretary of State for the Environment, 3 June 1981.

41. NRS, AD63/1514/7, G. Shaw to Patrick Mayhew, 21 July 1981; AD63/1514/8, correspondence between G. Shaw and P. Mayhew, 21 July 1981; AD63/1514/6, M. Rifkind to G. Shaw, 28 August 1981; Secretary, SHHD to M. Rifkind, 28 August 1981.

42. NRS, AD63/1514/7, George Younger to Michael Heseltine, 21 October 1981.

43. NRS AD63/1514/8, J. C. McCluskie to Lord Advocate, 18 November 1981.

44. Ibid., Michael Heseltine to George Younger, 23 November 1981.

45. According to the appeal judges, the prosecution had failed to prove that the material sold or displayed in the sex shops had been 'liable or likely to deprave and corrupt the morals of the lieges and to create in their minds inordinate and lustful desires' [NRS AD63/1514/8, Crown Office to Lord Mansfield, Minister of State in the Scottish Office, 2 December 1981].

46. NRS, AD63/1514/8, M. Heseltine to G. Younger, 23 November 1981.

47. Ibid., G. Younger to J. Halliday, Home Office, 21 December 1981. The position of Scottish law officers appeared to be vindicated when a number of these cases resulted in guilty pleas indicating that 'those involved [were] well aware they [were] breaking the law' [NRS, AD63/1514/9, Crown Agent to Lord Advocate, 1 February 1982].

48. NRS AD63/1514/8, G. Younger to J. Halliday, Home Office, 21 December 1981; AD63/1514/9, J. E. Fraser to M. Rifkind, 11 February 1982.

49. NRS, AD63/1514/11, minutes of meeting, 25 February 1982. Pressure was also coming from the Scottish media. See, for example, *Glasgow Herald*, editorial, 5 February 1982.

50. *Hansard* [HL], vol. 427, 2 March 1982, cols 1267–9.

51. These concerns were only heightened by news that Westminster City Council contemplated using their new powers to license ' "sex encounter" premises' [NRS, AD63/1514/9, Crown Agent to Lord Advocate, 1 February 1982]. The Church of Scotland's Committee on Social Responsibility remained

committed to an 'unequivocal' ban on sex shops [*Glasgow Herald*, 20 March 1982].

52. NRS, AD63/1514/12, minute from Solicitor's Office, 4 May 1982.
53. The act sought to restrict the display of indecent material to displays solely for an adult paying audience or to shops with warning notices and age restrictions [Durham, *Sex and Politics*, 81–2].
54. NRS, AD63/1514/10, J. Thornton to G. Younger, 18 February 1982; ibid., minute J. E. Fraser to M. Rifkind, 24 February 1982; AD63/1514/11, minute of meeting, 25 February 1982.
55. Civic Government (Scotland) Act 1982, c.45 Part III, section 45 and schedule 2.
56. Unlike the Local Government (Miscellaneous Provisions) Act 1982 in England and Wales, the Scottish measure did not provide for the licensing of sex cinemas. No sex cinemas had previously opened in Scotland and the Scottish Office considered that it was under no pressure to introduce separate licensing provisions [NRS, AD63/1514/13, G. P. H. Aitken (SHHD) to SSS, 17 June 1982].
57. A number of Scottish peers and MPs, such as Lord (Willie) Ross of Marnock and Donald Dewar, considered this clause to be duplicitous. They argued that local authorities should be given explicit powers to impose an outright ban on sex shops. The government remained constrained by legal opinion, however, that such a ban would necessitate a protracted and contentious debate over the relationship of the state to moral censorship and a substantive revision of the obscenity laws [*Hansard* [*HL*], vol. 435, 19 October 1982, cols 48–9; *Hansard* [*HC*], vol. 28, 28 July 1982, col. 1148].
58. Papers of Task Group on the review of licensing provisions contained in the Civic Government (Scotland) Act: Summary of Sex Shop Questionnaire, August 2001. Accessed following a Freedom of Information (hereafter FOI) request, 10 January 2014. The sex shops were *Erogenous Zone* in Bread Street, *Leather and Lace* in Drummond Street and Easter Road, and *Private Lives* in Elm Row.
59. Described by *The Scotsman* as 'Edinburgh's blind-eye approach to the sex industry' [*The Scotsman*, 26 February 2000].
60. *The Herald*, 23 September 2003.
61. The Drummond Street sex shop was later reported to stock explicit videos and DVDs that featured images of straight, lesbian and gay sex, as well as group sex. It also stocked sexually explicit magazines and books featuring hardcore nudity and sex. Its other wares ranged from thongs priced at £3.50 to a sex toy in the shape of a St Andrew's Cross priced at £500, along with a variety of exotic lingerie [*The Scotsman*, 18 April 2000; *Edinburgh Evening News*, 5 November 2004].
62. *Edinburgh Evening News*, 6 and 15 April 2000, 25 July 2000.
63. *Edinburgh Evening News*, 4 May 2002, 5 and 17 August 2002, 9 and 15 August 2005.

64. *Edinburgh Evening News*, 5 November 2004.

65. *Edinburgh Evening News*, 25 and 29 July 2000.

66. Ibid., 5 November 2004.

67. Unless otherwise stated, the following account is based upon *The Herald*, 14 May 2003, 16 June 2003, 9, 13, 19, 23 September 2003, 6 November 2003.

68. This formula was adhered to, despite the fact that, as early as 1983, the Town Clerk had ruled such a policy to be unlawful [*Glasgow Herald*, 22 April 1983]. As an additional deterrent, Glasgow imposed one of the highest fees for licences in Scotland. By 2001, Glasgow was charging more than £10,000 a year as compared with Edinburgh's £1,000 and the mean average for all Scottish local authorities of £846 [COSLA to Task Group on the Review of the Licensing Provisions contained in the Civic Government (Scotland) Act 1982, 17 May 2001. Accessed following an FOI request, 10 January 2014; *The Herald*, 19 September 2003].

69. *The Herald*, 25 February 2009, 10 March 2009.

70. *Aberdeen Press and Journal*, 19 December 2000, 28 February 2001, 23 and 27 August 2002, 22 February 2003, 8 August 2003.

71. *The Herald*, 23 September 2003.

72. Ann Summers outlets avoided licensing restrictions by claiming that only a small proportion of their stock on display consisted of 'sex articles'.

73. Task Force to Review Civic Government (Scotland) Act 1982: Papers of Sub-Group on Sex Shops – Summary of Sex Shop Questionnaire, 2001. Accessed following an FOI request, 10 January 2014.

74. Ibid., daft report of subgroup, 2001.

75. *A Report by the Task Force set up to review the licensing provisions contained in the Civic Government (Scotland) Act 1982*, November 2004.

76. *Longford Report on Pornography*, 387.

77. *Hansard* [*HL*], vol. 427, 2 March 1982, col. 1267; vol. 428, 16 March 1982, col. 560.

78. *Hansard* [*HL*], vol. 435, 19 October 1982, col. 50.

9

'Culpable and Reckless Conduct': Criminalising the Transmission of HIV in Scotland, 1983–2014

AN HISTORICAL PERSPECTIVE: THE LAW AND THE TRANSMISSION OF VENEREAL DISEASE IN SCOTLAND, 1900–83

On 13 February 2001, Stephen Kelly, thirty-three, went on trial at the High Court in Glasgow charged with 'culpable and reckless' conduct in having had sexual intercourse with his girlfriend, Anne Craig, thirty-four and a mother of three, at various addresses in King's Park and Ruchazie, Glasgow, between 1 January 1994 and 28 March 1994, while 'knowing or believing' he was infected with HIV, 'whereby she became infected with the virus to her permanent impairment, to the danger of her health and to the danger of her life'. Though there was no written judgment issued in the case of Stephen Kelly, legal commentators viewed his trial as 'something of a landmark' in the criminal law and as the 'first case of its kind' in the United Kingdom.[1] The case raised a range of key issues relating to confidentiality, disclosure, harm, risk and consent. In particular, it implied that the transmission of HIV might be regarded as a criminal injury, that non-disclosure of one's HIV serostatus might outweigh or 'vitiate' consent to sexual intercourse on the part of the appellant, and that liability did not necessarily depend on whether or not the disease was actually transmitted.[2] Nonetheless, arguably his prosecution can equally be viewed as but the latest in a long line of attempts to bring the Scottish legal system to bear on the wilful or careless transmission of sexually transmitted diseases.[3]

As we have seen in Chapter 3, there was clear precedent in Scots common law, dating back to the mid-nineteenth century, for the transmission of venereal disease (VD) to constitute an aggravated offence in cases of sexual offences against children. After 1910, perhaps in response to the moral panic that was sweeping Scottish cities over the issue of 'child outrage', law officers began to initiate an increasing number of prosecutions for this aggravated crime and a steady succession of such cases appeared before the Scottish High Courts up to the late 1930s.

In addition, during World War I, in response to heightened concerns over the impact of VD on the racial health and military efficiency of the nation, several attempts were made to penalise the careless transmission of the disease. In 1917 and 1918, criminal law amendment bills proposed to make it a criminal offence for a person suffering from VD in a communicable form to 'have sexual intercourse with any other person', 'to solicit or invite any other person to have sexual intercourse', or 'to wilfully communicate such disease in any manner to any other person'. Opinion in Scotland was divided over these proposals. Public health committees generally approved of a more punitive approach towards vectors of the disease. However, Scottish Office officials voiced serious reservations. They considered that, given the stigma of contracting VD, few people would accuse others of transmitting it. More seriously, it was felt that such coercive measures might deter sufferers from seeking treatment at the newly established clinics, and that prostitutes would avoid the official treatment centres for fear of prosecution. Moreover, as in England, while wanting to restrain and reform 'problem girls', and to regulate the behaviour of young, allegedly promiscuous 'amateur' prostitutes indulging in promiscuous and unsafe sex, many Scottish women's organisations were concerned at the likely discriminatory aspects of punitive purity legislation.

Their fears were borne out by the arbitrary use by military and police authorities of the Defence of the Realm Act (DORA), passed in 1914. In March 1918, under mounting pressure from Allied commanders to protect their troops from VD, the British government introduced Regulation 40D under the Act, making it an offence for any woman suffering from VD in a communicable form to have or to solicit intercourse with any member of His Majesty's Forces. In practice, the law operated in very similar ways to the notorious Contagious Diseases Acts of the 1860s. In order to establish their innocence, women were forced to undergo a medical examination. Conviction rested only on having intercourse while diseased and did not require proof of actual transmission. Nor was ignorance of infection held to be a legitimate defence, as three cases heard before Edinburgh Sheriff Court in August 1918 clearly indicated. There was a marked absence of safeguards against wrongful accusation, victimisation and infringement of civil liberties. As with the criminal law amendment bills, DORA 40D met with vigorous opposition from libertarian and feminist groups in Scotland. Moreover, given the few cases successfully proceeded against, Scottish law officers considered that the cost in social and political disaffection occasioned by the measure far outweighed its benefits to public health, and did not recommend that it be permanently incorporated in the criminal law. They were relieved when, in November 1918, faced by mounting opposition in Parliament and the media, and concerned not to alienate further the mass of newly enfranchised women, the government revoked the regulation.

Nonetheless, throughout the 1920s, a great deal of public and professional opinion in Scotland remained firmly in favour of more stringent legal controls of those infected with VD. In 1928, under the Edinburgh Corporation (Venereal Disease) Bill and the Glasgow-sponsored Venereal Disease (Scotland) Bill, it was proposed that Medical Officers of Health should be empowered to compel anyone believed to be infectious, and who refused to seek and sustain treatment, to undergo treatment by a qualified private practitioner or clinic and to continue it until certified cured or non-infective, under ultimate threat of prosecution and detention. Similarly, parents of infected children were to be subject to compulsory examination and treatment in the interests of family and public health.

These proposals aroused fierce public debate both at Westminster and in the counsels of Scottish local government, and became the focus for extensive pressure-group activity. They raised a range of fundamental and contentious issues relating to the liberty of the individual, to the role of the local state in the control of sexually transmitted diseases, to the medico-legal implications of compulsory treatment, and to the right of Scottish legislation to deviate from the diktat of Whitehall. As it transpired, the campaign for VD controls in Scotland proved abortive although, significantly, the Edinburgh Corporation Bill was defeated only after the Cabinet had imposed a three-line whip against the bill, an unprecedented step for private legislation.

The defeat of the Edinburgh Corporation Bill inevitably slowed the momentum of the Scottish campaign for VD controls. Yet, throughout the remainder of the interwar period, local authorities and public health committees continued to press the Department of Health for Scotland for additional powers to regulate those who ignored or defaulted from treatment and wilfully infected others;[4] demands that were to find increasing support from within the policy community faced with the exigencies of World War II. The increasing incidence of VD, and especially acute syphilis, in many Scottish urban centres from 1940 to 1941 elicited a growing call from local health authorities for more stringent measures to discipline those defaulting from treatment or identified as vectors of disease. After protracted negotiations, Defence of the Realm Regulation 33B was introduced in November 1942, providing for sexual 'contacts' named by two or more infected patients to be notified to Medical Officers of Health, with penalties of a fine and/or imprisonment for any contacts who failed to undergo examination and, where appropriate, a full course of treatment under a suitably qualified practitioner until pronounced free of VD 'in a communicable form'.[5] Though the eventual wording of DORA 33B was gender-neutral, successive drafts clearly reveal that it was intended to target a 'dangerous minority of infected women', casual prostitutes or 'good-time' girls who were held responsible for the major outbreaks of VD within the forces.

In the event, DORA 33B had a negligible impact on the incidence of VD and during 1943–4, a fresh campaign for the compulsory notification and treatment of persons infected with VD, with the prosecution of defaulters, was launched by Scottish local government, supported by leading Medical Officers of Health and venereologists, the Scottish Medical Advisory Committee, and the Church of Scotland. Strong representations were made in Cabinet by the Secretary of State for Scotland for new controls and legal sanctions but the greater attachment of the English medical establishment to voluntarist strategies prevailed. Nonetheless, in response to the renewed increase in acute syphilis and gonorrhoea that accompanied the end of the war and demobilisation, venereologists and public health committees in the major Scottish cities continued to press for the extension of emergency powers under Defence Regulation 33B after its expiry in 1947, and for additional controls by which to identify and contain 'the most dangerous and persistent spreaders of infection'. Scottish Office proposals were again overruled by Whitehall. The Ministry of Health argued that local authorities and medical practitioners in England were less committed to compulsory measures than their Scottish counterparts, that Scottish politicians had understated the possible damage that such measures might do to existing voluntary procedures, and that, given the likely impact of new forms of chemotherapy on infectivity, they had overstated the problem of 'default'. However the overriding concern was that to raise contentious issues relating to statutory controls and the legal obligation of patients and practitioners to disclose cases of venereal infection would be inopportune at a time when the government's energies were bent on securing agreement on a new National Health Service.

The issue of introducing more stringent controls to police and penalise those who wilfully or carelessly exposed others to VD continued to surface in Scottish public health reports in the 1950s and 1960s. As late as 1968, prompted by a rapid rise in the incidence of gonorrhoea and non-specific sexually transmitted diseases, Sir Myer Galpern, Member of Parliament for Glasgow Shettleston, sought to introduce a bill to provide for the compulsory examination and treatment of persons suspected of suffering from VD by the restoration of powers similar to those formerly contained in Defence Regulation 33B. A familiar range of arguments was marshalled against the bill, and especially its more punitive aspects.[6] They echoed the response of the Scottish Office to the many campaigns for VD controls that had been conducted in Scotland since the 1920s; that a punitive approach to VD transmission would discourage people from voluntarily seeking diagnosis and treatment; that, in practice, it would be discriminatory and reinforce sexual double standards; that it would compromise the trust and confidentiality upon which the relationship of medical practitioners and social workers to patients had traditionally been founded; and that criminalising certain aspects of 'wilful' sexual behaviour would prove legally problematic, facilitate false allegations and blackmail, endanger civil liberties, and contravene international conventions on human rights.

THE CRIMINAL LAW AND THE TRANSMISSION OF HIV/AIDS, 1983–2001

As we shall see, many of these objections were subsequently to feed through to HIV/AIDS policy-making in the 1980s. As in England, Scottish health officials were pressured by representatives of the tabloid press and the more conservative Presbyterian churches, along with moral activists within Scottish local government, to adopt a punitive approach to the transmission of HIV/AIDS. As in England, those favouring such an approach remained marginalised and policy was primarily shaped by a traditional, voluntarist, biomedical elite with the emphasis on counselling and education rather than on surveillance, social exclusion and legal sanctions.

Health officials within the Scottish Home and Health Department (SHHD) were sympathetic towards Whitehall measures to detain people in hospital who were highly infectious with AIDS and openly endangering the community. However, along with Scottish representatives on the newly appointed Expert Advisory Group on AIDS, established by the Department of Health and Social Security in 1985, they were not in favour of extending nineteenth-century powers under the Notification of

Diseases acts to AIDS, powers that would have compelled GPs to report all cases of AIDS and have enabled Medical Officers of Health to remove and isolate sufferers. It was felt that any form of compulsory notification and/or screening would merely fuel the moral panic surrounding AIDS while alienating high-risk groups such as the gay community and compromising their relationship with health professionals.[7] In the view of A. M. Macpherson, Assistant Secretary in the SHHD:

> ... on the basis of present knowledge, there is no point in limiting the freedom of a case of AIDS other than in exceptional circumstances where there is a risk of spread of blood. Limitation of sexual activities by statute is of course impracticable.[8]

Scottish health officials gave a cautious response to the Public Health (Control of Disease) Act 1984, and its associated regulations in 1985, that conveyed powers in England and Wales for the compulsory hospital detention of AIDS patients in exceptional circumstances.[9] They were relieved that, given the wording of previous Scottish health legislation, no new Act was needed north of the Border and that a provision that potentially could have ignited public debate around issues of civil liberties and social stigma could be handled discreetly purely by means of a departmental circular.[10]Subsequently, the thrust of Scottish evidence to the House of Commons Committee on AIDS in 1986 and 1987 was opposed to coercive measures to segregate infected individuals.[11] So-called 'revenge sex' was viewed as an exception that justified criminal proceedings. In addition, in January 1987, it was reported that the Solicitor General for Scotland and the Lord Advocate were considering the prosecution under Scottish common law of those prostitutes and drug addicts who, it was claimed, were deliberately and maliciously infecting others with AIDS.[12] Otherwise, however, there was general reluctance to deploy existing public health powers relating to infectious diseases or to associate the containment of the disease with the criminal law. Concern was expressed that this would inevitably infringe civil liberties and that a policy of 'isolation' was an 'illogical and inhumane approach to the problem'. Calls for more rigorous, targeted policing of high-risk groups, such as prostitutes, as a means of reducing their role as 'reservoirs of infection' met firm resistance from the majority of Scottish law officers. The views of the policy community in Scotland were broadly in accord with those of the Social Services Committee which recommended that policy should be inclusive and non-discriminatory and focus on the promotion of safe sex and harm reduction rather than the isolation of diseased and vulnerable individuals by means of public health directives and court proceedings, frequently demanded in the tabloid press.[13]

Moreover, despite the fact that a more politicised and interventionist approach to HIV/AIDS emerged in the early 1990s, provoked largely by the increased awareness of the spread of the disease to the heterosexual community,[14] coercive measures continued to be resisted. While there was a shift in emphasis from the promotion of safe sex to the provision of more systematic screening and surveillance, Scottish policy-making bodies, such as the newly established Ministerial Task Force on AIDS, sustained an inclusive, supportive and rights-orientated approach to sufferers, in line with the *Scotsman* and Scottish church leaders.[15] Both the remit and the recommendations of the task force were informed by a preventive rather than punitive ideology.[16] In contrast to the draconian provisions then being advanced in the charter of the Conservative Family Campaign, the report of the task force emphasised the need for a sensitive and flexible approach on the part of the police towards drug-users (specifically the provision of needle exchanges) and prostitutes in order to minimise risk behaviour, and close liaison between the police/ prosecuting authorities and AIDS support agencies.[17] Where new initiatives were recommended, as in the development of contact tracing, eliciting the voluntary co-operation of the patient was regarded as the priority rather than any element of coercion.[18]

In the following years, however, with the gradual fragmentation of the earlier consensus politics surrounding AIDS, a more *dirigiste* approach to HIV transmission emerged that was more disposed to restrict the civil liberties of the individual in the interests of public health. Compulsory notification and contact disclosure remained too contentious for health officials in Whitehall and the Scottish Office but more vigorous directives for routine screening and tracing were introduced, despite the opposition of some AIDS activists,[19] and the criminalisation of the 'reckless' or 'careless' transmission of HIV was increasingly aired as a policy option.[20]

This appeal to the criminal law, as distinct from public health regulations, as a possible means of policing the sexual behaviour of those infected with HIV was fuelled by a scatter of highly publicised cases in which it was alleged that innocent victims had been carelessly and knowingly infected.[21] The Scottish press accorded extensive coverage to the prosecution and sentencing in July 1997 of a Cypriot fisherman for infecting an English divorcee with HIV during what was reported to have been a 'torrid affair'.[22] However, it was the efforts of a 28-year-old Edinburgh man later that year to raise a prosecution against his former girlfriend for knowingly infecting him that really caught the media's attention and produced a wide-ranging public debate over the criminalisation of HIV transmission.[23]

Wayne Simpson, an unemployed former doorman, claimed that Stella Nelson had had unprotected sex with him in February 1996, in the knowledge that she was HIV positive. He was diagnosed as being HIV positive in July 1996 after he suffered from a series of unexplained rashes. The couple, both of whom were drug users, had begun an affair in September 1995 and continued to practise safe sex in her house in West Pilton until Simpson was sentenced to six months in jail for car-related crimes. After an 'emotional reunion' on his release, however, it was alleged that unprotected sex had taken place, leading to his infection and that Nelson had failed to reveal her condition during their two-year relationship. In what was described as making 'Scottish legal history', albeit reluctantly, the Lothian and Borders Police and Procurator Fiscal in Edinburgh investigated the case in conjunction with Crown Counsel.

The case raised a number of controversial legal and ethical issues relating to HIV disclosure and provoked a vigorous debate. Though broadly in agreement that there was an urgent need to clarify the law in what was variously described as 'a grey area' or 'uncharted waters', lawyers held mixed views on the desirability of recourse to the criminal law. The former Solicitor General for Scotland, Lord Cullen, called for an investigation by the Scottish Law Commission into the issue. He considered that Scottish criminal law was 'well known for its flexibility and capacity to develop according to changing social circumstances' and that a charge relating to the transmission of HIV might appropriately be 'framed within the boundaries of culpable and reckless conduct'.[24] George More, a leading criminal defence lawyer agreed, arguing that:

> It is the sort of thing where the public would be content with a prosecution because it is such a dreadful thing to do if someone's life was taken away by someone who didn't give a damn and was wicked enough to conceal it.[25]

At the same time, some legal ethicists, such as Professors Sheila McLean and Kenyon Mason, felt that, in such cases, proving the chronology and direction of HIV transmission would be problematic and raise the contentious issue of how far risk is accepted in any sexual relationship. Meanwhile, the Scottish Council for Civil Liberties warned that prosecutions might well infringe the right of the accused under the European Convention on Human Rights to a private 'sexual' life.

The Scottish medical establishment and Scottish churches condemned the wilful transmission of disease as morally wrong but did not favour the involvement of the criminal law. Medical opinion was mainly of the view that it would prove counterproductive as it would deter people from seeking an HIV test and accessing appropriate counselling and treatment. There was also considerable apprehension that medical confidentiality would be compromised and doctors forced to act as moral arbiters. For their part, the churches viewed the problem not as a legal but as a fundamentally moral transgression for which both partners were culpable in that sexual activity had not been 'restricted to within a stable family relationship'.

AIDS charities, such as the Waverley Care Trust, were equally apprehensive, claiming that the criminal law '[did] not have a place in sexual infection transmission'. They argued that there was a mutual responsibility for practising safe sex and that the threat of prosecution would merely drive sufferers away from the health services and lead to an escalation in undetected cases. It was also feared that the introduction of legal processes would encourage false allegations when relationships broke down acrimoniously.

In the event, the Crown Office declined to proceed with any prosecution in the case of Wayne Simpson, concluding that 'the evidence available would not justify criminal proceedings against any person'.[26] Meanwhile, however, the Strathclyde Police were actively investigating a similar case in which it was alleged that a Glasgow man had recklessly infected his girlfriend with HIV. In March 1997, the man appeared anonymously from Glenochil Prison, near Alloa, before a television audience of millions on ITV's *World In Action* and admitted to having had unprotected sex with a woman when he knew he was an HIV carrier. He confessed that:

> Effectively, I have ruined a life. I have taken a life ... My biggest regret is that I actually passed the virus on to somebody else. I know I should have told the girl I had the virus. But I had these feelings for the lassie that I have never felt for any lassie, and I just think now I'm sorry that I didn't tell her.[27]

After the programme, a woman, claiming to be the sexual partner referred to, complained to the Strathclyde Police. The Procurator Fiscal was persuaded that a charge of causing harm by 'culpable and reckless conduct' was justified. After a protracted process of trying to obtain the tape of the *World in Action* programme and other evidence from Granada Television, the interviewee, Stephen Kelly, was eventually brought to trial in February 2001.

THE TRIAL OF STEPHEN KELLY

During the subsequent court proceedings it transpired that Stephen Kelly and Anne Craig had met at a party in North Glasgow while Craig was on a short visit from Manchester.[28] Within twenty-four hours they had begun a sexual relationship and continued to have unprotected sex 'more or less every night' for weeks. Craig was aware that Kelly had been in prison in Glenochil following a conviction for assault and robbery and had previously been an intravenous drug-user. She claimed in court that she had specifically asked Kelly whether there was a need, other than the risk of pregnancy, for them to practise safe sex, and he had replied 'No'. He claimed that, when in jail, he had tested negative for HIV. In fact, he had become infected while in Glenochil Prison as a result of sharing contaminated needles. In the summer of 1993, he had tested positive and been given counselling about safe sex by an HIV nurse, one of a team of health workers from Ruchill Hospital, in Glasgow, sent to the prison following a serious outbreak of the HIV virus among prisoners.

Craig uprooted her family from England and moved to Glasgow to live with Kelly but, by early March 1994, Craig was feeling very unwell with flu-like symptoms and, shortly afterwards, Kelly concocted a story that he had been infected by a former girlfriend who was dying from Aids and that he had only just learnt that he was HIV-positive. He warned Craig that she 'would probably be infected because of the nature of the intercourse [they] were having'. Thereafter, Craig was referred to Ruchill Hospital and tested positive for the virus, with a prognosis that she might survive for as little as two years. According to her evidence, it was only at that point that Kelly admitted he had lied to her and had, in fact, contracted HIV from sharing needles in prison prior to their relationship.

Anne Craig testified that she was devastated by the news that she was HIV positive, 'fearing that she would die with nobody to look after her three daughters'. She claimed that her family and friends had deserted her and 'treated her like a leper' which left her even more dependent on Kelly. Though admitting that she had previously taken amphetamine and cannabis, she claimed that Kelly was the person who had introduced her to heroin as a means of coping with the situation and that, despite her attempts to end the relationship, it had continued for a further three years because of his intimidating behaviour and her fear of social isolation.[29] In October 1995 she had signed a letter accepting full responsibility for her condition and promising not to prosecute Kelly.

In court, however, she testified that she had been forced to sign it by Kelly's 'mind games' and 'emotional abuse'. In 1997, she and Kelly had separated and she had then approached the police with a view to bringing a charge against him.

In defending Kelly, Donald Findlay QC pursued a range of arguments. He questioned Professor Andrew Leigh Brown, a geneticist at Edinburgh University, with a view to establishing that, if two people had the same strain of the HIV virus, it was not possible to identify who contracted it first or who passed it to whom. He challenged, unsuccessfully, the admissibility of evidence on blood tests taken in prison on the grounds they had been conducted on the basis of strict anonymity. Above all, he cast doubt on the reliability of Craig's evidence and on her motives in seeking a prosecution. He put it to her that she had known that Kelly was HIV-positive when she originally slept with him, that she was already a drug addict and that 'they had been obsessed with one another in a world of drugs and it did not matter to them if it ruined both their lives'. He observed that Craig had not directed any blame at Kelly when she had initially used the counselling services provided by Ruchill Hospital and had instead conveyed the impression that she and Kelly were 'tackling "the most awful situation" as a couple'.[30] Findlay suggested that it was her sense of guilt, rather than justice, that was driving the case. In addition, in view of her application for Criminal Injuries Compensation, he questioned whether her real objective in pursuing Kelly was the prospect of financial gain.[31]

On 23 February 2001, in his closing remarks to the jury, Lord Mackay of Drumadoon told the jury that they had to be certain that not only had Kelly had unprotected sex with Craig despite knowing he was HIV positive but that he acted with 'total disregard for her health and well-being'. After hearing evidence for nine days, the jury of five women and ten men took just two hours to decide by a majority verdict that Kelly was guilty as charged and, on 16 March 2001, he was duly sentenced to five years' imprisonment, making British legal history. In passing sentence, Lord Mackay emphasised that the sentence reflected the gravity of the charge and the degree to which both Anne Craig's quality of life and life expectancy had been impaired. He left it to the prison authorities and Scottish ministers to decide whether a further deterioration in Kelly's condition should lead to an earlier than normal release.

THE AFTERMATH OF THE STEPHEN KELLY CASE: HIV/AIDS POLICY, 2001–15

The proceedings and outcome of the Stephen Kelly case elicited a varied response. The law correspondent of the *Glasgow Herald* welcomed the prosecution and conviction of Stephen Kelly as reflecting how 'flexible and imaginative' Scots common law could be 'in adapting to changing times and social conditions' by employing 'the tried and trusted' concept of 'culpable and reckless conduct'.[32] However, the case was considered by medical and legal experts and by AIDS-related charities to have far-reaching and concerning implications.

Professor David Goldberg, Deputy Director of the Scottish Centre for Infection and Environmental Health, described the guilty verdict as 'disturbing' because of its possible impact on the spread of HIV. In his opinion, the 'verdict might make people think twice about not having a test themselves but also notifying their partners that they were HIV-positive'.[33] According to Sheila Bird of the Medical Research Council's biostatics unit in Cambridge, the case raised a whole set of issues relating to partner notification and confidentiality, especially in light of the fact that Stephen Kelly's behaviour was far from unique and that Scottish studies had indicated that 20 per cent of patients did not confide in their partners following an HIV-positive diagnosis.[34] Professor Sheila McLean, an expert in medical ethics at Glasgow University also highlighted the dilemma created for health professionals by the conviction. While the disclosure of information to partners might be deemed in 'the public interest' and enable some doctors to have a clearer conscience, others would see it as a fundamental breach of confidentiality that potentially exposed their patients to criminal charges.[35]

The issue of confidentiality especially concerned Professor Andrew Leigh Brown, head of the Centre for HIV Research at Edinburgh University, whose HIV study was cited in securing the conviction of Stephen Kelly. He was 'appalled' that data relating to blood samples from Kelly and Craig, collected independently as part of his wide-ranging Medical Research Council-funded project on the molecular epidemiology of HIV, had been appropriated by the police and used in evidence, despite his protestations that this represented a serious 'invasion of human rights'.[36] The BMA's Scottish Council raised similar objections, arguing that years of building trust within the prison system that all medical data on inmates would remain strictly confidential had 'been destroyed at a stroke'. It was argued that, as a result, fewer inmates would come forward for testing with a consequent increase of HIV both in the prison population and the wider community.[37] Dr Andrew Fraser, Deputy Chief Medical Officer at the Scottish Home and Health Department was equally concerned at the likely impact on medical research of the type of disclosure to the police of personal health information that had occurred in the Kelly case and called for an urgent review of procedures.[38]

Meanwhile, echoing the view of many within the voluntary sector, both Charlie McMillan, the chief executive of Phase West, a Glasgow charity offering care and support to HIV sufferers and their families, and David Johnson, director of the Edinburgh-based Waverley Care Trust, voiced serious concerns about the 'criminalisation' of the issue, and questioned 'the assumption that the prosecution of Kelly would make HIV sufferers, who already suffered discrimination, more open about their condition'. On the contrary, along with many other representatives of HIV support groups, they feared that such cases would merely fuel the social stigma surrounding HIV/AIDS and that fewer people would seek an HIV test on the premise that ignorance of one's condition would ensure immunity from prosecution.[39]

A common thread to many of the concerns expressed immediately after the Kelly case was the belief that, far from being a deterrent, prosecution in such cases might actually increase levels of HIV/AIDS infection. A widely publicised article by Bird and Leigh Brown in the *British Medical Journal* in November 2001 appeared to confirm these fears. They predicted that as many as 40 per cent of likely victims might be prevented by the trial from taking an HIV test because a positive diagnosis could leave them open to future prosecution, potentially doubling the infection rate. In their view, the verdict had 'criminalised undeclared, but not untested, HIV transmission' and, far from protecting the public, the outcome of the Kelly case had 'endorsed abrogation of individual responsibility in sexual partnerships by asserting a legal duty of disclosure on an infected partner'.[40] Subsequently, both the theory and legal interpretation underpinning their paper were subject to criticism,[41] and, in 2002, returns from Scottish NHS laboratories appeared to indicate that the Kelly case had not had 'any apparent detrimental effect on the number of HIV tests carried out at either a national or local level'.[42] Nonetheless, the likely negative impact of criminal proceedings on testing and disclosure continued to be a widely held view within the social politics surrounding HIV/AIDS.

After 2001, two main strands of policy debate relating to legal issues surrounding the transmission of HIV/AIDS emerged. First, there was a protracted campaign to secure some form of legal protection for the police and health and social-care workers from the trauma of possible infection when injured by offenders and/or patients. Secondly, following a small number of further prosecutions for the 'culpable and reckless' transmission of HIV/AIDS, there was increasing pressure to clarify the law and to establish a set of clear and consistent guidelines for the prosecuting authorities.

In 2002, claiming that its members were at increasing risk when dealing with criminals and drug addicts infected with blood-borne infectious diseases such as HIV and hepatitis, the Scottish Police Federation petitioned the Scottish Parliament for legal powers to compel assailants to submit to blood tests and for details of their serostatus to be made available to the officers concerned. It was proposed that failure to comply with such tests would be a criminal offence. The aim was to try to reduce the anxiety surrounding the possibility that there had been a transmission of disease and to enable police officers to make an earlier and informed decision as to whether to risk the not inconsiderable side effects of the post-exposure prophylaxis then available.[43] Although, in 2003, the Federation's proposals were rejected in the Scottish Parliament when presented as an amendment to the Criminal Justice Bill, by early 2005 the Scottish Executive had accepted the need for action on the issue.[44] The Justice Minister wanted to broaden the scope of any measure to cover people 'working in the health services, the prison service, and social work' along with any member of the public. Under the new government proposals a dual system of mandatory blood testing was suggested where 'a person [had] come into contact with a bodily substance of another individual as a result of that individual allegedly committing a crime, and where as a result of that contact the applicant could reasonably believe that they might be at the risk of infection with a prescribed blood-borne virus'. In some cases, mandatory testing would form part of judicial proceedings under the criminal law, authorised by the Procurator Fiscal, with a positive serostatus perhaps being libelled as an aggravating factor in the assault charge. In other cases, where criminal proceedings were not involved, injured parties would have recourse to a newly created civil mandatory testing order issued by the Sheriff, failure to comply incurring a fine of up to £2,500 or up to twenty-eight days imprisonment.

In February 2005, these proposals were published in a consultation paper.[45] As responses were fairly evenly divided for and against new measures, in June a working group of experts was appointed to give further consideration to the issue. In their report, issued in March 2006, the group rejected the proposal to give victims of assault who were potentially exposed to a blood-borne virus legal power to access the medical records of their assailant.[46] It viewed the issue as predominantly one involving the civil rather than criminal law; as less a question of 'prosecuting an offender in the public interest' than of ensuring appropriate 'health care for the exposed person'. The group was persuaded by evidence from organisations such as Health Protection Scotland that mandatory testing would not reduce the actual transmission of HIV and that an improved system of pre- and post-incident counselling and psychological care by occupational health services and the NHS was likely to be far more effective in reducing the trauma of possible exposure to HIV. The immediacy with which post-exposure treatment was required was seen to be at odds with the inevitable delay encountered in securing a mandatory testing order. Weight was also attached to the evidence of Scottish agencies working with HIV sufferers that the introduction of mandatory testing with legal sanctions would endanger efforts to promote voluntary testing and damage the trust between the communities of those living with HIV/AIDS and the medical profession and police. The possibility of malicious applications for mandatory testing orders, with an associated abuse of the information obtained, were also considerations. Finally, the working group was sensitive to the need to comply with the European Convention on Human Rights and clearly considered that the possible benefits of legislation were insufficient to justify the degree of invasion into the private domain of the individual.

In the meantime, the Crown Office had authorised two further prosecutions involving the 'culpable and reckless' transmission of HIV. In the first case, in May 2005, Christopher Walker, a 34-year-old haemophiliac, was charged with repeatedly having sex with his girlfriend at his former home in Bellshill, Lanarkshire, between May 1999 and December 2002, despite knowing that he was infected with HIV and that it could be transmitted during sexual contact, to 'the danger of her health and life'. At a first hearing at the High Court in Paisley, the judge had called for psychiatric reports on the accused and subsequently at the High Court in Edinburgh ruled that Walker was insane and unfit to stand trial and ordered that he should be detained in a psychiatric hospital.[47]

The second more significant case involved Giovanni Mola, a 36-year-old Italian, variously described as a waiter or 'former chef', charged in July 2004 with 'endangering the health and life' of his former girlfriend during the period from September 2003 to February 2004 in that he failed to disclose his medical condition and refused to wear a condom during sexual intercourse despite 'knowing or believing' he was infected with HIV and hepatitis C.[48] Mola, who had contracted the diseases from another former girlfriend, claimed to have had 200 lovers, meeting them at Latin American clubs in Edinburgh. However, he failed to comply with a bail order imposed by Edinburgh Sheriff Court and to attend a preliminary hearing at the High Court in April 2005. Instead, he fled to Italy where he was imprisoned for other offences committed prior to his move to Scotland. The Crown Office immediately began extradition proceedings and secured his return for trial in 2007 by which time other former lovers had come forward to corroborate his predilection for unsafe sex.

At the trial at the High Court in Glasgow in February 2007 Mola pleaded not guilty and insisted throughout that he had worn condoms during his relationship with Miss X[49] but there was powerful evidence to support the prosecution. Not only had the transmission of both HIV and hepatitis occurred but the defendant and complainant were also found to share the same strain of the HIV virus. Mola was duly convicted on a majority verdict, sentenced to nine years imprisonment, and certified under the Sexual Offences Act 2003. The judge also recommended that Mola be deported on his release on 'grounds of public policy and public health'.

The case had important legal implications for the interpretation of criminality in relation to the transmission of HIV. As both James Chalmers and Matthew Weait have noted, in sentencing Mola, Lord Hodge made explicit reference to the distinction between failing to disclose known HIV status, which he held was not a crime per se, and the need to practise safer sex. His closing remarks therefore suggested that, in Scots law, the failure to disclose known HIV-positive status was not in and of itself something that could or should be used when determining whether someone has been reckless or not.[50]

When interviewed at the end of the trial, Detective Chief Inspector Adrian Lawrie of Lothian and Borders Police had been at pains to stress that the prosecution of Mola had not been about 'policing the sex lives of the public or criminalising people who [had] the horrible misfortune to contract the disease'. It was purely 'about an individual who through callous indifference [had] effectively handed a death sentence to a woman by knowingly infecting her'.[51] There were, however, aspects of the trial and its portrayal in the press that were concerning to HIV/AIDS charities and care workers. It was claimed that such prosecutions increased the stigma attached to HIV/AIDS by 'casting victims of the disease as criminals' and that they encouraged its spread by deterring people from talking about their condition and accessing counselling and treatment.[52]

A third case, that of Mark Devereaux, indicted in January 2010 on multiple charges of culpable and reckless conduct, was to prove even more controversial.[53] A 41-year-old chef who worked for an agency, travelling throughout the UK and abroad, Devereaux had been diagnosed as HIV-positive in 1994 and advised about the need to protect partners by practising safe sex. However, he subsequently admitted to having had unprotected sex with four different women in Tayside and north-east Scotland during the years 2003 to 2008 without telling them of the risks involved. One of the women, with whom he had a six-year relationship, was pregnant with twins when she discovered that he had infected her. When she was later informed that he had known of his HIV-positive condition for nine years, she decided to contact the police and to have an abortion. Significantly, although three of his 'victims' were reported to have escaped infection, their exposure to the risk of HIV was seen to justify criminal prosecution and to meet the criminal standard of recklessness necessary for a likely conviction. This was in marked contrast to the situation in England and Wales where the 'infliction of bodily harm' by the transmission of infection was necessary before criminal charges could be brought.[54] While admitting the charges, Devereaux claimed that he had been 'in denial' over his condition because he had suffered no ill health and had not required medication, but dispensary records from Ninewells Hospital in Dundee suggested otherwise. In February 2010, he was sentenced at the High Court in Edinburgh to ten years' imprisonment, reduced on appeal to eight years in view of his early admission of guilt.

The Devereaux case provoked strong criticism of the criminal justice system from Scottish HIV/AIDS organisations, led by HIV Scotland.[55] They deplored the extent to which media coverage of such prosecutions demonised defendants and reinforced the stigma surrounding the disease. Thus, while the BBC, STV and *The Scotsman* had adopted a fairly neutral approach to the trial, the *Scottish Sun*, the *Scottish Daily Record* and the *Daily Express* had variously described Devereaux as an 'HIV fiend', a 'callous predator' and 'HIV rat'. Particular concerns were also raised at the prospect of the case opening 'the door' for future prosecutions where there had been no actual transmission of HIV. The 'HIV sector' urged the Scottish government to revise the law so as to exclude such cases and to issue a 'clear statement of Scottish prosecution policy'. Public health authorities and HIV clinicians were generally in agreement, fearing that further cases would only alienate the HIV community, compromise the take-up of testing, tracing and treatment provisions, and undermine the notion of mutual responsibility for safe sex which lay at the heart of health-promotion initiatives.

In response, the Crown Office and Procurator Fiscal Service drew up a set of new policy guidelines for the prosecution of the 'intentional or reckless transmission of, or exposure to, sexually transmitted infections', issued in May 2012.[56] The guidelines were drafted in consultation with a range of interested groups including its own internal advisory groups on sexual crime and HIV, the Chief Medical Officer for Scotland, and officials from the Scottish Home and Health Department, consultants specialising in sexual health, and HIV agencies such as HIV Scotland. To ensure consistency in the interpretation of the law, all future cases of sexual transmission or exposure considered by procurators fiscal to merit criminal proceedings in the public interest were to be reported to the National Sexual Crimes Unit at the Crown Office, established in May 2009. A clear distinction was drawn between the intentional transmission of a sexually transmitted infection, which was held to constitute criminal assault, and reckless sexual behaviour that might incur a charge of 'culpable and reckless conduct'. The guidelines stressed, however, that, in the latter case, a high degree of 'recklessness' would be required for a prosecution to take place. Mere negligence was not sufficient. Something akin to 'criminal indifference to consequences was required'. There needed to be firm evidence that the victim had contracted the disease from the accused, using expert scientific and medical evidence, including detailed phylogenetic analysis. Proof was also needed that the accused had knowledge of his/her infection,[57] and corroboration that his/her subsequent sexual behaviour (for example, failure to disclose their medical condition or refusal to use condoms) was reckless.

Once satisfied that there was a sufficiency of evidence to prove knowledge and transmission, prosecutors had then to decide whether prosecution was in the public interest. The guidelines identified various factors favouring prosecution: when the accused had deliberately misled or concealed information from a partner; when the victim was vulnerable or had been coerced or exploited in some way; when the accused had not attempted to reduce the risk of transmission; and when the accused had a history of 'flagrant conduct' involving non-disclosure and unprotected sexual intercourse with several partners. In establishing this history, the prosecution might exceptionally use evidence of culpable and reckless conduct involving exposure alone. As in the Devereaux case, such evidence might be led, along with a charge of reckless transmission, to support the argument that the accused had displayed the necessary criminal disregard for the sexual health of his/her partners to justify the primary indictment. Nonetheless, the guidelines stressed that 'in cases involving exposure to sexually transmitted infections, where there ha[d] been no resultant transmission of the infection, prosecution would only be contemplated in exceptional circumstances'.

The guidelines were generally welcomed by HIV charities as a much-needed clarification of the law and prosecution policy. However, organisations such as HIV Scotland continued to question the value and ethics of criminalising the unintentional transmission of HIV and were strongly opposed to prosecutions based purely on evidence of 'exposure' on the grounds that it represented a potential violation of human rights. Since 2012, HIV Scotland has liaised annually with the Crown Office and Procurator Fiscal Service as part of monitoring the application and content of their guidelines. In particular it has campaigned for better support and guidance in relation to partner notification to pre-empt precisely those situations in which legal proceedings might arise.[58]

CONCLUSION

Any attempt to establish the social significance of the Stephen Kelly case and subsequent prosecutions in Scotland is problematic. Given the constraints on access to the files of the Crown Office and Procurators Fiscal Service,[59] as well as to Scottish court papers and transcripts, it is impossible to be certain as to what motivated the decision to initiate legal proceedings and to test the applicability of the charge of 'culpable and reckless conduct' to the transmission of HIV. It may well have been a response to public frustration at the ongoing threat of the HIV/AIDS epidemic, fuelled by a retributive tabloid press. Certainly, the prosecutions do not seem to have been part of any co-ordinated strategy by Scottish governance.[60] They were more likely to have reflected ad hoc initiatives by local police and prosecuting authorities.[61] Contemporary surveys revealed that it was those working in the criminal justice system who tended to be most unequivocal in their support for the application of the criminal law to both the intentional and reckless transmission of HIV.[62]

In this respect there appears to have been a dissonance between the prosecutions and the general thrust of HIV/AIDS policy being pursued by the Scottish government in conjunction with the AIDS charities and medical authorities. While issues such as compulsory screening, notification and contact tracing regularly appear as areas of debate within Scottish HIV/AIDS policy-making, the issue of criminalising HIV transference or exposure is notably absent.[63] Even the public health authorities that had formerly been at the forefront of Scottish campaigns for legal sanctions against irresponsible vectors of venereal disease were muted in their response and more inclined to embrace the more liberal and non-judgemental views of the voluntary sector. The sexual transmission of HIV was predominantly perceived as an issue of epidemiology, education and healthcare rather than criminality. Meanwhile, however, within the criminal justice system, as previously with homosexual offences, issues relating to sexual health and behaviour in the age of HIV/AIDS continued to be framed within legal discourses of criminal negligence and culpability that could at times both reflect and reinforce broader moral and stigmatising attitudes within Scottish society.

NOTES

1. See especially, Chalmers, 'Sexually transmitted diseases', 259–78. The first English prosecution took place in 2002.
2. Ibid., 263, 266–7.
3. Unless otherwise stated, the following section in based upon Davidson, *Dangerous Liaisons*, 31–7, 177–235, 273–7.
4. In the contemporary discourse surrounding VD such behaviour was represented as both dysgenic and a punishable offence.
5. For a detailed account of the genesis, implementation and demise of DORA 33B, see Davidson, *Dangerous Liaisons*, Ch. 9.
6. *Hansard* [HC], 774, 27 November 1968, col. 511; 780, 21 March 1969, cols 944–76.
7. NRS, HH61/1306, minutes of first meeting of the Expert Advisory Group on AIDS, 29 January 1985; minutes by R. G. Covell and J. G. Davies (SHHD), 21 and 26 February, 1985.
8. NRS, HH61/1207, minute by A. M. Macpherson, 19 March 1985.
9. For statutory and regulatory developments in England and Wales, see Weait, *Intimacy and Responsibility*, Ch. 1.
10. NRS, HH61/1207, minutes by S. M. Liddle and Departmental Solicitor, 4 and 5 March 1985; circular to Chief Administrative Medical Officers, 22 March 1985.
11. *3rd Report of House of Commons Social Services Committee: Problems Associated with AIDS*, 180, 195–6, 221–2, 230–1.
12. *The Guardian*, 22 January 1987. For a legal commentary on the possible implications of this proposal, see Farmer, Brown and Lloyd, 'Scots criminal law and AIDS', 389–93.
13. Berridge, *AIDS in the UK*, 147–52.
14. Ibid., 249–50.
15. *The Scotsman*, 28 August 1991.
16. NRS, HH61/493/1, minute by K. J. Mackenzie, 29 May 1991; Scottish Office Home and Health Department, *Report of Ministerial Task Force*,

HIV and AIDS in Scotland: Prevention the Key (St Andrew's House, 1992).

17. *Report of Ministerial Task Force*, 65–7; NRS, HH 61/1612, papers relating to the AIDS Task Force, 1991–92; HH61/1496/1, briefing note by P. M. Russell on 'Police Issues', 18 November 1991.

18. *Report of Ministerial Task Force*, 48–9. The task force resisted the suggestion of Scottish church leaders that GPs should be obliged to disclose a patient's HIV status to his/her family, arguing that 'ultimately the decision whether to pass this personal and sensitive information on is one which rests with the patient' [HH61/1495/1, minute by D. Tripp, 6 September 1991].

19. Thus, Derek Ogg of Scottish AIDS Monitor protested that a system of contact tracing would be nothing more than a policy of 'tracing criminals', whether they were 'drug misusers, consenting homosexuals under the age of 21, or prostitutes'. He argued that individuals needed reassurance about confidentiality, not a health system where they were 'nagged, tagged and bagged like rabbits with myxomatosis' [BBC Scotland, Focal Point, *Killing Without a Trace*, 15 October 1992].

20. Berridge, *AIDS in the UK*, 249–57; Coyle, 'A tale of one city', PhD thesis, 272–4; Weait, *Intimacy and Reponsibility*, 21–6.

21. Berridge, *AIDS in the* UK, 256–7.

22. *The Scotsman*, 30 July 1997; *The Herald*, 24 October 1997.

23. Unless otherwise stated, the following is based on *The Herald*, 24 and 25 October 1997, 14 November 1997, 4 March 1998, 9 April 1998, 17 October 1998; *The Scotsman*, 25 and 27 October 1997; 17 October 1998.

24. He cited as precedent the successful prosecution of a man in 1993 for failing to disclose that he was carrying a needle during a police search, thus injuring an officer and exposing him to the risk of infection.

25. *The Scotsman*, 25 October 1997.

26. It is possible that Simpson's lifestyle, the tempestuous and retributive nature of their relationship, and the fact that he had withdrawn his allegations when they had been temporarily reconciled, weighed against the case proceeding to court.

27. *The Herald*, 24 February 2001.

28. The following account is based on *The Herald*, 14, 15, 16, 17, 21, 23 and 24 February 2001; *The Scotsman*, 14, 16 and 24 February 2001; *Edinburgh Evening News*, 15 and 23 February 2001; Chalmers, 'Sexually transmitted disease and the criminal law', 259–78.

29. Craig later claimed that Kelly had 'set out with the clear intention of infecting her and sought to use the disease as a "weapon" with which he could trap her in a relationship' [BBC News Online, 16 November 2001, http://news.bbc.co.uk/1/hi/scotland/1659854.stm (accessed 2 January 2018)].

30. Findlay also raised the issue of whether she had worked as a prostitute after her diagnosis in order to buy heroin to fuel her drugs habit and that

of her boyfriend. This, she strenuously denied, but she did admit to having intercourse with Kelly at a later date in Barlinnie Prison when staff were allowing them more time together than normal during visits as they both had HIV [*The Herald*, 17 February 2001].

31. Donald Findlay also successfully challenged the admissibility of the video of the *World in Action* documentary as trial evidence on the grounds that the court lacked the opportunity to question exactly how it had been obtained and edited.

32. *The Herald*, 24 February 2001. He did foresee, however, that its very flex-ibility might bring it into conflict with recent human rights legislation.

33. *The Herald*, 24 February 2001.

34. Ibid.

35. Ibid.

36. Ibid., 17 March 2001.

37. Ibid., 26 February 2001.

38. NRS, HH57/222/3, memorandum by Dr A. Fraser, 21 March 2001. According to Fraser, the Strathclyde police had obtained by a court order details of Kelly's seropositive HIV diagnosis at Glenochil Prison in 1993 and the extent to which he had been counselled about safe sex. He also reported that by obtaining data on samples sent from the epidemiological study at Glenochil to the Medical Research Council laboratory, and aided by information published in the *British Medical Journal* on the sexual con-tacts of Glenochil prisoners, they were able to match the genetic make-up of the virus infecting both Kelly and Anne Craig.

39. *The Herald*, 24 and 26 February 2001, 17 March 2001; *Daily Mail*, 17 March 2001; *The Guardian*, 19 March 2001.

40. Bird and Leigh Brown, 'Criminalisation of HIV transmission', 1174–7; *The Herald*, 16 November 2001; *The Scotsman*, 16 November 2001.

41. Chalmers, 'Ethics, law and medicine', 448–51.

42. R. Fieldhouse 'No decline in HIV testing in Scotland following Stephen Kelly case', 10 July 2002, http://www.aidsmap.com/No-decline-in-HIV-testing-in-Scotland-following-Stephen-Kelly-case/page/1414440/ (accessed 2 January 2018). The number of tests recorded in Scotland in March 2001 was 16 per cent higher than in 2000 and represented the highest monthly total since national surveillance had begun in 1988.

43. Chalmers, *Legal Responses to HIV and AIDS*, 40–1.

44. Ibid., 41; *Edinburgh Evening News*, 20 February 2003, 24 February 2005; *The Herald*, 21 February 2003.

45. Scottish Executive Consultation Paper. *Blood Testing following criminal incidents*.

46. Scottish Executive, *Report of Working Group to address the needs of those potentially exposed to blood-borne virus*.

47. *The Scotsman*, 11 May 2005.

48. Unless otherwise stated, the following account of the Mola case is based on

The Herald, 27 April 2005, 10 May 2005, 19 January 2006, 2 February 2007, 8 February 2007, 6 April 2007; *The Scotsman*, 27 April 2005, 8 February 2007, 26 February 2007; *Edinburgh Evening News*, 6 April 2007.

49. For the first time in Scottish legal history, the judge, Lord Hodge, issued a wide-ranging order banning the media from identifying Miss X on the grounds that her mental health would have been put at serious risk if her name had been revealed during the trial [*The Herald*, 8 February 2007].

50. Weait, *Intimacy and Responsibility*, 34–5; Chalmers, *Legal Responses to HIV and AIDS*, 147–8.

51. *The Herald*, 8 February 2007.

52. *The Scotsman*, 8 and 26 February 2007; *Edinburgh Evening News*, 6 April 2007.

53. The following account is based upon *The Herald*, 20 January 2010, 26 February 2010, 30 June 2010; *The Scotsman*, 20 January 2010.

54. Chalmers, 'Ethics, law and medicine', 448–9. Between 2003 and 2012 there were twenty prosecutions in England and Wales involving the unlawful transmission of HIV under section 20 of the Offences Against the Person Act 1861.

55. BBC News Online, 20 January 2010 http://news.bbc.co.uk/1/hi/scotland/north_east/8469238.stm (accessed 2 January 2018); HIV Scotland had been established in 1994 as the Scottish Voluntary HIV and AIDS Forum, a charity co-ordinating HIV/AIDS initiatives in Scotland in response to the recommendations of the Scottish Office AIDS Task Force.

56. Crown Office and Procurator Fiscal Service, *New Prosecution Policy on Intentional or Reckless Transmission of, or Exposure to, Sexually Transmitted Infections*. An additional consideration was a desire to ensure some degree of consistency with English prosecution policy, guidelines for which had initially been issued in 2008 by the Crown Prosecution Service.

57. This would usually involve diagnostic evidence, but evidence of 'wilful blindness' on the part of the accused to their condition might also be led by the prosecution.

58. *The Herald*, 2 May 2012; HIV Scotland, *HIV Policy in Scotland: A Stock Take of Relevant Policy and Law*, March 2014.

59. Access to the relevant files within the Crown Office and Procurator Fiscal Service was requested under the Freedom of Information (Scotland) Act 2002 but rejected on the grounds that it would contravene the Data Protection Act and might 'influence the behaviour of persons to avoid detection and prosecution for offences'[Crown Office and Procurator Fiscal Service to R. Davidson, 25 November 2015].

60. According to HIV Scotland, 'the small number of high-profile cases' had not been 'the result of a Government policy to prosecute people for passing on HIV'. They had begun 'because prosecutors tested existing laws to see if they could be applied to HIV' [HIV Scotland, *Prosecutions for HIV and STI Transmission and Exposure*, leaflet, 21 March 2013].

61. Similarly, evidence would suggest that prosecutions in England tended 'to happen rather haphazardly' and depended 'on how a particular police officer deal[t] with a complainant' and how prosecutors then communicated and decided how best to proceed. Prosecutors did not feel constrained by Home Office guidelines [Dodds et al., 'Grievous harm', 3-4, 19].
62. Ibid., 8.
63. See, for example, Coyle, 'A tale of one city', PhD thesis.

10

Conclusion

The most notable contrast between the early and late twentieth-century studies in this volume is the degree of exposure of 'illicit and unnatural' sexual practices in the press. As the early chapters illustrate, except for cases involving prominent local personalities, such as the well-known VD quack, 'Professor' Abraham Eastburn, or the abortionist, Professor George Bell Todd, there was very little newspaper coverage of trial proceedings in the period 1900–30. Indeed, as late as 1950, this silence which, as Foucault has observed, constitutes a powerful discursive practice,[1] continued to prevail in the Scottish press. Law reports continued to excise explicit details of offences, such as the sexual practices performed or depicted in film and literature. In contrast, although the social historian of sexuality is severely restricted in access to late twentieth-century Crown Office and High Court records, newspaper coverage in part compensates for this. Details of cases involving sexual offences were fully reported, often with sensational headlines and explicit discussion of intimate sexual practices and preferences. Indeed, in some instances, as with the madam, Dora Noyce, and the sex-shop owner, John Cameron, sexual entrepreneurs exploited this media coverage to their own advantage. Furthermore, as in the cases of brothel-keeping, sex shops and the wilful transmission of HIV, detailed exposure of court proceedings in the press not only reinforced the moral panic that had initiated legal action in the first place but served to strengthen the call for additional measures to regulate and/or penalise such practices.

At the same time, there are significant areas of continuity. A number of important aspects of the relationship between the law, sex and society recur throughout the volume. One outstanding feature of the case studies is the degree to which the legal process, far from being autonomous, was very much a social construct. In many instances, the law both reflected and reinforced contemporary moral concerns that occupied public and professional debate. For example, the prosecution of 'Professor' Eastburn was a product of the moral panic surrounding VD during and immediately after World War I, and of lobbying by the social hygiene and social purity movements. The increasing number of aggravated charges of sexual assault on young girls after 1910 stemmed from similar concerns over the impact of VD on social order and racial progress, from fears that the 'pernicious delusion' of a 'virgin cure' was rife in society, as well as from the growing resistance of feminist groups to the perceived escalation in 'child outrage'. Likewise, the prosecution of abortionists in the period 1900–30 was in part driven by contemporary fears of family breakdown and population decline. Later in the century, police action against sex shops was part of a more general panic of Scottish church and civic leaders at what was perceived to be the growing social evil of pornography. Similarly, the criminalisation of certain forms of HIV transmission in Scotland at the start of the new millennium arguably grew out of the judicial response to media coverage that sensationalised the threat of individual vectors who deliberately failed to protect their sexual partners from infection.

In addition, these studies confirm the view of recent historians that rather than a monolithic, 'neutral arbiter of justice', the law is 'multi-faceted' and involves the interaction of numerous individuals within the political, legal and forensic communities with different perspectives 'on the law's tenor and reach'.[2] Within this framework of analysis, certain figures are seen to play a significant role in determining patterns of enforcement over time and space. This is especially true of the procurators fiscal who were responsible in Scotland for initiating prosecutions. Fiscals such as J. Drummond Strathern and James Adair dominated legal proceedings in Glasgow and Edinburgh in the early decades of the twentieth century. It was Strathern who initially pressed for the prosecution of Eastburn under the Venereal Disease Act 1917. Likewise, it was Adair, with his intense desire to protect Scottish morality and close affiliation to the National Vigilance Association, who pushed for a proactive police campaign against all forms of vice and unnatural practices.[3] Other fiscals, as we have seen in the studies on child sexual abuse, bestiality, brothel-keeping and sex shops, were highly responsive to the concerns of local church and civic leaders. In some instances, as with cases of bestiality, because of the social taboo surrounding the sexual act, a fiscal might try to avoid legal proceedings for fear that a trial might pollute the whole community by association. More usually, local moral outrage precipitated police action and legal proceedings.

The decision to charge Stephen Kelly for 'culpable and reckless conduct' in wilfully transmitting HIV may also have reflected the personal agenda of an individual prosecutor under pressure from the local media and civic leaders, rather than a more systemic shift in the mindset of the judiciary and Scottish policy-makers. In this respect these studies echo Stephen Robertson's view of the North American experience that the decision to prosecute was to a significant extent a 'social decision'; 'a complex and contingent set of choices, priorities and responses shaped by neighbourhood pressures as well as the law'.[4]

A further central theme of the volume is the pivotal role, or rather roles, of the medical profession in framing and implementing the prosecution of 'illegal and unnatural' sexual practices. In particular, the studies highlight the process by which medical expertise, armed with new technologies of microscopy and bacteriology, was accorded an increasingly authoritative role within the legal process. In the first half of the twentieth century a small coterie of forensic medical experts and pathologists, led by John Glaister senior and junior, Henry and Harvey Littlejohn and John Anderson, came to dominate legal proceedings in Scotland, whether they related to child sexual assault, bestiality, abortion, or homosexual offences. Their reports and precognitions over many decades, often recast at the behest of Crown Counsel and procurators fiscal in order to strengthen the prosecution case, were critical in securing convictions. However, while historians have explored the contribution of this group to the development of forensic medicine in Scotland,[5] we remain relatively ignorant of their underlying social philosophy and its likely impact on the interpretation of evidence and shifts in medico-legal responses to sexual practices.

What evidence we do have suggests that they were reluctant to embrace new theories that accorded priority to the psychological forces shaping sexual behaviour. Thus, the study on bestiality reveals little indication of engagement with the work and insights of the early sexologists in the field of sexual deviation, and the limited psychiatric evidence that was submitted tended to be presented within a eugenic framework of analysis of 'moral' degeneracy. Similarly, John Glaister senior approached his forensic work as a keen eugenist, believing that crime stemmed fundamentally from 'moral inadequacy' and 'low moral fibre' among the poor rather than social deprivation and psychological disturbance.[6] Later in the century, while more receptive to the psychiatric and psychotherapeutic treatment of certain homosexual offenders increasingly advocated by medical witnesses for the defence in High Court cases, John Glaister junior continued to adhere in practice to traditional taxonomies of deviance and to treatment regimes that favoured cure or sublimation rather than sexual expression and empowerment.

Other members of the medical fraternity, less embedded within the legal process, had a more uneasy relationship with the law. There was an enduring struggle between the legal and medical profession over the issue of disclosure and confidentiality, especially in matters relating to the sexual history and sexual health of patients. In part, this reflected the determination of the medical profession to preserve its autonomy and the sanctity of the doctor–patient relationship. In addition, as in the prosecution of cases of child sexual assault and abortion in early twentieth-century Scotland, doctors were sometimes reluctant to divulge information on the VD status of patients, fearful of being sued for damages or concerned that it would deter infected patients from seeking treatment at a VD clinic. This concern was to underlie the opposition to the introduction of compulsory notification and screening for sexually transmitted diseases for the rest of the century. Again, the treatment of homosexual offenders in the period 1950–80 reveals an ongoing struggle between a judiciary who viewed homosexual behaviour as fundamentally a criminal act and psychiatrists and psychotherapists who viewed it as a disease shaping sexual identity. Moreover, the process of criminalising the wilful and reckless transmission of HIV at the turn of the new millennium reveals similar tensions between the medical and legal professions over the appropriate level of intrusion by the state into the sexual behaviour of individual citizens based on the use of confidential medical information.

A pathological attitude to sexual gratification and diversity, framed by either an explicit or implicit ideal of conventional, heterosexual reproductive sex within marriage, also characterised the legal response to several issues explored in these studies. Underlying early twentieth-century efforts to criminalise VD quackery and to impose a public-health system of clinics was a concern to police the sexual behaviour of promiscuous groups in society that were allegedly functioning as irresponsible vectors of the disease. Brothel-keeping and prostitution were viewed as a threat both to the morals and health of civil society and to the integrity of Christian marriage. Sex shops posed similar challenges. With their increasingly explicit pornographic materials and titillating sex aids, they were viewed as 'depraving and corrupting the morals of the lieges' and of pandering to the basest instincts of sexual perverts and predators. Moreover, as with homosexuality, there was a strong inclination on the part of moral vigilantes within the Scottish cities to associate the sexual proclivities of the regular patrons of sex shops with pederasty. Finally, public pressure on the Scottish judiciary to prosecute the wilful and reckless transmission of HIV was undoubtedly driven in part by moral outrage at the sheer sexual indulgence and alleged mindless promiscuity of the parties involved.

In many of the studies, the social response to 'illicit and unnatural' practices is seen to embrace a distinctive and, at times, protective ideology of male heterosexuality. In the first half of the twentieth century legal and medical authorities in Scotland regularly interpreted 'abnormal' and transgressive male sexual behaviour as reflecting exceptionally deprived and dystopian lifestyles that bred immorality and deviance. Viewing child 'abusers' as moral degenerates and 'lustful ruffians' on the margins of society, despite clear evidence to the contrary, served to weave a narrative that sought to protect the family and prevailing ideals of male sexuality within the working-class home. Bestiality was also largely comprehended by the judiciary and medical experts as outwith the normal parameters of male sexual behaviour, and the liminal status of offenders duly emphasised in court proceedings.[7] Abortion cases involved a more varied presentation of male sexuality. Scottish courts were very reluctant to charge husbands with responsibility for their wives' abortions, and, where an abortion involved a married woman, the husband's participation was regularly played down in framing a prosecution case. In contrast, when an abortion involved a single woman, her male partner/lover was assumed to have been actively involved, vigorously investigated, and, on occasions, included in the indictment along with the abortionist. Conventional ideals of masculinity were, of course, most openly challenged by homosexual offences. The study of the medical treatment of offenders after 1950 would suggest that, while the Scottish judiciary was made increasingly aware of psychiatric advances in the understanding of homosexual behaviour, it continued to view it as intrinsically antisocial, as an issue of criminal wilfulness rather than medical dysfunction, and a threat to a stable and fertile civil society based on 'normal' male heterosexuality.[8]

This volume also reveals enduring, discriminatory perceptions of female sexuality entrenched within the legal process in twentieth-century Scotland. In the early decades, however innocent a victim of child sexual assault a young girl might be, once violated she represented a sexual danger to others with an innate predisposition to prostitution, necessitating segregation from society. On the surface, the analysis of abortion cases accords women substantial agency in effecting self-treatment and thereafter exploiting social networks to gain access to abortionists. However, the decision not to prosecute those undergoing an abortion was predominantly a function of the need for corroborative evidence and did not validate the behaviour of the so-called 'victims'. Forced to give evidence, their sexual history was exposed in court to the lasting detriment of their reputation while the men responsible for their condition often emerged unscathed. Similar double standards operated where the law sought to police prostitution. While Dora Noyce and the residents of the Danube Street brothel were regularly prosecuted, their male clients were rarely charged. The debate over sex shops was ostensibly gender-neutral but the underlying assumption of their opponents was that the pornography and sex toys conveyed an image of female sexuality that church and civic leaders viewed as a threat to the moral fabric of Scottish society. Products that artificially stimulated women's sexual pleasure or facilitated their self-arousal were regarded as particularly subversive.

Another theme common to several of the case studies is the ongoing struggle to balance the right of the law to intrude on the domain of private morality in the interests of public order, public decency and public health against the preservation of civil liberties. Thus, the Venereal Disease Bill in 1917 was vigorously opposed in the House of Commons on the grounds that, at a time when venereology was in its infancy as a specialty, it was wrong to usurp the right of the infected individual to choose the source of his/her treatment. Proposals for the regulation of sex shops also raised more general issues relating to censorship and the right of individuals to indulge their sexual appetites. Meanwhile, the infringement of the civil liberties of homosexuals by the law, and by medical treatments often imposed as part of the process of plea bargaining, was central to the campaign of the Scottish Minorities Group in the 1970s for the decriminalisation of homosexual acts in Scotland. However, it was the proposed criminalisation of HIV transmission at the dawn of the new millennium that perhaps encountered most resistance on the grounds of its threat to the basic human right of a private sexual life as laid down in the European Convention on Human Rights.

Finally, from a comparative perspective, the distinctiveness of Scots law and of the Scottish legal system forms a common thread through many of these studies. The more stringent requirements of proof in respect of corroboration in Scotland and the more limited admissibility of written confessions, rather than any libertarian sentiments, served to constrain the Crown Office and Procurator Fiscal Service in conducting their investigations, framing their indictments and presenting the prosecution case. As in the case of illegal abortions and homosexual offences, this explains the curious paradox of a society reputed for its

moral conservatism recording disproportionately fewer criminal prosecutions compared with England and Wales.[9] The greater reliance in
Scotland on common rather than statute law in many cases involving
sexual offences, such as those involving illegal abortion, also enabled a
more flexible approach to 'illicit and unnatural practices'. Moreover,
even when statutory powers were invoked, there was a strong legal
tradition in Scotland of relying on local powers under the Burgh Police
(Scotland) Act 1892 and later provisions of local acts and corporation
orders. This was a tradition zealously guarded by local magistrates and
law officers as reflecting community values rather than some distant
directive from London and subsequently embraced within the Civic
Government (Scotland) Act 1982. It was most clearly reflected in the
response of Scottish governance to the arrival of sex shops north of the
Border and its determination to regulate them in accordance with local
sensitivities rather than the predilections of policy-makers in Whitehall
and Westminster. Evidence suggests that, as in 1900, a distinctive relationship between the law, sex and society prevailed in Scotland as it
entered the new millennium.

NOTES

1. Foucault, *The History of Sexuality*, Vol. 1, 27.
2. Cook, 'Law', 66.
3. On Adair's agenda in the interwar period, see especially, Merrilees, *The Short Arm of the Law*, 73–4, 115; Settle, *Sex for Sale*, 159, 173.
4. Robertson, 'What's law got to do with it?', 179.
5. See especially, Crowther and White, *On Soul and Conscience*; Duvall, 'Forensic medicine in Scotland, 1914–39', PhD thesis.
6. Crowther and White, *On Soul and Conscience*, 52.
7. In later cases involving the prosecution of sex-shop owners, male customers were similarly portrayed as abnormal in their sexual proclivities.
8. As late as 1978, sodomy and bestiality were paired in the taxonomy of crimes listed in Scottish legal textbooks as both involving 'unnatural carnal connection' [See, for example, Gordon, *The Criminal Law of Scotland*, second edition, Ch. 34].
9. The Wolfenden Committee described the number of prosecutions in Scotland for homosexual offences committed in private with consenting adult partners as 'infinitesimal' [*RWC*, 50].

Sources and Select Bibliography

ARCHIVE SOURCES

Central Government Archives

National Records of Scotland:

AD15, Crown Office precognitions.
AD63, Parliamentary Bills' Files, Series B.
Census Records.
CS46, Court of Session: Warrants of the Register of Acts and Decrees, 5th Session.
CS258, Court of Session: Unextracted Processes.
CS275, Court of Session: Bill Chamber, Processes in Actions of Suspension and Interdict.
ED11, Child Care Files.
ED15, Approved Schools and Remand Home Files.
HH43, Scottish Home and Health Department, Licensing Files.
HH57, Prison and Borstal Services, General Files.
HH60, Criminal Justice and Procedure Files.
HH61, Local Authority Health Services (Health and Welfare) Files.
JC9, High Court Minute Books.
JC13, Minute Books of West Circuit Court of Justiciary.
JC14, Glasgow Second Court Minute Books.
JC15, Books of Adjournal.
JC26, High Court of Justiciary Processes.
JC31, Justiciary Appeals Processes.
JC34, Criminal Appeals.
JC36, Trial Transcripts.
SC39, Edinburgh Sheriff Court Records.
Statutory Registers of Births, Deaths and Marriages.

The National Archives, Public Record Office, Kew

HO345, Home Office, Papers of Wolfenden Committee on Homosexual
   Offences and Prostitution.

Local Government Archives

Edinburgh City Archives

Burgh Court Records.
Edinburgh City Police, Annual Reports.

Medical Archives

British Medical Association Archives: Committee on Homosexuality and
   Prostitution, Minutes and Agenda.
Lothian Health Services Archive.
Royal College of Physicians of Edinburgh Archive.

Other Archives

Church of Scotland Archives (Charis House, Edinburgh): Working Party on
   Obscenity, Papers and Correspondence.

PRINTED SOURCES

Official publications

Public general acts and regulations

Criminal Law Amendment Act 1885 (48 & 49 Vict. c.69).
Burgh Police (Scotland) Act 1892 (55 & 56 Vict. c.55).
Immoral Traffic (Scotland) Act 1902 (1 & 2 Geo. 5, c.20).
Venereal Disease Act 1917 (7 & 8 Geo. 5, c.21).
Children, Young Persons, Bill 1924 (Bill 37).
Judicial Proceedings (Regulation of Reports) Act 1926 (16 & 17 Geo. 5, c.61)
Criminal Justice (Scotland) Act 1949 (12,13 & 14 Geo.VI, c.94)
Indecent Display (Control) Act 1981 (1981, c.42).
Civic Government (Scotland) Act 1982 (1982, c.45).

Local and private acts

Edinburgh Municipal and Police Act 1879 (42 & 43 Vict., c.cxxxii).
Edinburgh Corporation Order Confirmation Act 1933 (23 & 24 Geo. V, c.v).

Dundee Corporation (Consolidated Powers) Order Confirmation Act 1957 (6 & 7 Eliz. 2, c.xxxvi).
Glasgow Corporation (General Powers) Order Confirmation Act 1960 (8 & 9 Eliz. 2, c.iii).
Edinburgh Corporation Order Confirmation Act 1967 (1967, c.v).

Reports and minutes of evidence (annual)

Scottish Board of Health, *Annual Reports.*
Scottish Home Department/ Scottish Home and Health Department, *Criminal Statistics Scotland, Annual Reports for 1950–74.*

Reports and minutes of evidence (occasional)

Report on the Practice of Medicine and Surgery by Unqualified Persons, PP 1910 (Cd. 5422) XLIII.
Royal Commission on the Poor Laws and Relief of Distress, Oral and Written Evidence from Scottish Witnesses, PP 1910 (Cd. 4978) XLVI.
Local Government Board, Report on Venereal Diseases by Dr R. W. Johnstone, PP 1913 (Cd. 7029) XXXII.
Royal Commission on Venereal Diseases, Reports and Minutes of Evidence, PP 1914 (Cd. 7475) XLIX, PP 1916 (Cd. 8189) XVI, PP 1916 (Cd. 8190) XVI.
Local Government Board for Scotland, Venereal Diseases: Circulars issued on 31st October 1916 (Edinburgh, HMSO, 1916).
Joint Select Committee of the House of Lords and the House of Commons on the Criminal Law Amendment Bill and Sexual Offences Bill, Minutes of Evidence, PP 1918 (142) III.
Joint Select Committee on the Criminal Law Amendment Bill, Criminal Law (no. 2) Bill and the Sexual Offences Bill, Minutes of Evidence, PP 1920 (222) VI.
Report of Departmental Committee on Sexual Offences against Children and Young Persons in Scotland, PP 1926 (Cd. 2592) XV.
Report of the Inter-Departmental Committee on Abortion (London: HMSO, 1939).
Scottish Advisory Council on the Treatment and Rehabilitation of Offenders, *Psycho-Therapeutic Treatment of Certain Offenders with Special Reference to the Case of Persons Convicted of Sexual and Unnatural Offences* (Edinburgh: HMSO, 1948).
Report of the (Wolfenden) Committee on Homosexual Offences and Prostitution, PP 1956–57 (Cmnd 247) XIV.
Report of Committee on Obscenity and Film Censorship, PP 1979–80 (Cmnd 7772) 49.
3rd Report of House of Commons Social Services Committee: Problems

Associated with AIDS, Volume 2, Minutes of Evidence, PP 1986–87 (HC 192) 19.
Report by the Task Force set up to Review the Licensing Provisions Contained in the Civic Government (Scotland) Act 1982 (Edinburgh: Scottish Government, 2004).
Scottish Executive, *First Report of Working Group to Address the Needs of those Potentially Exposed to Blood-borne Virus*, 7 March 2006.

Other central government publications

Parliamentary Debates (Hansard), House of Commons Official Reports (London: HMSO).
Parliamentary Debates (Hansard), House of Lords Official Reports (London: HMSO).
Scottish Executive Consultation Paper. *Blood Testing Following Criminal Incidents where there is a Risk of Infection: Proposals for Legislation*, 24 February 2005.
Crown Office and Procurator Fiscal Service, *New Prosecution Policy on Intentional or Reckless Transmission of, or Exposure to, Sexually Transmitted Infections*, 1 May 2012.

Local government reports

Edinburgh Public Health Department, *Annual Reports.*

Church reports

Free Church of Scotland, *Acts and Proceedings of General Assembly.*
Free Presbyterian Church of Scotland, *Proceedings of Synod.*

Other printed reports, proceedings and leaflets

Pornography: The Longford Report (London: Coronet Books, 1972).
HIV Scotland, *Prosecutions for HIV and STI Transmission and Exposure*, 21 March 2013.
HIV Scotland, *HIV Policy in Scotland: A Stock Take of Relevant Policy and Law*, March 2014.

Medical journals

British Medical Journal.
Edinburgh Medical Journal
Lancet

Scottish newspapers and journals

Aberdeen Press and Journal.
Edinburgh Evening News.
Edinburgh Review.
Glasgow Herald (1900–92).
Linlithgow Gazette.
Scottish Daily Record.
Scottish Review.
The Herald (1992–).
The Scotsman.

Books and articles

Abrams, L., *The Orphan Country: Children of Scotland's Broken Homes from 1845 to the Present Day* (Edinburgh: John Donald, 1998).

Abrams, L., *Oral History Theory* (Abingdon and New York: Routledge, 2010).

Anderson, M., 'Population and family life', in A. Dickson and J. H. Treble (eds), *People and Society in Scotland: Volume III, 1914–1990* (Edinburgh: John Donald, 1994), 1–47.

Anderson, M., 'The demographic factor', in T. M. Devine and J. Wormald (eds), *The Oxford Handbook of Modern Scottish History* (Oxford: Oxford University Press, 2012), 30–61.

Anderson, M. *Scotland's Populations from the 1850s to Today* (Oxford: Oxford University Press, 2018).

Anderson, M., and D. Morse, 'High fertility, high emigration, low nuptiality: adjustment processes in Scotland's demographic experience, 1861–1914', *Population Studies*, 47 (1993), 5–25, 319–43.

Angus, J. W., *A Dictionary of Crimes According to the Law of Scotland,* third edition, (Edinburgh: W. Green and Son, edited by C. A. Macpherson and J. Mill, 1936).

Bancroft, J., *Human Sexuality and Its Problems* (Edinburgh: Churchill Livingstone,1989).

Bates, V., ' "So far as I can define without a microscopical examination": venereal disease diagnosis in English courts, 1850–1914', *Social History of Medicine*, 26 (2013), 38–55.

Beirne, P., 'On the sexual assault on animals: a sociological view', in A. N. H. Creager and W. C. Jordan (eds), *The Animal/Human Boundary: Historical Perspectives* (Rochester: University of Rochester Press, 2002), 193–227.

Berridge, V., *AIDS in the UK: The Making of Policy, 1981–1994* (Oxford: Oxford University Press, 1996).

Bird, S. M., and A. J. Leigh Brown, 'Criminalisation of HIV transmission: implications for public health in Scotland, *British Medical Journal*, 323 (2001), 1174–7.

Bollinger, G. and A. F. Goetschel, 'Sexual relations with animals (zoophilia): an unrecognised problem in animal welfare legislation', in A. M. Beetz and A. L. Podberscek (eds), *Bestiality and Zoophilia: Sexual Relations with Animals* (West Lafayette: Purdue University Press, 2005), 23–45.

Bondi, Liz, 'Sexing the City', in R. Fincher and J. M. Jacobs (eds), *Cities of Difference* (New York and London: The Guildford Press, 1998), 177–200.

Brend, W. A., *A Handbook of Medical Jurisprudence and Toxicology* (London: Charles Griffen and Co., 1915).

Brown, J., 'Scotland and the Abortion Act: historic flaws, contemporary problems', *Juridical Review* (2015, part 2), 135–51.

Brown, J. S., 'A comparative study of deviations from sexual mores', *American Sociological Review*, 17 (1952), 135–46.

Burridge, H. A., *An Introduction to Forensic Medicine for Medical Students and Practitioners* (London: H. K. Lewis and Co., 1924).

Cant, B., (ed.), *Footsteps and Witnesses: Lesbian and Gay Lifestories from Scotland*, (Edinburgh: Polygon, 1993).

Chalmers, J., 'Sexually transmitted diseases and the criminal law', *Juridical Review*, 5 (2001), 259–78.

Chalmers, J., 'Ethics, law and medicine: the criminalisation of HIV transmission', *Sexually Transmitted Infections*, 78 (2002), 448–51.

Chalmers, J., *Legal Responses to HIV and AIDS* (Oxford and Portland: Hart Publishing, 2008).

Collins, A.-M., 'Woman or beast? Bestiality in Queensland 1870–1949', *Hecate*, 17 (1991), 36–42.

Collins, M., 'The pornography of permissiveness: men's sexuality and women's emancipation in mid twentieth-century Britain', *History Workshop Journal*, 47 (1999), 99–120.

Collins, M., *Modern Love: An Intimate History of Men and Women in Twentieth-Century Britain* (London: Atlantic Books, 2003).

Cook, M., 'Law', in H. G. Cocks and M. Houlbrook (eds), *The Modern History of Sexuality* (Basingstoke: Palgrave, 2006), 64–86.

Crowther, M. A. and B. White, *On Soul and Conscience: the Medical Expert and Crime: 150 Years of Forensic Medicine in Glasgow* (Aberdeen: Aberdeen University Press, 1988).

Crozier, I. D., 'Taking prisoners: Havelock Ellis, Sigmund Freud, and the construction of homosexuality, 1897–1951', *Social History of Medicine*, 13 (2000), 447–66.

Crozier, I. D., '"All the appearances were perfectly natural": the anus of the sodomite in nineteenth-century medical discourse', in C. E. Forth and I. D. Crozier (eds), *Body Parts: Critical Explorations in Corporeality* (New York and Oxford: Lexington Books, 2005), 65–84.

Davenport-Hines, R., *Sex, Death and Punishment: Attitudes to Sex and*

Sexuality in Britain since the Renaissance (London: Fontana Press, 1990).

Davidson, R., ' "A scourge to be firmly gripped": the campaign for VD controls in interwar Scotland', *Social History of Medicine*, 6 (1993), 213–35.

Davidson, R., *Dangerous Liaisons: A Social History of Venereal Disease in Twentieth-Century Scotland* (Amsterdam and Atlanta: Rodopi, 2000).

Davidson, R., ' "The cautionary tale of Tom": the male homosexual experience of Scottish medicine in the 1970s and early 1980s', *Journal of Scottish Historical Studies*, 28 (2008), 122–38.

Davidson, R., 'Psychiatry and homosexuality in mid-twentieth-century Scotland: the view from Jordanburn Nerve Hospital', *History of Psychiatry*, 20 (2009), 403–24.

Davidson, R. and G. Davis, *The Sexual State: Sexuality and Scottish Governance, 1950–80* (Edinburgh: Edinburgh University Press, 2012).

Davidson, T., (ed.), *And Thus Will I Freely Sing: An Anthology of Gay and Lesbian Writing from Scotland* (Edinburgh: Polygon, 1989).

Davies, C., 'Sexual taboos and social boundaries', *American Journal of Sociology*, 87 (1982), 1032–63.

Davis, G. and R. Davidson, ' "A fifth freedom" or "hideous atheistic expediency"? The medical community and abortion law reform in Scotland', *Medical History*, 50 (2006), 31–3.

D'Cruze, S., *Crimes of Outrage: Sex, Violence and Victorian Working Women* (London: Northern Illinois University Press, 1998).

de Blécourt, W., 'Cultures of abortion in The Hague in the early Twentieth Century', in F. X. Eder, L. A. Hall and G. Hekma (eds), *Sexual Cultures in Europe: Themes in Sexuality* (Manchester and New York: Manchester University Press, 1999) 195–212.

de Blécourt, W., 'Prosecution and popularity: the case of the Dutch Sequah, 1891–93', in J. Woodward and R. Jütte (eds), *Coping with Sickness: Medicine, Law and Human Rights – Historical Perspectives* (Sheffield: EAHMH, 2000), 75–89.

Dewar, T. F., 'On the incidence of venereal disease in Scotland', *Edinburgh Medical Journal*, XXX (1923), 313–36.

Dodds, C., P. Weatherburn, F. Hickson, P. Keogh, and W. Nutland, 'Grievous harm: use of the Offences Against the Person Act 1861 for sexual transmission of HIV', *Sigma Research Briefing Paper*, October 2005, 1–36.

Douglas, M., *Purity and Danger: An Analysis of the Concepts of Pollution and Taboo* (London: ARK edition, 1984).

Durham M., *Sex and Politics: The Family and Morality in the Thatcher Years* (London: Macmillan, 1991).

Ellis, H. H., *Studies in the Psychology of Sex*, vol. 5 (Philadelphia: F. A. Davis Co., 1906).

Encyclopaedia of the Laws of Scotland, Vol. 5 (Edinburgh: William Green and Sons, 1928).

Evans, D., 'Tackling the "Hideous Scourge": The creation of the venereal disease treatment centres in early twentieth-century Britain', *Social History of Medicine*, 5 (1992), 413–33.

Farmer, L., P. Brown and J. Lloyd, 'Scots criminal law and AIDS', *Scots Law Times* (1987), 389–93.

Ferguson, A. H., 'Speaking out about staying silent: an historical examination of medico-legal debates over the boundaries of medical confidentiality', in I. Goold and C. Kelly (eds), *Lawyers' Medicine: The Legislature, the Courts and Medical Practice, 1760–2000* (Oxford: Hart Publishing, 2009), 99–124.

Ferris, P., *Sex and the British: A Twentieth-Century History* (London: Michael Joseph, 1993).

Fisher, K., ' "Didn't stop to think, I just didn't want another one": the culture of abortion in interwar South Wales', in F. X. Eder, L. A. Hall and G. Hekma (eds), *Sexual Cultures in Europe: Themes in Sexuality* (Manchester and New York: Manchester University Press, 1999), 213–32.

Foucault, M., *The History of Sexuality, Volume 1: An Introduction* (London: Penguin Books, 1990 reprint).

Fudge, E., 'Monstrous acts: bestiality in early modern England', *History Today*, 50 (2000), 20–5.

Gane, C. H. W., *Sexual Offences* (Edinburgh: Butterworths, 1992).

Glaister, J., *A Textbook of Medical Jurisprudence, Toxicology and Public Health*, first edition (Edinburgh: E. and S. Livingstone, 1902).

Glaister, J., *A Textbook of Medical Jurisprudence and Toxicology*, fourth edition (Edinburgh: E. and S. Livingstone, 1921).

Glaister J. and J. Glaister Jr, *A Textbook of Medical Jurisprudence and Toxicology*, fifth edition (Edinburgh: E. and S. Livingstone, 1931).

Gloag, W. M. and R. C. Henderson, *Introduction to the Law of Scotland*, ninth edition (Edinburgh: W. Green and Son, 1987).

Golla F. L. and R. S. Hodge, 'Hormone treatment of the sexual offender', *Lancet*, CCLVI, vol. 1, 11 June 1949, 1006–7.

Gordon, G. H., *The Criminal Law of Scotland* (Edinburgh: W. Green and Son, 1967).

Gordon, G. H., *The Criminal Law of Scotland*, second edition (Edinburgh: W. Green and Son, 1978).

Hall, L., 'Articulating abortion in interwar Britain', *Women's History Magazine*, 70 (autumn 2012), 13–21.

Hand, W. D., *Magical Medicine: The Folkloric Component of Medicine in Folk Belief, Custom and Ritual of the Peoples of Europe and America* (Berkeley and London: University of California Press, 1980 edition).

Haste, C., *Rules of Desire: Sex in Britain: World War 1 to the Present* (London: Chatto and Windus, 1992).

Henderson, D. K., *Psychopathic States* (London: Chapman and Hall, 1939).

Henderson, D. K., *Society and Criminal Conduct*, Morison Lecture (Edinburgh: Royal College of Physicians of Edinburgh, 1955).

Henderson, D. K. and I. R. C. Batchelor, *A Textbook of Psychiatry for Students and Practitioners*, ninth edition (London: Oxford University Press, 1962).

Herzog, D., *Sexuality in Europe: A Twentieth-Century History* (Cambridge: Cambridge University Press, 2011).

Higgins, P., *Heterosexual Dictatorship: Male Homosexuality in Post-War Britain* (London: Fourth Estate, 1996).

Holden, A., *Makers and Manners: Politics and Morality in Post-War Britain* (London: Politico's, 2004).

Holmes, L., 'A tale of three cities: regulating street prostitution in Scotland', *Scottish Affairs*, 52 (2005), 71–88.

Houlbrook, M., *Queer London: Perils and Pleasures in the Sexual Metropolis, 1918–1957* (Chicago and London: University of Chicago Press, 2005).

Jackson, L. A., 'The child's word in court: cases of sexual abuse in London, 1870–1914', in M. L. Arnot and C. Usborne (eds), *Gender and Crime in Modern Europe* (London: Psychology Press, 1999) 222–37.

Jackson, L. A., 'Family, community and the regulation of sexual abuse: London 1870–1914', in A. Fletcher and S. Hussey (eds), *Childhood in Question: Children, Parents and the State* (Manchester: Manchester University Press, 1999), 133–51.

Jackson, L. A., *Child Sexual Abuse in Victorian England* (London and New York: Routledge, 2000).

Jamieson, L., 'Changing intimacy: seeking and forming couple relationships', in L. Abrams and C. G. Brown (eds), *A History of Everyday Life in Twentieth-Century Scotland* (Edinburgh: Edinburgh University Press, 2010), 76–102.

Jivani, A., *Its Not Unusual: A History of Lesbian and Gay Britain in the Twentieth Century* (London: Michael O'Mara Books, 1997).

King, M., G. Smith and A. Bartlett, 'Treatments of homosexuality in Britain since the 1950s – an oral history: the experience of patients', *British Medical Journal*, Vol. 328, 21 February 2004, 427.

King, M., G. Smith and A. Bartlett, 'Treatments of homosexuality in Britain since the 1950s – an oral history: the experience of professionals', *British Medical Journal*, Vol. 328, 21 February 2004, 429.

Knight, P., 'Women and abortion in Victorian and Edwardian England', *History Workshop*, 4 (1977), 57–68.

Krafft-Ebing, R. von, *Psychopathia Sexualis* (Philadelphia and London: F. A. Davis Co., 1892 edition).

McCulloch, R., *My Fare City: A Taxi-Driver's Guide to the Capital* (London: Serendipity, 2003).

Macdonald, J. H. A., *A Practical Treatise on the Criminal Law of Scotland* (Edinburgh: William Patterson, 1867).

Macdonald, J. H. A. and N. D. Macdonald, *A Practical Treatise on the Criminal Law of Scotland*, third edition (Edinburgh: William Green and Sons, 1894).

McLaren, A., 'Abortion in England, 1890–1914', *Victorian Studies*, 20 (1977), 379–400.

McLaren, A., 'Illegal operations: women, doctors, and abortion, 1886–1939', *Journal of Social* History, 26 (1993), 797–816.

McLaren, A., *Twentieth-Century Sexuality: A History* (Oxford: Blackwell, 1999).

Mahood, L., *Policing Gender, Class and Family: Britain 1850–1940* (London: UCL Press, 1995).

Mahood L. and B. Littlewood, 'The "vicious girl" and the "street-corner" boy: sexuality and the gendered delinquent in the Scottish child-saving movement, 1850–1940', *Journal of the History of Sexuality*, 4 (1994), 549–78.

Massie, A., *Edinburgh* (London: Sinclair-Stevenson, 1994).

Maxwell-Stuart, P. G., ' "Wilde, filthe, execrabill, detestabill and unnatural sin": bestiality in early modern Scotland', in T. Betteridge (ed.), *Sodomy in Early Modern Europe* (Manchester: Manchester University Press, 2002), 82–93.

Meek, J., *Queer Voices in Post-War Scotland: Male Homosexuality, Religion and Society* (Basingstoke, Palgrave Macmillan, 2015).

Merians, L. E., 'The London Lock Hospital and the Lock Asylum for Women', in L. E. Merians (ed.), *The Secret Malady: Venereal Disease in Eighteenth Century Britain and France* (Lexington: University Press of Kentucky, 1996), 128–48.

Merrilees, W., *The Short Arm of the Law: The Memoirs of William Merrilees, OBE: Chief Constable, The Lothians and Peebles Constabulary* (London: John Long, 1966).

Moran, L. J., *The Homosexual(ity) of Law* (London and New York: Routledge, 1996).

Mort, F., *Capital Affairs: London and the Making of the Permissive Society* (New Haven and London: Yale University Press, 2010).

Munro, K., *Manual of Medicine* (London: Bailliere, Tindall and Cox, 1903).

Newman, D., 'The history and prevention of venereal disease', *Glasgow Medical Journal*, 81 (1914), 164–78.

Norrie, K. McK., 'Abortion in Britain: one act, two laws', *Criminal Law Review*, (1985), 475–95.

Ogston, F., *Lectures on Medical Jurisprudence* (London: J. and A. Churchill, 1878).

Parker, G., ' "Is a duck an animal?": an exploration of bestiality as a crime', *Criminal Justice History*, 7 (1986), 95–109.

Porter, R., *Quacks: Fakers and Charlatans in English Medicine* (Stroud: Tempus, 2000).

Robertson, S., 'Signs, marks, and private parts: doctors, legal discourses, and evidence of rape in the United States, 1823–1930', *Journal of the History of Sexuality*, 8 (1998), 345–88.

Robertson, S., 'What's law got to do with it? legal records and sexual histories', *Journal of the History of Sexuality*, 14 (2005), 161–85.

Rorie, D., *Folk Tradition and Folk Medicine in Scotland: The Writings of David Rorie, edited by D. Buchan* (Edinburgh: Canongate Academic, 1994).

Ross, J. E. and S. M. Tomkins, 'The British reception of Salvarsan', *Journal of the History of Medicine and Allied Sciences*, 52 (1997), 398–423.

Rydström, J., 'Sodomitical sins are threefold'; typologies of bestiality, masturbation and homosexuality in Sweden, 1880–1950', *Journal of the History of Sexuality*, 9 (2000), 240–76.

Rydström, J., *Sinners and Citizens: Bestiality and Homosexuality in Sweden, 1880–1950* (Chicago and London: University of Chicago Press, 2003).

Sacco, L., *Unspeakable: Father–Daughter Incest in American History* (Baltimore: Johns Hopkins University Press, 2009).

Settle, L., 'The social geography of prostitution in Edinburgh, 1900–1939', *Journal of Scottish Historical Studies*, 33 (2013), 234–59.

Settle, L., 'The Kosmo Club case: clandestine prostitution during the interwar period', *Twentieth Century British History*, 25 (2014), 562–84.

Settle, L., *Sex for Sale in Scotland: Prostitution in Edinburgh and Glasgow, 1900–1939* (Edinburgh: Edinburgh University Press, 2016).

Simpson, A. E., 'Vulnerability and the age of female consent: legal innovation and its effect on prosecutions for rape in eighteenth-century London', in G. S. Rousseau and R. Porter (eds), *Sexual Underworlds of the Enlightenment* (Manchester: Manchester University Press, 1987), 181–205.

Smart, C., 'A history of ambivalence and conflict in the discursive construction of the "child victim" of sexual abuse', *Social and Legal Studies*, 8 (1999), 391–409.

Smart, C., 'Reconsidering the recent history of child sexual abuse, 1910–1960', *Journal of Social Policy,* 29 (2000), 55–71.

Smith, F. B., *The People's Health 1830–1910* (London: Croom Helm, 1980).

Smith, R. and B. Wynne (eds), *Expert Evidence: Interpreting Science in the Law* (London: Routledge, 1989).

Spongberg, M., *Feminizing Venereal Disease: The Body of the Prostitute in Nineteenth-Century Medical Discourse* (London: Macmillan Press, 1997).

Stockley, D., 'The increasingly strange case of abortion: Scots criminal law and devolution', *Edinburgh Law Review*, 2 (1998), 330–7.

Taylor, A. S., *Medical Jurisprudence* (London: John Churchill, 1861).

Taylor, K. J., 'Venereal disease in nineteenth century children', *Journal of Psychohistory*, 12 (1985), 431–64.

Thomas, C., ' "Not having God before his eyes": bestiality in early modern England', *The Seventeenth Century*, 26 (2011), 149–73.

Tomkins, S. M., 'Palmitate or permanganate: The venereal prophylaxis debate in Britain, 1916–26', *Medical History*, 37 (1993), 382–98.

Usborne, C., *Cultures of Abortion in Weimar Germany* (New York and Oxford: Berghahn Books, 2007).

Walton, H. A. and E. Reeder, *The Eastburn Family* (Doylestown, PA: Intelligencer, 1903).

Wardrop, K., *Psychiatry and Probation* (London: Institute for the Study and Treatment of Delinquency, 1971).

Waters, C., 'Havelock Ellis, Sigmund Freud and the State: discourses of homosexual identity in interwar Britain', in L. Bland and L. Doan (eds), *Sexology in Culture: Labelling Bodies and Desires* (Oxford: Polity Press, 1998), 165–79.

Waters, C., 'Disorders of the mind, disorders of the Body Social: Peter Wildeblood and the making of the modern homosexual', in B. Conekin, F. Mort, and C. Waters (eds), *Moments of Modernity: Reconstructing Britain 1945–1964* (London and New York: Rivers Oram Press, 1999), 135–51.

Watson, D., *Gonorrhoea and its Complications in the Male and Female* (London: Henry Kimpton, 1914).

Weait, M., *Intimacy and Responsibility: The Criminalisation of HIV Transmission* (Abingdon: Routledge-Cavendish, 2007).

Weeks, J., *Sex, Politics and Society: The Regulation of Sexuality since 1800*, second edition (London: Longman, 1989).

Weeks. J., *Sex. Politics and Society: The Regulation of Sexuality since 1800*, fourth edition (Abingdon: Routledge, 2018).

Westwood, G., *Society and the Homosexual* (London: Gollancz, 1952).

Wheeler, A. and W. R. Jack, *Handbook of Medicine and Therapeutics* (Edinburgh: E. and S. Livingstone, 1908).

Unpublished theses and articles

Coyle, H., 'A tale of one city – A history of HIV/AIDS policy-making in Edinburgh, 1982–1994', PhD thesis, University of Edinburgh, 2008.

Duvall, N. A., 'Forensic medicine in Scotland, 1914–39', PhD thesis, University of Manchester, 2013.

Innes, S., 'Love and work: feminism, family and ideas of equality and citizenship, Britain 1900–39', PhD thesis, University of Edinburgh, 1998.

Jones, E., 'Abortion in England, 1861–1967', PhD thesis. University of London, 2007.

Macaulay, K. E. C., 'Birth control knowledge in Scotland, 1900–1975, MD thesis, University of Glasgow, 2015.

O'Neill, J., 'Youth, sexuality and courtship in Scotland, 1945–80', PhD thesis, University of Edinburgh, 2015.

Radio, television and theatre productions

'Killing Without a Trace', BBC Scotland, Focal Point, 15 October 1992.

'17 Danube Street', BBC Radio Scotland, 19 December 2005.

Hector Macmillan, *Capital Offence: The Tail of One City*, Script, Glasgow University Library, Special Collections, STA H.p Box 1/11.

Index

Note: *italic* page numbers indicate a figure; **bold** page numbers indicate a table